An illustrated History of Rallying

Contents

Introduction

In 1985 the motor car will celebrate its 100th birthday, for it was in 1885 that Karl Benz's frail petrol-powered tricycle made its first hesitant trip along the streets of Mannheim, Germany. The world's first motoring competition took place in 1894; and ever since that earliest 'rally', men and machines have been racing 'against the clock'.

I am often depressed to realize how little the average motoring enthusiast knows about the long and distinguished history of rallying. It could be that memories are very short; yet clearly many people believe that 'real' rallying began with the Twin-Cam Escort, and that no rallies of note were promoted before the Second World War! Granted, there are very few rallying writers, so perhaps it is our fault. There has, in fact, been no complete book to chronicle the development of rallies *and* rally cars over the years. This book, therefore, has been written to fill that gap.

Basically, what is a rally? We all have our own ideas. The problem is that, from time to time, and from place to place, rallying means different things to different people. Let's look at the Concise Oxford Dictionary definition:

'Rally: 1, Reassemble, get together again after rout or dispersion, (cause to) renew conflict; bring or come together as support or for concentrated action; revive by effort of will, pull oneself together . . . 2. Act of rallying, reunion for fresh effort; recovery of energy . . .'

Not much help there, though that first phrase might be applicable to what usually happens afterwards! I think, therefore, that I must start with a cliché, and go on to better things. Rallying is not what it used to be. A typical Old Hand's comment, but on this occasion quite justified. Unlike pure motor racing, which is essentially the same sort of business now as it was at the beginning of the century, old-time rallying would be almost unrecognizable to the glossy-jacketed rally watcher of the 1980s. Only the most basic of its principles – that competitors are racing 'against the clock' rather than against each other – has remained.

In the beginning, too, it was not even called rallying; the events that really qualify as the sport's ancestors were invariably known as 'trials'. Although I cannot vouch for one obscure earlier event that was given no publicity, apparently the first actually to use the word 'rally' was the original *Rallye Automobile vers Monte Carlo*, held in January 1911. Very soon after this, rallies and trials became rather different forms of motor sport.

At first, therefore, a trial-which-was-really-a-rally was all about reliability and the maintenance of a time schedule, rather than a matter of outright speed. Even by the early 1900s, in spite of the legends which have grown up, cars had become sufficiently reliable to be required not only to complete a testing course but also to adhere to a strict time schedule. Thus even at this stage in motoring history they were 'against the clock', and any lateness (*or* earliness) was penalized. In case of ties, or in order to separate crews with equal penalties, special tests were usually included, often at the end of the road section of the event, when a car had to demonstrate its hill-climbing ability or perhaps its straight-line performance.

In events such as the early Monte Carlo rallies, weather conditions were often severe enough to produce a result without recourse to artificial tests, while in the Alpinefahrts road conditions and severe gradients had the same effect. However, as cars and their special equipment continued to improve, as factories gave more backing to events and as road surfaces became smoother and more stable, rally drivers often found it very easy to complete the road sections without penalty. By the 1920s and 1930s, therefore, a rally frequently had to be settled by the special tests, which became increasingly involved and were marked more and more severely. Even in those days some cars were developed with motor sport very definitely in mind: the SS100, for all that William Lyons denied it, was an excellent example, while the astonishingly advanced BMW 328 sports car was another.

After an enforced six-year interval during the Second World War, and a further delay for the repair of damaged roads and the restoration of petrol supplies, top-class rallying came back with a vengeance. More and more 'works' teams – whether official or clandestine – appeared, their specifications began to drift well away from 'standard', and perhaps for the first time the concept of providing service cars began to develop.

Even in the 1920s and 1930s the more dedicated crews had been accustomed to reconnoitre, or even practise, before the important rallies. Gradually, with greater prestige at stake and with factory backing assured, this became usual procedure. Yet it was not until 1960, when Mercedes-Benz virtually 'won' the Monte Carlo with their month-long training in advance of the event, that the idea of serious full-scale practising won general acceptance.

Incidentally, although it has often been claimed that John Gott and the BMC team of the 1950s developed the 'pace notes' system, we should never forget that Stirling Moss attributed his famous Mercedes-Benz victory in the 1955 Mille Miglia to the assiduous practice *and note-taking* which he carried out, with Denis Jenkinson, in the weeks before the race.

By the 1950s, too, at least four rather different types of rallying had evolved, each of which was best tackled with a different breed of car. For the true professionals and their factory cars, there were the great Alpine and Liège 'road races', which demanded very high speeds on open public roads, while for the masochists there were the 'off-road' endurance events held in the more open, less developed countries. Growing steadily in popularity, but still not widely accepted, were the 'special stages' rallies of Scandinavia, while in Britain and North America events were being decided on intricate navigational puzzles, split-second time-keeping and manoeuvring tests. A 'road race' driver needed a Mercedes-Benz, Porsche or Jaguar sports car to be competitive, while in the wilderness he depended on something tank-like such as a VW Beetle or a Peugeot. Special stages events were invariably run over loose surfaces, where traction (from rear-engined or front-drive cars) was at a premium. For the 'naviga-

tional' rallies, any car with a modicum of performance and good driving-test ability would do the job.

Small wonder, therefore, that at this time a determined and analytical driver could win an event in almost any type of car and that the 'homologation special' had not even been invented. He could win (or at least compete) in something really fast and strong such as one of the aforesaid European 'Grand Tourers', but by picking and choosing he might also achieve success in a massive Holden, a thoughtfully prepared DKW or even an old-fashioned Ford, not to mention a front-drive Saab or Dyna Panhard, a rear-engined Renault or VW, a nippy but spidery 'special', a big Volvo or simply a 'Maigret' Citroen. In many events it was not uncommon to see Bentleys and Rolls-Royces entered for certain categories – and winning them – nor was it a disgrace for 'works' Aston Martins to be humbled by the weather or by the handicaps.

Handicaps, such a valuable and popular means, during the 1940s and 1950s, of giving a level chance to the most unlikely cars, rapidly went out of favour in the 1960s when factory teams let it be known that they were not interested in competing against the intricate ingenuity of organizers as well as against their rivals.

Except in North America, and in the more specialized type of European club events, the navigational rally was swept away in the 1960s. In most parts of the rallying world, drivers (not to mention owners) of expensive cars saw no reason why their best efforts should be negated by the mistakes of the men sitting beside them. It also became embarrassingly clear that events could be won and lost by a mathematical, intuitive route-finding genius, and that the car and driver combination could be incidental.

By the 1960s it was obvious that even on rough road events it was no longer enough to have a car which was strong if it was too slow. All over the world, but initially in Europe, the need for high performance became paramount. Professionalism spread rapidly, as did sharp practice and – sometimes – downright cheating. Not only was it an advantage to have a practising 'barrack-room' lawyer in the team, but it also helped to have a car of doubtful legality.

Contrary to popular belief, it is not the BMC Cooper S which qualifies as the first of the 'homologation specials'; that honour probably goes to the supercharged Bentleys of the late 1920s (especially developed for production car racing), and to several extremely special German cars of the 1930s. Some of the 1950s Dyna-Panhards and Renaults, as entered by works-backed teams, were so rapid as to be almost embarrassing, while there are even well-documented cases of 'ordinary' cars such as Jowett Javelins being thrown out of European events for using non-standard items.

In later years, however, it was BMC, with the Austin-Healey 3000s and the Mini Cooper Ss, Ford with the Lotus-Cortina, and Renault with the R8 Gordini, who truly set the 'homologation special' scene. Before long every manufacturer committed to the sport had to follow suit. There was nothing remotely standard about a 'works' Triumph Spitfire, Volvo PV544, or Alfa Romeo GTZ, for incidentally, it was not only Ferrari (with the mid-engined 250LM) who were refused homologation in the 1960s.

By the end of the 1960s, public opinion and the many politicians who manipulate it, had, with a few exceptions, forced open-road rallying out of Europe. To fill the vacuum the 'special stages' version of rallying progressively took over. From the end of the 1960s cars were allowed to carry advertisements, and big-time sponsorship of machines and drivers quickly followed. Spectators soon became used to seeing cars promoting everything from milk to pipe tobacco, cigarettes to whisky, cosmetics to fork-lift trucks, and airlines to oil companies. Famous events began to be submerged (though, in truth, clinging for survival) beneath the gloss of commercial sponsorship. It was L'Équipe who helped to pay the bills for the Tour de France, while the Sun, then the Daily Mirror, and, currently, the Lombard finance house did the same for the RAC rally. The Daily Mirror supported one marathon and Singapore Airlines another. Major events received financial aid from tobacco concerns, tyre companies, purveyors of drink and even local authorities.

In the 1970s, indeed, part of the sport was to spot the cars and the drivers who were hiding cheerfully behind such a colourful facade. Some teams made money at the periphery with a change of sponsor ('Well, we've changed the colour schemes, so now we can start selling different jackets . . .'), and some altered their entire programme to suit marketing needs.

Meanwhile, the cars that competed and won became more and more exciting, less and less standard. Conventional machines, no longer having any chance of victory, had to give way to cars built and sold purely for rallying. There was a rash of rear-engined or front-wheel-drive machinery in the 1960s, and although some mid-engined cars were also developed in the 1970s, only Lancia (with the magnificent Stratos) capitalized on it.

By the end of the 1970s the most successful rally cars once again adhered to the 'classic' layout, with front engines but driven rear wheels. The fashion had swung from Mini-Cooper S to Alpine-Renault and on to the Lancia Stratos, but was back to the Fiat Abarth 131 Rallye, the Ford Escort RS and the Opel Ascona 400. The detail specification of all cars, however, had become steadily more sophisticated. There was really no comparison, say, between the layout of the first of the 'works' Escorts of 1968, and the last magnificent RS models of 1979. For whereas an 'homologation special' rally car of the 1960s tended to retain its standard mass-production body shell and basic suspensions, the Supercars of the late 1970s and early 1980s used little more than the basic structure of the machines from which they were developed. It was Ford, in 1970, who started the 16-valve band wagon rolling (in the RS1600), after which every competitive car really needed 4-valve cylinder heads to stay in the race. Fiat used acres of bolt-on glass-fibre panels to lighten their 131 Abarth shells, and that process is still being adopted by rival teams. If the regulations of the 1980s permit it, turbocharged engines may well be necessary. In any case, it certainly looks as if specialized, low-production, mid-engined cars might prove the winning combination in the 1980s.

All this, of course, is typical of the way that the rallying scene has been transformed in the last 20 or 30 years. Cars, drivers and financial involvement have changed out of all recognition. At the end of the 1950s, for instance, it was rare for any driver to command a sizeable fee for his services, and many drove for nothing but meagre expenses; in 1980 it is rumoured that the first £100,000-a-year professional drivers have arrived.

In the 1950s, too, it was still possible for a factory to campaign lightly modified mass-production cars with great success: Rootes, with their Rapiers, Citroen with their DS19s, and Mercedes with their 220SEs are all perfect examples. By the end of the 1970s it was essential to have a specialized (and *very* sophisticated) car for every type of event, to stand a chance of winning, and, if possible, a specialized driver as well. A strong but standard car could no longer win, or even be entered for any of the classic rough-road rallies against respectable opposition. Back at the beginning of the 1970s Ford found they had misjudged the pace of the Safari with the best of their Twin-Cam Escorts (and needed a lot more power to win the following year). Later in the decade there was nothing very 'showroom' about the Datsuns which performed so well in Africa and Australasia.

Rallying has now been in existence for more than 80 years, and at top level it is still a growing international sport. It used to be said of emergent nations that one of their first priorities was to establish a new airline; nowadays they seem equally anxious to set up their own Grand Prix and promote a major international rally! This explains the inception, during the 1970s, of a World Rally Championship, recognized not only by Europe but by the whole world of motoring; and this is why the World Champion rally driver is now acclaimed as a true superstar.

Not that this should mislead the reader. The glamour and excitement of modern rallying is still more to do with cars and drivers than with events. No true enthusiast can fail to respond to the excitement and colourful urgency of a modern international event, the sheer technical élan and bravado of a world-class Scandinavian,

or the thrilling sight and sound of a well-driven Stratos in full cry.

Nevertheless, I promise you (not merely because I have read about it but because I have also been lucky enough to see it), that the spectacle of a big Healey going flat-out or of Ian Appleyard's inspired use of a Jaguar XK120, once brought the same familiar tingles to the back of my scalp. The Monte-winning cars of the 1940s and 1950s may look relatively drab and elephantine today; but that's not important, since they were right for their time. No matter what form it has taken, rallying has always been an enthralling and demanding business.

I am eagerly looking forward to the new rally car of the 1980s. Will the next 'winner' be something like a turbocharged mid-engined car, a four-wheel-drive model, or something technically sophisticated backed by a large concern? Whatever develops – whether it is what we now know as 'Group 5' or perhaps even 'Group 1' – the rallying scene will surely be as exciting and unpredictable as ever.

The cars, the people and the events may change, but the sport itself provides continuity. Rallying was *the* sport when I was a schoolboy. Later on I became a participant and it has interfered with my private and business life for the past 30 years. Will I still be as committed and involved when the 21st century dawns? I hope so.

GRAHAM ROBSON

1 | The Rallying Pioneers

It is easy to pinpoint the date and location of the world's first motoring competition but less simple to identify the first rally. The problem is not one of research but of definition; it all depends, of course, on what we mean by the term 'rally' – something which has exercised the more analytical motoring enthusiasts for generations. In the 1950s and 1960s, for instance, the fact that certain long-distance events bore a strong resemblance to the town-to-town races of the 1900s did not trouble anyone. Some of the most demanding endurance events in Britain and Europe were called 'trials', but by almost any modern definition they were unquestionably rallies. Even in the 1970s, when the trans-continental marathon events matured, it was difficult to distinguish between a race described as a rally (London–Mexico or London–Munich), and a virtual rally officially called a race (such as the Argentinian road races).

One thing, however, is absolutely certain. As soon as motor cars were put on sale, competitions began to be promoted. That was inevitable, for *homo sapiens* has always been a competitive animal. Races on foot, on horseback, in chariots, in ships or even in trains, have underlined the same thing – that personal athletic contests do not satisfy his desire to establish a 'pecking order'.

The first properly organized motor contest of all time was the *Concours des Voitures sans Chevaux* (literally, a test for horseless carriages), promoted by the French newspaper *Le Petit Journal* in 1894, which ended with an 80-mile reliability run from Paris to Rouen and back. According to the regulations, it was supposed to be a 'trial' of the type that later came to be known as a rally. There was, however, one major snag: although it was not designed as a speed contest, most of the competitors made a race of it!

On that occasion, the fastest time between the two cities was set up by the Comte de Dion, driving a steam-powered device, who achieved a mere 11.6mph average speed. Although that may not sound very exhilarating, it was, after all, the first motoring event ever, and considered a great achievement for its day. The really significant outcome, however, was that during the event four of the eight steam-powered machines broke down completely, while all 13 of the new-fangled petrol-powered cars finished the course.

Out of this affair grew the Automobile Club de France, and it was not long before the administrative home of world motor sport was also established in Paris, where, sometimes in an atmosphere of considerable acrimony, it has remained ever since. Setting up the governing body in France was logical enough, as most of the early, very primitive production cars were being built in that country (even though it was Benz and Daimler, both in Germany, who had separately developed the world's first motor cars), and many of the newly introduced motor-sporting events took place there.

The world's first official motor race was staged in July 1895, on the open public highway, over the formidable racing distance of 732 miles from Paris to Bordeaux and back. The hero of that event, unquestionably, was Emile Levassor, who drove a staid-looking, upright 4hp Panhard et Levassor, without rest or relief driver. The race took no less than $48\frac{3}{4}$ hours, of which only 22 minutes were spent in involuntary stops. Levassor, who was perched up high, completely exposed, on a car virtually without suspension and certainly with no weather protection, covered the distance 8 *hours* faster than the next competitor, averaging an overall 15mph.

The roads throughout were loose, unmade and often appallingly dusty, and Levassor had to battle his way through two periods of darkness with virtually no form of guiding illumination. Officially, it might have been a race, but it certainly has the look of a splendid marathon rally run!

Next we must turn our attention to Britain, to a welcome change in the original anti-motoring climate of public opinion and to the events of the legendary 'Emancipation Day' of 14 November 1896. To commemorate an alteration to the law (finally abandoning the

Emancipation Day, November 1896, when phenomenal public interest was shown in the first-ever London–Brighton run. There is one car in the foreground, but it is significant that every other vehicle in the street is either man-powered (bicycles) or horse-drawn

requirement for a man to be employed to walk ahead of the earliest 'autocars', thus warning the public of the approach of these dangerous inventions) and – it must be stressed – to publicize his motoring products, that commercial adventurer Harry Lawson asked his own Motor Car Club to organize an 'Emancipation Run' from London to Brighton.

This first British trial or rally proved a real damp squib of an event. The occasion offered spectacle, chaos, farce *and* sharp practice (as was often the case when Lawson was involved), and many prominent pioneering British motorists boycotted the affair. By all accounts, several cars which reached the finish at Brighton never

started from London; on the other hand, several cars which began the day under their own power, ended it at Brighton on the train. For all that, it made headlines and certainly celebrated, with some style, the arrival of relatively unfettered motoring in Britain. It was the first British long-distance event and was undoubtedly a form of rally. Happily, the successors to this run are still held every November.

For some time, however, the London–Brighton run remained something of an isolated event, a one-year wonder, not being taken up in Europe, where the sporting accent was firmly on the tremendously stirring, red-blooded town-to-town races. Because the latter were held on normal roads from which other traffic was not wholly banned, and because they went directly from one place to another (rather than lapping a circuit), they were really 'rallies' even though they were called 'races', but with the accent on all-out speed rather than reliability. There was no question, for example, of maintaining a target average speed; the challenge was merely to get from place to place as fast as possible.

As the power and durability of the cars increased and as the size of engines grew, speeds in these town-to-town races rose rapidly and spectacularly. Paris–Bordeaux–Paris, remember, had been won at 15mph. A year later, in 1896, Paris–Trouville was won at 28.2mph, and by 1900 the Paris–Bordeaux 'classic' was won at 48.4mph, a 300 percent increase in a mere five years. In 1902, Marcel Renault showed that a car of his family's own design could not only last the course but also perform better than any other car with a larger engine, when it completed the mountainous Paris–Vienna road race in just over 26 hours, at a running average of nearly 39mph. This event surely had the makings of a long-distance rally with a vengeance, for in addition to showing endurance and speed, the cars had to cope with the rough surfaces and twisting routes of Switzerland and Austria.

A year later, in 1903, came the Paris–Madrid race, which changed everything. Public interest in this type of motor sport was by now so intense that the run from Paris to Bordeaux was watched by tens of thousands of milling, uncontrollable spectators. In the dust of a hot summer's day, tragedy was almost inevitable. Between Paris and Bordeaux, 342 racing miles,

there were literally dozens of accidents, and at least 15 fatalities involving competing crews and spectators. The outcry was immediate. The race was stopped at Bordeaux, the cars were unceremoniously dragged by horses to the railway station, and Gabriel's stupendous 65.3mph drive in the 60hp Mors remained a sad criterion by which all turn-of-the-century races came to be judged.

It was also a signal to promoters and car manufacturers that they would have to turn their attention to other types of motor sport, more acceptable to public opinion and the authorities. For many years to come, motor racing would either have to be held on tracks or on road circuits specially closed for the occasion. The open road would only be available for reliability trials, with high speeds either suppressed or carefully disguised.

In the meantime, rallying as we know it had effectively begun, in Britain, with the Thousand Miles Trial of 1900. Organized by Claude Johnson (later to achieve lasting fame with

One of the brand-new 45hp Daimlers, all ready to compete in the 1906 Herkomer Trial. The owner was Mr R. Stotesbury. Surely those lady passengers, well cocooned against the dust, were not proposing to act as co-drivers?

A big four-seater Mercedes tourer competing in one of the speed tests included in the route of the 1908 Prince Henry trial

Rolls-Royce but then secretary of the Automobile Club of Great Britain), it was virtually a forerunner of the RAC Rally, for the AC of GB was shortly to be rechristened the Royal Automobile Club. Compared with the London–Brighton run of 1896, which had been a flop, and an over-publicized flop at that, the Thousand Miles Trial of 1900 was an enormous success. Britain, by this time, had a fledgling motor industry, even if some firms and their supporters were more sound and fury than substance, which partly explains why there were 200 tentative entries but only 65 actual cars starting. Among these 65 cars, however, were several examples of what we would now call 'works' teams.

The date that really matters, therefore, is 23 April 1900, when the event got under way from Hyde Park Corner in London. The star-studded list of drivers or entrants included notable personalities like the Hon C. S. Rolls, Herbert Austin, George Lanchester, Charles Jarrott, S. F. Edge, Alfred Harmsworth (of Fleet Street fame) and J. D. Siddeley, the future Lord Kenilworth.

Although there were 11 running days in the event, the longest single sector was from Edinburgh to Newcastle. The route, in outline, was mainly over unsurfaced roads (even if they *were* nominally main roads they were still something of a challenge), taking in Bristol, Birmingham, Manchester, Kendal, Carlisle, Edinburgh, Newcastle, Leeds, Bradford, Sheffield, Lincoln, Nottingham, and a final run to the Princes Skating Club in London.

The Thousand Miles Trial was not just a reliability tour, for the target average speeds were 12mph in places (which was *very* sporting, for that was as high as any instantaneous speed allowed anywhere in Great Britain!), and there were special trials over sections of road in the Lake District, southern Scotland and Derbyshire, with a genuine flat-out speed trial on the private roads of the Welbeck estate in Nottinghamshire.

It was the intrepid Hon Charles Rolls (later to found Rolls-Royce Ltd) whose Panhard was fastest at Welbeck, where his car achieved a sparkling 42.55mph. Rolls, in fact, was also the outright winner of the Trial and won the Gold Medal. It was a tough event, and only 23 of the 65 starters managed to complete the course. Two new marques which did much to further their reputations were Daimler (who won the team

It was all so different 75 years ago – this is the Scottish 2000 Mile Trial of 1907, and the road section is Devils Elbow

prize) and Wolseley (for whom Herbert Austin was then technical chief and one of the team drivers), while Napier and Lanchester were also prominent.

The Thousand Miles Trial, however, was not an unqualified success, for it attracted the kind of comment from unbelievers which is familiar to modern rallying enthusiasts. In particular, there was complaint about speeds, not only those achieved on the open road but also the target averages which had been set. Not unreasonably, people wanted to know how the target average could be 12mph when this was also the British overall speed limit. The immediate result was that British trials had to be organized with rather lower target speeds, and even though the overall speed limit rose to 20mph in 1903, tradition ensured that no British trial or rally would be won 'on the road' for the next 40 or 50 years.

In 1901, therefore, the AC of GB announced that if they were to organize another long trial, it would either have to be in Ireland or on the continent of Europe. A 1200 mile event was suggested, from London to Bordeaux via Southampton, Le Havre and Paris (with a stop-over in Bordeaux to watch the Gordon-Bennett race), but nothing came of it. The Club had difficulty, indeed, in organizing any kind of trial, for their 1902 proposal to arrange a 650-mile event, as a series of 'out-and-back' runs from Crystal Palace to southern coastal resorts, also fizzled out at the discussion stage. It was not until September 1903, by which time the speed limit laws had been eased, that another 'Thousand Miles Trial' was held. This followed the suggested 1902 pattern, with eight daily 'out-and-back' runs, centred on Crystal Palace. The main competitive criterion was that cars were to complete each day's run non-stop, or be penalized accordingly, and AC of GB observers were carried to ensure this. The primitive cars, however, did not prove all that reliable; of the 104 that started, only four managed to complete the entire event without an involuntary halt of any nature.

The Scottish Automobile Club (which in due course became the RSAC) envisaged sterner stuff than this, and in 1902 set up the stiff challenge of a two-stage 'non-stop' trial from Glasgow to London, split only by a night halt in York. In deference to the law of the land, the target average speed was only about 11mph. Endurance and dogged determination, however, were the main requirements. The 'time permitted for the Glasgow–York run (by way of Carlisle and Scotch Corner) was 22hr 50min; the rather more straightforward York–London run was allowed 18hr 20min. Perhaps because of this, the event (held in April) attracted only five competitors, of whom three finished; honours went to the De Dion driven by Stocks and Talbot-Crosbie.

Britain's sporting motorists responded better to the Scottish club's event in subsequent years, for the 1903 trial attracted 22 cars and the 1904 trial 29. In 1903 seven motorcyclists had entered

A line up of cars for the legendary 1000 Miles Trial of 1900. The driver of the car A17, a 12hp Panhard, was the Hon. C. S. Rolls

as well, but this category was dropped as it was almost impossible to observe their 'non-stop' abilities over long distances. In 1904 the overnight break was placed at Leeds, and there was a standing-start hill-climb test on Woodcock Hill, now better known as the A411, between Elstree and Stirling Corner on the Great North Road, to establish a final classification.

It is clear that organizers were already trying to give everyone an equal chance, for the incredibly complex formula used to assess performance on the hill-climb test involved the car's weight, gearing, engine size and diameter of road wheels! By now, however, some form of eliminating test was certainly needed, for 'non-stop' certificates were awarded to eight entrants, and it was with a touch of pride that

The Autocar, reporting the event, commented that all eight were petrol-driven vehicles – from which it may be assumed that the august journal did not approve of 'steamers'!

There were, too, interesting signs of activity from overseas. At the end of the year the Motor Union of Western India organized an 880-mile trial, starting from Delhi and finishing at Bombay. Featuring a run on Christmas Day, it was mainly comprised of 'non-stop' observation mileage, but also included driving tests, something known as motor musical chairs ('which requires no description', as *Autocar* whimsically commented), and a so-called Gretna Green affinity race in which 'competitors had to drive to a given point where each was given an envelope with the name of the lady he had to

bring back in his car, the ladies being hidden in bushes two hundred yards away . . .'.

India was obviously not yet ready for *serious* rallying. Europe, however, undoubtedly was. With the demise of the town-to-town trans-European races, trials began to come into their own. The term 'rally' had not yet been invented, but the German Herkomer Trophy event, held in Bavaria in August 1905, certainly showed all the familiar features of a rally as we know it. The event's full and ponderous title was the 'International Herkomer Competition for Touring Cars', for which Professor Hubert von Herkomer had offered a personally designed trophy. A renowned artist, he also proposed painting portraits of the winners of each of the five events involved.

The Herkomer Trophy was to be no ordinary reliability trial. It included a road section of 1000 kilometres, occupying more than three days and encompassing Munich, Baden-Baden, Nuremberg and Regensburg, plus speed trials and a speed hill-climb in the week-long itinerary. There was a specified route, frequent controls and carefully defined target averages. The whole event was subject to such complex regulations that many competitors could hardly understand what they were expected to achieve, and there seemed to be as much arguing with officials and post-event negotiating as there was actual motoring.

Things were little better in 1906, but this did not seem to deter competitors. In 1905 there had been 102 starters, but on this occasion 133 crews faced the starter at Frankfurt-on-Main in June. The entry was notable not only for the presence of Prince Henry of Prussia (in a Benz) and Victor Lancia (in a 24hp Fiat), but also for a 13-car British entry, comprising a round dozen Daimlers, mainly 'works' sponsored, and a single Argyll. The rules regulating car entries were interpreted very liberally when it suited the organizers, which may explain why Hieronimus was allowed to start in a 90hp two-seater racing Mercedes, and why several German crews appeared to have cars with extremely skimpy and non-standard bodies.

The 1906 itinerary took competitors through Bavaria and much of Austria, and it included famous passes such as the Brenner, a hill-climb at Semmering, and speed tests in Forstenrieder Park near Munich. One regulation required all cars to climb the Semmering road with four passengers, or with an equivalent amount of

A smoky start from Paris for one of the very first pre-First War Monte Carlo Rallies. There isn't much interest from spectators

sandbagging. As H. Massac Buist, the distinguished motoring writer of the day, commented: '. . . as there was no check as to whether the ballast was being carried at the finish, one was not surprised to come across sandbags at the side of the road at various stages on the way up . . . .'

For British competitors the final straw came at the speed test near Munich, when it was realized that the handicap formula required the 45hp Daimlers to reach more than 160mph (and the 90hp Mercedes over 200mph) to beat Dr Stoess's small 18hp Horch which, as a result, easily won the Trophy. The best British placing was tenth by Grigg's 35hp Daimler, which was more favourably handicapped, while Mrs Edward Manville took eleventh place, and as the only lady competitor in the event became the first ever winner of a well-deserved *Coupe des Dames*. The whole thing, however, was so devoid of natural justice that the magisterial Buist commented: 'I am in a position to state that the British team, that has been so kindly welcomed and whose going over was rightly deemed by the committee to be a great honour, will be conspicuous by its absence next year.'

And so it was. The Herkomer, which had promised to become a major European trial, degenerated into nothing more than a glorified national event, dominated by cars from Opel, Mercedes, and Benz, not to mention the 18hp Horch with which Dr Stoess had won the 1906 Trophy. Rather late for credibility, the rules regarding lightweight or 'temporary' bodies were tightened up. Several cars were eliminated for having unpainted shells, while the Opel and Adler 'works' machines, initially thrown out for having lightweight coachwork, were reinstated after agreeing to carry ballast throughout. Would this concession have been made to foreigners? Observers thought not.

In the meantime, the Scottish AC's trial went from strength to strength, for in 1905 it took on the pattern which would remain familiar until the 1960s – a tour over several days of the spectacular and demanding Highlands, including hill-climbs and other tests intended to produce results not assured by the sheer slog over roads which were not made up until the end of the 1920s. Forty-three cars faced a four-day event, which started from the club's famous headquarters in Blythswood Square, Glasgow, took in night halts at Dundee, Aberdeen and Pitlochry, and finished back in Glasgow.

The roads themselves – even so-called 'main roads' like that connecting Aviemore in the north with Pitlochry in the south – were often in loose and evil condition, and speed hill-climb tests were thrown in to pose more serious problems at Cairnwell Hill (near the Spital of Glenshee), at the Devil's Elbow, and at Loch-na-Craig, near Aberfeldy. Even by 1905, however, rally cars were becoming more reliable. In four days only seven cars were forced to retire,

several recorded 'non-stop' runs throughout, and the event had to be decided by the hill-climbs. Fastest of all was Tom Thornycroft, driving one of his own 24hp models, in a performance which upset at least one reporter enough to remark that the winner '. . . did not appear to err on the side of carefulness or consideration'. Aggressive driving, it seems, was not invented in recent years.

Throughout Europe, however, it was rapidly becoming evident that cars were by now too sturdy and reliable to be sorted out by simple road sections. It has often been pointed out that design engineers spent the first years of the 20th century simply making cars go, but that thereafter they made them go beautifully. More difficult events, or entirely different types of event would be required in order to satisfy everyone. There was to be much controversy about it all in the ensuing years – a period that saw, on the one hand, the appearance of *true* endurance rallies and on the other, the proliferation of *Concours d'Élégance* events. Which would prove more popular?

Competitors in the Glasgow–London Trial of 1902, in the courtyard of a British hotel at the start of the day's run

2 | Rallying at Speed or Rallying in Style?

The Herkomer Trials, although ultimately unsuccessful, had not been promoted in vain. They were, after all, the first real international trials of any stature, and they certainly sparked off discussion about the future form of long-distance events for road cars. In addition, their promise *and* their mistakes inspired Prince Henry of Prussia to do better.

Prince Henry had competed without success in the 1906 Herkomer Trial, expressing disapproval of the complex regulations and unfair handicap, and being appalled at the way in which unscrupulous works drivers attempted to get round them. The prince was not only an aristocrat, a great sportsman and a talented driver, but also a fervent patriot, and as such he was not prepared to see Germany's sporting reputation damaged by the Herkomer's shortcomings. Before the end of 1907, therefore, he enlisted the aid of the Imperial Automobile Club of Germany, collected trophies and money prizes from all sides, and announced that the *Prinz Heinrich Fahrt* (Prince Henry Trial) would be held in June 1908. It was to be the first of several 'Prince Henry Tours' in which factory cars competed and which gave rise to several models carrying its name.

The 1908 event, a milestone in more ways than one, started from Berlin and finished in Frankfurt-on-Main; and the seven daily runs passed through towns such as Stettin, Kiel and Hamburg. Compared with the Herkomer Trials, the rules were simple but nonetheless strict. Club observers were carried in each car, which had to be four-up during the speed tests and at least three-up at all other times. Engine sizes (and, indirectly, their power) were limited by a rule restricting cars to four-cylinder or six-cylinder units, with an absolute maximum piston area of 679 sq cm. (For comparison, the piston area of a 2.0-litre Escort RS was 254 sq cm.) Marks were lost for unreliability (involuntary stoppage, replenishment of cooling water, and other details), while there were speed and hill-climb tests to produce a final result.

The first event was a great success, with 130 cars facing the starter on 9 June. One interesting condition, designed to preclude the building of special 'competition only' cars, was that all machines had to certify that they had completed more than 2000km before the start of the event. As a cynic might have predicted, this did not work, and it became obvious that an event framed for 'touring cars driven by gentlemen' was being dominated by professionals in near-racing cars. So what is new about homologation arguments and the use of highly paid drivers in the 1970s?

Indeed, it was Fritz Erle, driving a factory-prepared 50hp Benz tourer, who won that first Prince Henry tour outright – a man who was already in charge of that company's racing department and who would stay with the firm until his retirement in the 1930s. Poegge's Mercedes took second place, with Paul's Adler third. Erle's car was not only reliable but also fastest on all the speed tests.

There was no way, it seemed, of eliminating disguised racing cars from the Prince Henry trials, which were held on only three occasions entirely in Germany. A glance at the famous names in the last of those events, the 1910 trial run from Charlottenburg to Hamburg, is illuminating: once again Erle was present in a Benz, Dr Ferdinand Porsche had one of his Austro-Daimlers, Jenatzy had a Mercedes, while Percy Kidner and A. J. Hancock drove 'Prince Henry' Vauxhalls. Porsche's very fast and special Austro-Daimler won the event, hardly surprising since Porsche had designed it specifically for the purpose. Fischer's almost identical car was second, Henney's Benz third, and Erle's Benz was also well placed.

Although there was one other Prince Henry Tour, in 1911, it was an entirely different event. Taking in Germany and Great Britain, it was really no more than a lengthy, leisurely and highly prestigious holiday trip for 60 selected

Famous driver and famous car. Dr. Ferdinand Porsche, driving the 'works' Austro-Daimler to victory in the 1910 Prince Henry Trial

crews. Prince Henry was related to King George V, whose Coronation was taking place that year; so it seemed appropriate that something like a goodwill tour should be arranged.

In the meantime, those interested in motoring for sport rather than motoring for style, had found new pursuits, one in the form of the first wintry marathon trek to Monte Carlo, the other, the exciting run through the Austrian mountains. Although the Monte would achieve everlasting fame, the Alpine Trial was to prove of greater significance.

The first Alpine Trial of all held in 1909, had been a parochial affair, but the 1910 event was thrown open to foreign crews, and encompassed a four-day route from Vienna to Radstedt, Klagenfurt, and Graz before returning to Vienna, a total of 530 miles. In the years that followed, it became one of the original mountain-storming classics. It was, to some extent, the model for the Alpine Trials of the 1930s, and it was a real test of car reliability, agility and performance. Austria was then a larger country than it is today, embracing most of the Dolomite

areas and the coastal region near Trieste which now belongs to Jugoslavia. In the 1913 trial, for example, cars were faced with an assault on famous passes such as the Tauern, Katschberg, Brenner, Rolle, Pordoi, Falzarego, Wurzen, Predil and Loibl – any of which were still being described as difficult by rally drivers in the 1950s. Cars, of course, had now become so much stronger, faster and sturdier than those built a mere ten years earlier, that this sort of route was needed to achieve a definite result. In 1914, incidentally, the route was different but no less difficult, and even included a timed climb of the notorious Turracher Hohe, which was incredibly steep, rough, loose-surfaced *and* pitted with cross-gullies; even as late as the 1950s, when it was used as a section in the French Alpine rally, there were complaints that it was still too tough.

Every year the Austrian Alpine trial became more demanding – a supreme test of cars, driving and the craft of rallying. Until the 1920s it was the most difficult in the world. By 1914, when it took place only weeks before the outbreak of the First World War, it had expanded to take in 1800 miles of mountain roads in a week-long contest and included no fewer than 19 tests of speed and reliability on passes which became bywords among the sporting fraternity

James Radley's magnificent performance, in the 1914 Alpine Trial, in an 'Alpine Eagle' Rolls-Royce 40/50hp, must rank as one of the epic performances of all time. In every way, he put up best overall performance

throughout Europe. There were severe penalties for servicing or replenishing the car at unauthorized points. It was so tough that works teams came from all over Europe to prove their worth – some more successfully than others.

Rolls-Royce, of all people, thought it necessary to enter a team of cars in 1913, partly because a privately entered car driven by James Radley had failed the Katschberg hill-climb test in 1912, due to the overall gearing being too high. The 1913 Rolls-Royce Silver Ghosts – known as 'Alpine Eagles' because of their very special nature – were developed with revenge in mind, having evolved from continental tests carried out by the factory engineers after the 1912 debacle. Compared with Radley's 1912 car, the Alpine Eagles had more than 150 care-

fully developed modifications, including major items such as a new four-speed gearbox, and delightful minor touches like the steam-water separator in the form of a polished tower mounted on top of the radiator cap. No detail was spared, even though the Silver Ghost had already proved its worth in 1907 with flawless performances, in quick succession, in the Scottish 2000 Miles Trial, the 750-mile Scottish Reliability Trial, and a 15,000 mile open-road observed endurance run, all by the same car!

The three 1913 team cars were driven by E. W. Hives (later to become the company's chairman), Jock Sinclair (a test driver), and C. C. Friese, who was based at the company's Vienna workshops. James Radley was also supplied with an identical chassis and ran once again as a private owner.

The result testified to the diligence of the engineers at Derby. One car – that of Friese – completed the gruelling event without loss of marks, while that of Hives lost a single mark, because the driver accidentally stalled the engine

*Capt. Von Esmark's Durkopp car in the 1912
Monte Carlo Rally*

on the exit from a *parc fermé* after a night halt.
The hapless Sinclair finished the event with
penalty, partly due to a damaged gearbox incurred when his car was rammed by a non-
competing Minerva in Wiener Neustadt.

Friese's Rolls-Royce was one of nine cars of
the huge entry which was completely unpenalized, and was awarded a silver medal for
the feat. However, it was a team of three Audis,
driven by Lange, Graumuller and Obruba,
which won the team prize, all three being unpenalized. Other unpenalized cars included a
Minerva-Knight, a Horch, a Laurin-Klement,
a Raba and a Benz.

It was enough for Rolls-Royce, who promptly
withdrew from competition. Radley, however,
who had been penalized in the 1913 event when
his car would not start after a night out in the
open at more than 4000 feet, took along the
same machine in 1914 and set up an outstanding

performance in a field of no less than 78 competitors, including teams of all the top Europeans.
That 1914 entry list is almost a 'Who's Who?'
of Edwardian thoroughbreds, with teams from
Fiat, Minerva, Darracq, Austro-Daimler, Audi,
Puch, Hansa, N.A.G., Benz and others. Mercedes would probably have entered, too, but
had their hands full with preparation for the
French Grand Prix at Lyons.

Radley, in true 1960s 'professional' style, con-
ducted a recce of the sections he did not like,
especially the Turracher Hohe, which seems to
have caused as much concern before the start as
the most horrifying stage or speed test in a
latter day Monte or Liège–Sofia–Liège. It was
time well-spent, for the Rolls-Royce was the
fastest and most reliable car in the event.
Radley, starting from number five, was invariably running at the head of the field. Not only
was he first on the road, but fastest on the
Katschberg hill-climb (sweet revenge after his
failure in 1912!) and on the 5-kilometre speed
trial, in which his big car averaged nearly

69mph. A glance at the results, obligingly printed in full by *The Autocar*, shows that Radley's Rolls-Royce was one of 16 cars to finish without penalty, several of the others being Audis, which had performed so well in the previous year, though the Rolls-Royce was the only large-engined car to keep up with the schedules.

It is hard to imagine how very forbidding the Alpine Trial must have seemed to competitors and observers of the period, but the pictures that survive tell their own story. Not only were the mountain passes every bit as difficult as they look, but their surfaces were almost all loose (and slippery, if the weather was bad). The cars, though infinitely more reliable and lively than at the beginning of the Herkomer Trial period, were still open tourers (which must have made life miserable in any conditions less than ideal), and most were very hard sprung and none too comfortable when being driven four-up, as the regulations demanded.

To complete up to 250 miles a day for 10 days, with only two of those days allocated to rest, and to tackle a total of 27 named passes, many of which were timed, or at least observed for a non-stop performance, demanded real stamina of car and crew. It is true that there was a scheduled night's rest after every run, but the cars were left to stand out in the open. Remem-

M. Maidee's taper-bonneted Delage, rallying to Monte Carlo in great comfort in 1912

ber that in 1914 there was no such thing as an electric starter motor, nor were crews allowed to lift the bonnet to make cold starting adjustments before leaning on the starting handles. The life of tyres was still somewhat suspect, even on the most patrician of cars, and mending a puncture often meant not simply taking off the wheel but changing the tyre on a fixed rim. Cars such as the big Rolls-Royce weighed well over two tons, had no power assistance to the steering and were equipped only with rear brakes. Lights were more for decoration than for effect (not that this mattered very much on the Austrian Alpine, which had no night sections and was held in June), and closed cars with their attendant creature comforts were never used. Although I am full of admiration for the pace, bravery and skills of the modern rallying superstars, I challenge anyone to dispute that the heroes who tackled mountain rallying in the 1910s were in any way inferior.

The overall pace, of course, was very different in those days, not only because the cars themselves were much slower and heavier, but because the organizers intended it to be that way. It was not always a competitive disaster if a few seconds, or even a few minutes, were lost in a mishap. Schedule average speeds of up to 20mph were, admittedly, pretty difficult in mountainous areas but could be beaten easily elsewhere. There usually seemed to be time enough for a bite to eat at controls. Service cars and trade support were quite unknown, even among the

factory-sponsored teams; indeed, the whole business was friendlier and run in a more genuinely amateur spirit.

Meanwhile, however, the world's first 'rally' had been promoted. It had taken nearly 20 years for the term to be employed, and it was first applied to an event with very little competitive character. For strictly commercial reasons, the Société des Bains de Mer, in Monaco, had invented the 'Rallye Automobile vers Monte Carlo'. The authorities of the tiny principality of Monaco had realized not only that there were more and more motor cars being built but that their little country was very short of custom in the winter months between January and March. The rally was thus designed to attract rich motoring enthusiasts to the Mediterranean at a time of year when they were most needed.

The first Monte of all time, therefore, was a very leisurely event, something of a 'go-as-you-please' contest, with starting points at Paris, Geneva, Boulogne, Vienna, Brussels and Berlin. All cars were asked to rally to Monaco on 28 January 1911, but there were no intermediate controls. As an example, the distance from Berlin to Monaco was quoted as 1055 miles, for which 7 days 2 hours were allowed; the overall target average speed was 10kph (6.2mph), which allowed plenty of time for the drivers and their chauffeurs to eat and sleep in hotels along the way.

Despite the novelty of the challenge and the ease of the schedule, only 23 entries were received and only 20 cars actually started. Then, as later, the French took the keenest interest in the event, so there was great rejoicing when the winner, chosen as much for the magnificence of his car as for its performance, proved to be Henri Rougier, who had used a French Turcat Mery car fitted with a lofty limousine body.

A year later there was a much larger entry – 90 cars, of which 60 actually started. In 1912 there were nine starting points, the winning and second-place cars both setting off from Berlin (then, as later, in an event where ice and snow could affect road conditions, choice of starting point could be a matter of luck). Once again the winning car was French, a Berliet, driven by Julius Beutler, while the German combination of Captain von Esmark (Durkopp – built at Bielefeld) took second place.

The Monte's problem, at this stage, was that it fell between two stools. On the one hand, it was not truly competitive, so the 'professionals'

Lt. Knapp's decorated Fiat in the 1912 Monte Carlo Rally

would not drive in it. On the other hand, it failed to persuade the rich dilettante motorists to stay in Monaco out of season; traders in the principality found to their cost that rally crews tended to disappear soon after the rally had officially finished. Certainly there was no great rush to support another event after 1912.

In 1914, of course, the assassination of the Archduke Franz Ferdinand, in Sarajevo, precipitated the outbreak of the First World War, bringing all motor sporting activities to an immediate halt. It ended the period which might now be described as the dawn of motoring and motor sport. Cars that had once struggled to keep going at all, with little pretence to performance or agility, had been replaced by magnificent machines which were not only fast, but strong and nimble into the bargain.

The period had not, however, seen any stabilization in the sport of open-road competition which we can now call rallying. In 1914, the most exciting and demanding events in Europe were those following the pattern of the International Alpine Trial, but these had already begun to be dominated by factory-supported teams using professional or semi-professional drivers.

Undoubtedly, more sporting drivers would have been interested in tackling events of this kind had they been organized, at reasonable

J. Ledure's Bignan – Monte Carlo Rally 1924

cost, in their own countries. In Britain, however, the overall speed limit of 20mph on all roads, and the anti-motoring attitude habitually demonstrated by police and judiciary, meant that nothing could possibly be organized there. The alternative – the *only* alternative – was to continue arranging reliability trials, usually entailing many miles of boring low-speed driving, a few speed tests or 'non-stop' hill-climbs and an increasing amount of rough-road motoring. After the initial novelty had worn off, it was not really surprising that interest in long-distance events such as the Scottish Reliability Trials began to wane. Indeed, the Scottish event was abandoned in 1910 due to lack of entries, and no further events were promoted until the 1920s.

After the end of the First World War, in 1918, there was, inevitably, a further long pause while things returned to normal. There were several good reasons why serious motor sporting events continued to be suspended. Long-distance trials were usually enjoyed only by the well-to-do, often providing opportunities for conspicuous high spending; and at a time of national and economic disaster, particularly in France and Germany, this type of extravagance was politically unacceptable. Furthermore, roads in many areas had been neglected or damaged and were generally in appalling condition, while the supply of new cars was very restricted until the early 1920s.

For a time, therefore, nothing much happened. In Britain, motor sport was confined to a modicum of racing at Brooklands (the only available venue), the occasional very gentle long-distance trial, and the promotion of a few *Concours d'Élégance* events at fashionable seaside resorts. On the continent of Europe, where there had been so much more damage and suffering, all was chaos for a while. The Austrian economy was in no state to support the revival of the famous Alpine Trial, and the Monte Carlo Rally appeared to have been dropped. Conditions in Germany were so bad in every respect, but particularly in the financial sphere, that the country's battered car industry could underwrite only a little motor racing. While Mercedes were building cars to enter, and win, the Targa Florio long-distance races of the early 1920s, they could raise no enthusiasm for trials.

Not everything, however, was quite the same as before, for the French now invented a demanding long-distance event designed to suit their roads and their new cars – the Paris–Nice Trial. This linked the nation's capital with one of its most fashionable Mediterranean resorts, took advantage of the fact that there was a network of fine roads (some in the plains, some in the mountains) which had not been damaged by the war, and recognized the emergence of a whole series of fine French *Grande Tourisme* cars – from concerns like Delage, Delahaye, Hotchkiss, Voisin and Chenard-Walcker.

Compared with the Monte Carlo Rally, which had still not been revived, Paris–Nice was an altogether more exacting test of man and machine. For French sporting enthusiasts it temporarily replaced the Monte. Nice, incidentally, was no stranger to motor sporting events, for it had staged Speed Weeks at the very beginning of the century, the 1901 event being noted for the sensational first appearance of the Mercedes 60hp car.

The Paris–Nice organizers did not at first require high-speeds from competitors, but were sticklers for absolute reliability. In 1923, for instance, the 758-mile route was split into four days' running, each divided into morning and afternoon sessions. That may not sound too bad, even at a target average speed of 25mph, but the real catch was that almost every conceivable mechanical component (including engine and transmission) was sealed, as was the bonnet, before the start. This meant that the cars had to tackle several days' arduous winter driving without any attention whatsoever. Even so, a high proportion of the runners usually reached the Riviera without penalty, and further special tests (including, in 1923, that favourite of the day, a top gear slow-driving test) were necessary.

A year later, Paris–Nice was much more of a performance test. Twenty-two competitors faced the starter in Paris, with all the obligatory seals in place, and reached Nice by way of a 300-mile run to Lyons, a short three-hour dash from Lyons to Grenoble, and a final gruelling day's run to Nice through the Alpes Maritimes over the snow-covered main road passes. On that final day, apparently, many competitors decided not merely to complete the run on time but to go as fast as possible. Some of the quickest cars reached Nice less than six hours after leaving Grenoble and averaged more than 60kph (37mph) in the process.

Once at Nice, cars had to tackle cold start, turning, and slow-running tests, followed by a speed test up La Turbie hill (which was still being used by Monte Carlo Rallies of the 1960s), a kilometre sprint, and a high-speed braking test. These last two trials, incidentally, took place on the famous Promenade des Anglais at Nice, in front of all the luxurious hotels. In 1924 there were class wins for Darracq, Peugeot and Voisin,

with *The Autocar*'s revered Continental Correspondent, W. F. Bradley, in charge of one of the successful 2-litre Darracq sports cars.

It was much the same story again in 1925, when competitors treated the last day's 205-mile run from Grenoble to Nice as an impromptu winter road race. As there was a massed start from Grenoble, it was always something of a mad scramble to the top of the first big hill – the Col de la Croix Haute; and it was won on this occasion by a privately owned Darracq 14hp model, which took a mere 1hr 15min for the 42 miles, including starting up from cold and manoeuvring out of the storage garage. For 1925, that was a remarkable performance. Class winners (there was no outright winner in this event) included Bugatti, Voisin, Darracq, Georges-Irat, Lancia and Austro-Daimler.

There was little British interest, as yet, in postwar European motor sport, and at this stage in the development of long-distance road events the French were undoubtedly dominant. Participation by British works teams, even in British events, had received a severe blow in 1925, when the industry's trade body – the Society of Motor Manufacturers and Traders – had opposed any trials which could be used by the manufacturers for 'advertising'. This produced the extraordinary situation of all 'trade' entrants being ordered to withdraw from the Scottish Six Days Trial in mid-event, leaving only six genuinely private entrants to carry on to the finish. For 1926, therefore, the SMMT proposed forbidding 'trade' entries in all road trials organized in Great Britain – a move that instantly reduced them to minor and unimportant status.

Compared with what was afoot in Europe, all this was parochial. The mid-1920s saw two world-class events revived and refined, and at the start of the 1930s more events were added to the list. It is fair to say that modern rallying began, or was reborn, with the first competitive Monte Carlo Rally of 1924, and that the tradition of high-speed open-road motoring was confirmed anew with the revival of the International Alpine Trial. A pattern was about to develop.

3 | 1920s and 1930s – The Pattern Develops

By the mid-1930s, international rallies in Europe were taking on an attractive, coherent shape. Several of these events are still promoted today, even if in considerably modified form. But modern rallying, based on performance and driving ability rather than vehicle reliability and flashy styling, had begun even earlier. In my opinion the most significant year was 1925 – when the Monte Carlo Rally reverted to its traditional January date and when talks first began to convert the Alpine Trial from an Austrian event into one embracing several countries.

Throughout the 1920s, many so-called sporting motorists still liked to enter their cars for *Concours* events. Such gatherings really have no place in this book, except as a passing reference, since the accent was almost entirely on the looks of the cars and the equipment carried. To win any class of a *Concours*, a motorist merely had to buy, choose, or commission an elegantly designed body shell for his car, making sure that it was presented to the judges in the glossiest, smartest possible condition. Gimmicks were

In the Monte Carlo Rallies of the mid-1920s, the only prominent British marque was AC. This is the Hon. Victor Bruce's tourer, pictured before the start

quite acceptable and, indeed, few *Concours d'Élégance* events were ever won by standard production machines. In truth, this sort of thing was not a *motoring* event at all, as a car's road manners or capabilities were never tested in the course of the day; even a real lemon, if beautifully maintained and prepared, could win – and many did.

Cars of the 1920s (nowadays, of course, known as 'Vintage' cars), were often thoroughly reliable unless shamefully neglected, so the long-distance 'reliability trial' began to lose ground to more serious events. In Britain, events like the Exeter and Land's End Trials attracted shoals of entries but also resulted in dozens of unpenalized 'clean' sheets. Even the inclusion, later in the 1930s, of rather more freakish rough-surfaced hill-climbs, did not transform the situation. Indeed, the awards list for such an event was often reminiscent of the conclusion of the Caucus Race in Lewis Carroll's *Alice in Wonderland*: 'Everybody has won, and all must have prizes.'

The Monte Carlo Rally was actually revived in 1924, although in that year it was held in March so that the competing cars could arrive in 'Monte Carlo Week', which traditionally launched Monaco's social season. The problem was that potential entrants were far more interested in the challenge of wintry roads than in the social glitter of Monte Carlo. By March all but a few roads were absolutely clear, even of ice-patches, removing the bad-weather risk. Consequently, there were very few entries and the 1924 Monte was a complete flop. The organizers immediately took the hint. In 1925, and every year after that, the rally was held in January.

Interest was sustained as the years passed, and by the 1930s the Monte Carlo Rally was undoubtedly the most famous winter motoring event in the world. In 1925, however, it was not yet too rigidly defined. Points were awarded for the distance covered on the way to Monaco, the number of passengers carried and the average speed attained (up to a maximum of 30kph or

18.6mph). In view of the distance rule, therefore, it was no surprise that the event was won by a gargantuan 40hp Weymann-bodied Renault, driven by M. F. Repusseau, which started from Tunis in North Africa, followed the Mediterranean coast westward to Tangier, crossed by ferry to Spain and drove to Monte Carlo by way of Madrid and San Sebastian, clocking up 2400 miles on arrival. As *The Autocar* succinctly commented in its report: 'As points were given for distance covered, one point per 25 kilometres, and for the number of persons carried, the big Renault, with six aboard, had an advantage over the others.'

There were, however, disadvantages as well. At the end of the rally, there was a three-kilometre speed hill-climb up the Mont des Mules (just inland, in France), followed by a 50-mile regularity run over a circuit including the Haute Corniche, the Col de Braus, Sospel and Menton. Fastest of all up the hill was Mme Mertens's Lancia Lambda, which had also started from Tunis, but only carried two passengers. Repusseau's huge Renault, faced with the tight hairpins of the Col de Braus, reputedly had to reverse on 39 separate occasions, and lost a lot of time on the regularity run. Even so, his 'six-up' feat was just enough to give him the outright victory over the gallant Mme Mertens, and two other cars which had likewise started from Tunis were third and fourth.

There was only one all-British entry – that of the Hon Victor Bruce in a six-cylinder AC Tourer, which started from Glasgow and (because of the limited mileage covered) was placed 12th overall of the 32 competitors. His route, incidentally, which had to be declared in advance, was via Manchester, London, Folkestone, ship to Boulogne, Paris, Lyons and Avignon – 1222 miles, for which he was allowed (and achieved) 65 hours.

In 1926, the incredible happened. With no professional support, and with little preparation of any nature, Victor Bruce took another AC 2-litre tourer on the event, started from John O' Groats and won the event outright. Apart from James Radley's outstanding Rolls-Royce Silver Ghost performance in the 1914 Alpine Trial, this was the first overall win by a Briton, driving a British car, in a major European trial or rally. Most modern rallying enthusiasts know that British cars and teams dominated the Monte in the 1960s, but few realize how rarely the event has been won by a British driver. Victor Bruce's

Road rallying, abandoned for a time, returned to British roads in 1928. Donald Healey won the first event, which finished at Bournemouth, but it was F. F. Austin's Morris Cowley which won the rally which was centred on Southport in September

achievement is sometimes shrugged off as insignificant by those who look upon all 'Vintage' cars as primitive freaks, so it is worth recalling that the second all-British win occurred in 1931 (when Donald Healey used an Invicta), and that the next did not come until 1952, when Sydney Allard pulled it off in a car of his own manufacture.

Vasselle's winning Hotchkiss, pictured on arrival at Monte Carlo in 1932. Did they really drive all the way dressed like that?

A Lanchester being slung aboard the SS Maidstone, *at Folkestone, on the Monte Carlo Rally in 1933. The cross-channel trip was part of the romance of those friendly days. Also in the picture are a Lagonda and a Sunbeam*

In 1926, when Bruce won the event out of 45 starters, only 24 of whom finished, the overall target average speed had been raised to 35kph (21.7mph), but distance still featured high in the marking. Of the 18 starting points, all but three were less than 1000 miles from Monaco. John O' Groats was 1529 miles from the finish, but Bruce ought to have been comfortably out-distanced by M. E. P. Malaret (six-cylinder Darracq), who elected to start from Paris, drive to Marseilles, ship the car to Tunis, and then follow the victorious 1925 Renault's route back to Monaco. The fates, however, did not smile on him; fording a river in Spain, his engine flooded and he later had to retire when the engine seized a big-end bearing.

Bruce, in fact, tied for first place with Bus-seinne's Sizaire Frères, but beat the latter by eight points on the same Col de Braus regularity test which had been used in 1925. It is interesting to note that both cars had 2-litre engines; then, as now, this seemed about the right size for the job – not too small to be underpowered, and not too large to be overweight.

From now on, despite fairly slow acceptance at first, the Monte Carlo Rally became increasingly popular in Britain. In 1927 there were three British runners – Mrs Victor Bruce, starting from John O'Groats, Cecil May (AC) from Glasgow and Captain Francis Samuelson (750cc Ratier – smallest car in the event) from Doncaster. There were still no intermediate time controls in the itinerary, so a competitor, with luck, could make considerable gains on the schedule speeds and enjoy two, or even three short nights in bed. Mrs Bruce, for instance, was allowed about 70 hours to get from the northern tip of Scotland to the Mediterranean, that time allowance to include the crossing of the Channel.

The Bruces, incidentally, obviously changed their ACs every year, for on this occasion the sports chassis was equipped with a Weymann saloon body and carried yet another registration number. As before, the order of merit was based not only on the maintenance of a target speed but also on distance covered. Mrs Bruce's tenacious driving, in what was not at all a fast car by modern standards, was rewarded by sixth place overall (and, of course, the *Coupe des Dames*) but she was beaten, not on merit, by five other crews who had started from even farther away. The most popular, though not the most distant starting point, was Koenigsberg in East Prussia (a journey of 1638 miles), and the first three cars, led home by Lefebre-Despeaux's 1.1-litre Amilcar, all started there. On this occasion there were 52 starters and 45 finishers.

In 1928 the weather was poor (thus for rallying ideal!) but in 1929 it was by far the worst yet experienced. Starting points ranged from Lyons (322 miles to the Riviera) to Athens (2291 miles), the most popular being Riga, in Latvia (1834 miles); and 12 British crews elected to start from John O'Groats. The British individualists, incidentally, included Mrs Victor Bruce, who had chosen Riga, and Donald Healey (Triumph Super Seven) who would have started from that city had he been able to get there through the snow, but decided instead to begin his rally from Berlin! Even without the very severe weather, this particular Monte Carlo event was designed to be more rigorous than ever, as the deciding test now comprised two loops (or 100 miles) of the Col de Braus circuit.

Even in Britain, conditions were terrible – so bad that many of the competitors had a struggle even to get to John O'Groats in the first place. Only five of the 12 cars starting here reached Dover in time to catch their appointed cross-channel ferry, mainly because of the awful ice and snow layers which spread across Scotland. Mrs Bruce, co-driven as usual by her husband, but this time driving an Arrol-Aaster, was unable to reach Riga to start, and was forced, like Donald Healey to choose the Berlin start point (more than 500 miles nearer to Monte Carlo) instead.

In Europe, not only was there deep snow and ice, but vast blankets of fog to make the going tough. In the event, only 24 cars from the original entry of 93 managed to reach the finish

The first RAC Rally of all, in 1932, was distinguished by a slow-*driving test. Lt-Col. Loughborough's Lanchester, complete with fluid flywheel, took more than five minutes to complete the 100 yards of sea-front at Torquay – and won the event*

inside time limits, though stragglers continued to trickle in for days. Poor Donald Healey flogged his way across Germany, Belgium and France, had time in hand at Fréjus, but was misdirected on to the 'wrong' Corniche from Nice, arriving at his destination just two minutes too late.

Surprisingly enough, the route from one of the more 'wintry' starting points, Stockholm, was passable, if very difficult, for Dr Van Eijk, who won the event in his big American Graham-Paige, followed by Szmick's Weiss-Manfred (an obscure Hungarian car with an 875cc two-stroke engine), and Visser's Lancia. Van Eijk's drive, by all accounts, was something of an epic, for it included a roll into a field, retrieval by a team of horses and rebuilding of the battered saloon body in a local service station, followed by a frantic dash across southern Sweden to catch a ferry to Denmark. The car then had to be dug out repeatedly from snow drifts before crossing into France and heading for Monaco. Target average speeds, incidentally, had been increased once again; the highest which could be nominated by a competitor was now 40kph (24.8mph). Of the

One of Britain's truly 'professional' amateur rally drivers for many years was Tommy Wisdon, here seen hurling his Talbot up the Stelvio Pass in the Alpine Trial of 1934, with a Bugatti struggling to keep up

British crews, A. H. Pass's Sunbeam (which had started from John O'Groats) put up the best performance, with Samuelson's 18/80 MG second, and Leo Cozen's Sunbeam third.

Although Victor Bruce's AC victory of 1926 had been virtually ignored by the press – the Monte, at the time, was still making its name – there could be no overlooking Donald Healey's great triumph in 1931. It was not the redoubtable Cornishman's first important rallying success (he had, for example, already won the Brighton national rally and was a formidable competitor in all types of long-distance open-road event); and his 1930 Monte Carlo Rally performance, when he urged his Triumph Super Seven saloon into seventh place, had really been rather special. His Monte win, however, put him firmly in the limelight – a position he did not relinquish until the 1950s, when he drove his last record car.

Donald Healey must surely rank with the best British rally drivers of all time, his talent being on a par with more modern idols such as

Ian Appleyard, Peter Harper or Roger Clark. His competition career began in the 1920s when, among other things, he 'discovered' the famous Blue Hills Mine trials section for the Motor Cycling Club's use. By the 1930s he was a potential outright winner in major trials and rallies, and even in the late 1940s he was good enough to be battling for *Coupes des Alpes* in the Alpine rallies. Healey was not, however, merely a competition driver. In a brief period with Riley he helped conceive the Riley Imp/MPH/Sprite family of sports cars, he was technical chief at Triumph from 1934 to 1939, and from 1946 onwards he masterminded the production of cars carrying his own name. Every Austin-Healey (*and* every post-1961 MG Midget) owes something to the genius of this remarkable man.

Healey's big win in 1931, however, really heralded the start of his competition career as a works driver, for the $4\frac{1}{2}$-litre low-chassis Invicta was supplied by Sir Noel Macklin, who owned Invicta at Cobham. It was a difficult rally that year (most Montes of the 1930s seemed to be run in bad weather), and as Healey was not only using a starkly equipped two-seater open sports car, but also chose to start from Stavanger in Norway (2260 miles from the finish), his courage and fortitude can be imagined. Co-driven by fellow-Cornishman Lew Pearce (who would become one of his works drivers at Triumph, later in the 1930s), Healey averaged well over 30mph on the long run down from Northern Europe, set up the best time of the rally in the Mont des Mules hill-climb test and crowned it all by being fastest in the acceleration and braking test mounted on the harbour side in the picturesque port of Monaco.

It was a year when more than 120 competitors started their journeys from points as distant as Athens in Greece, Tallinn in Estonia and Lisbon in Portugal. There were 21 starters from John O'Groats, which on this occasion had a considerable disadvantage on the 'mileage' handicap, but no fewer than 30 cars started from Stavanger, where the 'distance' bonus was highest of all. It was a measure of the difficulty of winter motoring in Europe during the 1930s that 14 teams elected to start from Athens but that only seven managed to reach that city at all and none completed the rally.

This concentration on Donald Healey's performance should not detract from another fine British effort – that of Victor Leverett in a Riley Nine saloon. Leverett, like Healey, started from

In the 1930s, British rallying was still rather a leisurely business except for the driving tests. Here is George Goodall, a director of Morgan, hurling his 4/4 Morgan through a test on the sea front at Hastings in the 1937 RAC Rally

In Britain's RAC Rally of the 1930s, the most unlikely-looking cars could win awards. In 1933, Weston's P1 Rover won its class, and was fastest in this acceleration and braking test

Stavanger, nominated a running average of 35kph (21.8mph), achieved this, and triumphantly won the 1.1-litre division of the event.

By now the Monte Carlo Rally was no longer merely an adventure for the enthusiastic amateur, as several factories lent cars to silver-spoon drivers, while the 1931 entry included racing drivers such as Louis Chiron and J-P. Wimille, André Boillot, Laurie Schell, the 1928 winner Jacques Bignan (in a six-cylinder Fiat), and S. C. H. 'Sammy' Davis of *The Autocar* in a big Armstrong-Siddeley saloon. It is worth noting, incidentally, that the best overall performance (though not the fastest acceleration time) in the acceleration and braking test was set up by T. C. Mann's 'blown' 2-litre Lagonda.

The 1930s were successful and glamorous years for the Monte Carlo Rally. On more than one occasion the annual entry approached 200 cars, and while the 'handicap' system favouring the longest possible approach run to Monaco was gradually tamed down, there was no compensating increase in the amount of competitive motoring near the finish.

One must remember, of course, that in those days there were no studded tyres to conjure grip from icy surfaces, nor was it really practical to use a locked differential, so that heavy deposits of snow and ice could only be tackled successfully with chains (which often broke at higher speeds) or with shovels and a lot of brute force. In a year blessed by really wintry conditions (something for which the organizers prayed), the drivers who urged their cars to Monaco inside the time limits were real artists in car control, and as many epic drives were completed in the 1930s as have ever been notched up since.

By the beginning of the 1930s, too, the rally's *Concours de Confort* had become an important section for prestige-seeking manufacturers. This was, in fact, a cross between the *Concours d'Elégance* and the judging of special rally-style equipment. Many cars were entered with this solely in mind, though all cars had to complete the entire road section before becoming eligible, ensuring at least that they were practical and driveable machines.

The rules regarding eligibility for the rally itself, however, were not always very carefully written, with the inevitable result that cars became more freakish year by year. It was probably the irrepressible Donald Healey who started the rot in 1932, when his Invicta appeared wearing the monstrous balloon tyres on special wheels; and by 1934, when he was working at Triumph and using their cars in the competition, he was even having special bodies built as well. In 1935 he went one better, using a supercharged Triumph prototype which had not been, and never would be, put on sale. But that wasn't all, for in 1936 he used the same prototype in un-supercharged form, which made it a real one-off in every respect! In those years, incidentally, Healey finished second overall in 1932, third in 1934 in a special Triumph Gloria, crashed and wrote off the Dolomite prototype in 1935, and finished eighth in 1936. He crashed another Triumph in 1937, after which his fellow-directors at Triumph suggested that he should be with them more often. . . .

Bodywork reached such extremes in 1936 that the event was almost won by Colonel Berlescu's Ford-based special, which wrapped a much modified V8 chassis in a stark two-seater open sports body, had twin-driven rear axles, half-tracks that could be fitted at will, and wooden skis which could be attached under the front wheels! Had it not been for one mistake in

British rallies and reliability trials often included stop and re-start tests on steep hills. Godrey Imhof's Singer Le Mans is tackling such an exercise at Torquay in the 1936 RAC Rally

the driving test at the end of the event, the resourceful colonel would have won – but he was never given another chance. The rules were hastily rewritten for 1937, and only standard coachwork was allowed afterwards.

Although the target average speed of the early 'outer' road sections of the rally remained unchanged at 40kph (25mph) throughout the 1930s, it was not long before the use of precisely placed intermediate controls began to ensure that something approaching steady progress was maintained. By 1934 the last 1000 kilometres of each route were being set at 50kph (31mph), and from 1936 a feature of the last few hours from a common meeting point (Avignon in 1936 and 1937, Grenoble in 1938 and 1939) was a lengthy, strict regularity run over the mountains at averages between 50kph and 60kph (31mph and 37mph). Even in 1939, however, it was still worth 500 points to start from Athens compared with 496 marks from John O'Groats or from Umea in Sweden; since the winner was usually decided on fractional errors in regularity or in driving tests, the wrong choice of starting point could be fatal – even though the Athens route was often a gamble.

Following Healey's great win in 1931, there were high hopes of another British victory in the Montes of the 1930s, but it was not to be. The best placing was second overall in 1932 (again by Healey in an Invicta) and second overall in 1935 (by Jack Ridley, driving a works Triumph Gloria). Almost every winner started from Athens or from Stavanger, for by the end of the decade the approach routes had become relatively settled.

The 1939 event was in many ways, typical. The imposition of intermediate controls had virtually equalized the mileage between start points, with the Palermo route, by way of Ljubljana, Vienna and Dijon, being the longest, at 2542 miles. The target average for the last 1000km was 50kph, while the common meeting point was Grenoble. From Grenoble to Monaco the famous 'Winter Alpine' route was used, by way of Sisteron, Digne and Grasse, including the Col de Leques, which was to become even more noted as an eliminating test in later years. Finally, there was an acceleration and braking test on the *quai*, followed by a short flat-out hill-climb test, over one kilometre, at Eze. There were 135 entrants, of whom 38 were British.

As the decade progressed, French-built cars became more and more prominent, and it was

For British manufacturers, the team prize was a prestigious RAC Rally award to win. Singer were victorious, at Bournemouth in 1934, with sports cars driven by (left to right) the Barnes brothers, the Langley brothers, and by W. J. B. Richardson

usually French drivers who made the headlines. A young man called Jean Trevoux was co-driver of the winning Hotchkiss in 1934, finished second overall in 1938, and tied for first place in 1939, all in Hotchkiss cars. He also went on to win the 1949 and 1951 events outright, thus completing a hat-trick which was not to be matched until Sandro Munari repeated it in the 1970s.

M. Vasselle won the event twice in succession – in 1932 and 1933 – both times in Hotchkiss cars, and along with Gas's victory in 1934 this gave Hotchkiss four victories in eight years. A big Renault won once, a Delahaye twice (counting the tie for first place in 1939), and V8-engined European Fords twice. These winning performances were also backed up in depth, for Mme Schell drove Delahayes into third place in 1935 and second place in 1936, while Quatresous's Renault was also third in 1938.

By the end of the decade, the Monte Carlo Rally had become *the* motoring event most likely to interest the media – magazines, news-papers and radio stations – and a successful car could expect good publicity. Although few British manufacturers actively supported competition departments in those days, such publicity for their products did not come amiss. For that reason, many of the so-called privately entered cars had been prepared by the factories and were loaned to well-known or otherwise newsworthy competitors. In 1939, for the last prewar Monte Carlo Rally, the British works or assisted entries included a vast 25hp Wolseley limousine for B. W. Fursdon, a V12 Lagonda for Charles Brackenbury and Alan Good, a Humber Super Snipe for Lord Waleran, a Daimler for 'Sammy' Davis, a 3½-litre SS-Jaguar for Jack Harrop, a Vauxhall for Stanley Barnes, another Vauxhall for Mrs 'Bill' Wisdom, a Morris for Bill McKenzie (then, as later, one of the more knowledgeable of Fleet Street's motoring writers) and a Ford 8hp saloon for Tommy Wisdom.

The rally was not lacking in incident, for not only did Trevoux's Hotchkiss and Paul's Delahaye tie for first place at the end of the event, but they were also level even before the final hill-climb test, and both had started the event from Athens! In the end, Fursdon's Wolseley won the *Prix d'Honneur* in the coachwork competition, while the Lagonda was adjudged the best convertible in the contest.

Toughest of all the 1930s events was probably the Alpine Trial, which moved its locale from year to year. Two special-bodied Mercedes-Benz two-seaters are here seen climbing the French Galibier pass in the 1933 event

Meanwhile, however, the Monte's reputation among sportsmen, if not in the press, had been eclipsed by the rebirth of the famous Alpine Trial, and by the arrival of a new trans-European rally known as the Liège–Rome–Liège. By putting all the accent on hard motoring, pass-storming and a modicum of endurance, rather than on average-speed-keeping and driving tests, these events made the Montes look rather ordinary, even in winter weather.

The Austrian sporting authorities had not been able, during the 1920s, to restore their own Trial to the standard that had electrified the sporting world in prewar years; but they eventually had the brainwave of cooperating with neighbouring national clubs to organize an even more difficult event, incorporating not only the mountains of Austria but also those of countries such as Italy, Switzerland and France.

It was not until 1925 that their plans were made public, and next year the first International Alpine Trial (the word 'Austrian' had been dropped) was held. The 1926 event was still not up to the standard of the 1913 and 1914 events, even though the Austrian club organized the affair, but it started and finished in Milan, taking in six long stages by way of Nice, Geneva, Zurich, Munich and Merano during the first week of July. Clearly it was not difficult enough, and for 1927 various acceleration and braking trials were included in the 3000km (1860 mile) route. Thereafter, the Alpine became more and more difficult, more and more attractive to manufacturers anxious to prove the worth of their cars, and more and more famous among the best and bravest of drivers. Even in 1928, 99 cars started an event which opened in Milan and ended in Munich. In these trials the team contest was as important as that for individuals – the winning teams in 1928 being Adler, Brennabor, O.M. and Minerva. As in the Monte Carlo rallies of the period, it was Mrs Victor Bruce in an AC who put up the best British performance. Even by the standards of the Alpine Rallies of the 1940s and 1950s, incidentally, this event was no picnic, for the largest and fastest cars (Mercedes-Benz, Austro-Daimler and Hispano-Suiza) were often asked to average 50kph (31mph) over mountainous and sometimes un-surfaced roads.

The popularity of the 'Alpine' sparked off rallying interest and promotion in other coun-tries. In Italy, for example, which hosted the first International Alpines of the 1920s and was the home of the famous Mille Miglia, founded in 1927, San Remo promoted its first rally in 1928. The Alpine Trial, which became the Alpine Rally, fizzled out at the beginning of the 1970s, but the San Remo is now Italy's most important rally, and a World Championship qualifier at that.

In the 1930s, the International Alpine Trial went from strength to strength, though it naturally suffered from the political and military upheavals involving Germany and Italy towards the end of that troubled decade. Teams of cars which completed the event without penalty on the road sections were awarded a *Coupe des Alpes*, while individual clean sheets were re-warded by a *Coupe des Glaciers*. After the Second World War, the *Coupe des Glaciers* disappeared, as did the team *Coupe*, and individual clean sheets were rewarded with a *Coupe des Alpes*.

In 1932, even at the depths of the business depression hanging over Europe, more than 100 cars started the Trial from Munich. For once it was not a very destructive course, for 27 *Coupes des Glaciers* were awarded, 17 of them to British drivers in British cars. It was the year in which a team of Roesch-type Talbots, entered for the first time, won a *Coupe des Alpes* for an abso-lutely faultless performance, with the Hon Brian Lewis, Tim Rose-Richards, and Norman Garrad at the wheels. Brian Lewis (who later inherited the family title, becoming Lord Essendon) was already an established racing driver, as was Tim Rose-Richards, but Norman Garrad's claim to real fame would come after the Second World War, when he directed the fortunes of the Rootes competition department for 16 distinguished years.

From so many splendid performances it is difficult to pick out the best. Donald Healey and Charles Needham both won *Coupes* in their 4½-litre Invictas, as did all three works Arm-strong-Siddeley tourers driven by Cyril Sidde-ley himself and 'Sammy' Davis, by Humfrey Symons and by *The Autocar*'s continental correspondent W. F. Bradley. Among the smaller cars to gain *Coupes* were the 'chain-gang' Frazer Nash of H. J. Aldington, Mike Couper's Lagonda, Margaret Allan's Wolseley and Jack Hobbs's Riley Nine. It was a year in which the event started in Munich, finished in Sanremo, and took in the mountains of five countries, including real monsters like the 9000ft Stelvio, along with the Galibier and the Allos, all of which still figured prominently in Alpine rallies of the 1960s.

There were other names in the finishers' list which, although unsuccessful on this occasion, were all – then or later – famous for other activities, including Major Tony Lago (Arm-strong-Siddeley), Ledwinka (Steyr) and Dick Seaman (MG Midget).

In 1933 it was a much more strenuous affair, attracting 132 competitors, but resulting in only two absolutely unpenalized individual runs, for Delmar's Bugatti and Carrière's Alfa Romeo. A taxing five-day route started from Merano, on the edge of the Dolomites, and finished at Nice, on the Mediterranean, just in time for the surviving crews to watch the Nice Grand Prix. It was August – high summer in the Alps – and the organizers (French on this occasion, for the job was reallocated among the consortium of clubs every year) had no mercy on the 'tourists' and novices in the entry. Only 30 cars were unpenalized after the first day's run, and a mere seven were still 'clean' after two days. During the event, three timed speed hill-climbs up the Pordoi, Stelvio and Galibier passes helped to sort out any ties.

There were British teams of cars from Riley, MG, Singer, Frazer Nash and SS, of which the MGs (K-Type Magnettes for Watkinson, Welch and Tommy Wisdom) and the 1½-litre Rileys (two of the Riley family and T. C. Griffiths) both won their group. The Frazer Nash and Singer teams finished intact, respectively behind the Rileys and the MGs, but the SS1s were out of luck, as Symons's and Margaret Allan's cars both suffered from blown engines (which had been rather injudiciously tuned by the factory in a 'last-minute' programme of preparation), leaving Charles Needham's car to finish alone.

Three of the German 2-litre Hanomags entering
Parc Fermé *at the end of a day's run in the 1936
Alpine Trial. By this time, the Nazi influence on
German teams was very obvious*

It was in 1934, however, that British teams
and cars really shone again. Most distinguished
of all were the beautifully prepared and immacu-
lately driven Talbot 105s (the famous trio of
cars registered BGH 21, BGH 22 and BGH 23,
driven by Tommy Wisdom, Hugh Eaton and
Mike Couper), which finished unpenalized,
winning a manufacturer's *Coupe des Alpes*, and
effectively finishing equal first with teams from
Germany and Britain. The other splendid
British performance, of course, was that of the
Triumph team of much-modified Southern
Cross tourers. Like the Talbots, the team put up
an unsullied performance, and the *Coupe des
Alpes* went to cars driven by Victor Leverett,
Charles Ridley, and Colonel Holbrook (who
was managing director of the Triumph con-
cern).

That year no fewer than seven factory teams
gained maximum points over the 1800-mile

route from Nice to Munich, one that included
all the usual hair-raising cols and hill-climbs,
along with a 10-km speed test along the Italian
autostrada near Venice, and an assault on the
Turracher Hohe, which appeared not to have
been improved since the Alpine Trial had last
visited it in the 1910s!

A team of SS1s did better on this occasion
(with Douglas Clease, a well-known *Autocar*
journalist, driving one of the cars, and Charles
Needham another), while Donald Healey (in
his new position as technical chief at Triumph)
won an individual *Coupe* in a Southern Cross,
as did Maurice Newnham, who was shortly to
become Triumph's managing director in succession to Colonel Holbrook. As the event finished
in Germany, at a time when German national-
ism was fiercer than ever, there were strong and
well-drilled teams from Adler, BMW, Opel
and Wanderer, all of whom achieved maximum
performances.

Fascist and Nazi activities caused such concern
among Germany's and Italy's European neighbours that there was no chance of the Alpine
Trial being held in 1935, but it returned in 1936,

organized by the Swiss, running from Lucerne to Interlaken by daily stages to Lugano, St Moritz, Thun, Lucerne and Basle.

The political upheavals (which also had their effect at the Berlin Olympics the same year) discouraged many entries, and the field was down to 74 cars, of which a mere eight were British. *The Autocar*, in its report, was quick to spot the real significance: 'In 1933 there were 53 of our people competing, and when the Trial was last held, in 1934, we were represented by 45 cars. . . . The Germans have been quick to profit by the apparent apathy of British drivers and manufacturers, and two-thirds of the entry is German – fifty cars including two German-built Fords.' The only serious British entries, in fact, came from Humfrey Symons (Wolseley), Donald Healey (Triumph Vitesse saloon), Tony Rolt (Triumph Southern Cross) and Tommy Wisdom (2½-litre SS100 sports car): before the end of the event, it was the gritty and experienced Wisdom who made most of the headlines.

The SS100 was a works-prepared car (registered BWK 77), which later became even more famous as a Brooklands and hill-climb machine. It had never previously been seen in a European rally (the model had only been announced the previous autumn) and was so strikingly styled that many scoffed at it as being merely a poseur's boulevard-special. They could not have been more wrong. The redoubtable and talented Wisdom, crewed as always by his wife Elsie (usually known as 'Bill'), never actually achieved fastest time of day on any of the speed hill-climbs or on the kilometre sprint near St Moritz, but was edged out only by Descollais's very rapid and very special Type 57 Bugatti saloon. In his class he was quite outstanding, so that his *Coupe des Glaciers* was almost a formality. Donald Healey, in the Vitesse with the still-secret 2-litre overhead valve Triumph engine (announced a few weeks later), also won a *Coupe des Glaciers*, but the youthful Tony Rolt was not quite so lucky, as his 2-litre Southern Cross was not as highly prepared, nor was he so experienced in Alpine motoring.

As might have been expected from the massive German entry, teams from Ford, Hanomag, Adler and DKW won *Coupes des Alpes* in the various performances. Rolt was in good company as one who had lost time – one of his rivals was a young man called Huschke von Hanstein, driving a Hanomag, who would

Trevoux, who later became the driver to beat in Monte Carlo rallies, shunting his Alfa Romeo coupé in the promenade test of the 1935 event

later become famous as the Porsche racing manager.

Nevertheless, German domination and nationalistic fervour ensured that there was little further interest from other countries, and by 1939 the event had sunk into obscurity. Not until 1946, when the French Marseilles club revived the ideal of a pass-storming event, would the Alpine Trial be reborn, and renamed as the Alpine Rally or *Criterium de la Montagne*.

In the 1930s, too, the Liège–Rome–Liège marathon, which would become so renowned in postwar years, was struggling to become established. The Belgian organizers realized, from the start, that they could only develop a truly difficult international event by approaching other countries. Even in 1931, when it was first held, the event took in German, Austrian, Italian and French roads. The entry was very restricted at first (only 22 cars in 1933, of which nine finished), but its popularity soon grew, and before 1939 any Liège entrant knew in advance that he would be required to drive virtually without rest from Liège to Rome and back, with no special speed tests on the way, but having to tackle the highest, toughest, most demanding mountain roads in between. No competitor ever recorded an unpenalized run in a prewar Liège, and if the organizers had their way, no one ever would. When Johnny Claes achieved the impossible, after the Second World War, in the 1951 marathon, the committee were positively ashamed of themselves!

In 1938, Trevoux was the master of his craft, and drove this big French Hotchkiss to second place in the Monte, being narrowly beaten by a Ford

J. Paul's Delahaye tied for outright victory in the 1939 Monte Carlo Rally with Trevoux's Hotchkiss. Here it is seen on the speed hillclimb at Eze

While all this exciting mountain motoring was going on, however, rallying in Britain was being left far behind. It was not that British cars and drivers could not stand the pace – Donald Healey and Tommy Wisdom had already disproved this many times – but that the local countryside was unsuitable, roads too good *and* too crowded, and legislators appalled at the idea of fast open-road motoring of any sort. It is worth remembering that, until the end of 1930, it was illegal for anyone to drive at a speed faster than 20mph on any British road. However, this overall speed limit was almost universally ignored by the end of the 1920s, especially by competitors in the Monte Carlo Rally making their way from the north of Scotland to the Channel ports.

The SMMT's ban on 'trade' involvement in British trials and rallies, which came into force in 1925, meant that no 'works' or even garage entries could openly be made. One immediate consequence, for example, was that the hitherto popular Scottish Six Days' Trial was cancelled because only two entries were received! For a time, therefore, open-road motor sport in Britain virtually disappeared, and had it not been for the MCC's long-distance trials (Exeter, Lands End and Edinburgh events) would have sunk without trace.

One thing the British did love, however, was a *Concours d'Élégance*. The industry, after all, was graced with a number of fine coachbuilders always anxious to show off their expertise. But a *Concours* had nothing to do with motoring and everything to do with style. It was the looks of the car, not the performance, which influenced the judges. In many *Concours* events the cars never moved during the judging; at some, the motoring was confined to a low-speed parade past the judges.

Nevertheless, the rebirth of British rallying owed something to *Concours* events, for it was thanks to a couple of *Concours* in 1928 that things really got moving again. In July of that year, the Bournemouth 'Rally' included an optional motoring section, in which cars drove to Bournemouth from as far afield as John O'Groats, at a maximum average speed of 20mph. Those driving the longest distance were awarded the highest marks. Should we be surprised to learn that it was Donald Healey, in his Triumph Super Seven, who took the premier award?

Two months later there was a similar event,

with an equivalent road section, concentrated on Southport. Twenty British start points were nominated, along with points at Brussels and Paris. The 'rallying point' was at Clitheroe in Lancashire, after which a strict average speed of 20mph had to be maintained, including the passage through Preston. No crews appear to have started from either of the overseas points, most electing to drive from John O'Groats or Land's End, though at least one half-hearted entrant actually started from Clitheroe! In this event it was F. F. Austin's flat-nose Morris Cowley saloon which gained highest marks.

Further events of this type were held in the next few years – Donald Healey, for instance, won the Brighton Rally in 1930 in another Triumph – but there was no attempt to introduce a British Monte Carlo Rally: not, that is, until *The Autocar* (admittedly acting as a 'front' for the RAC itself) started running leading articles on the subject towards the end of 1931. The result was the very first RAC Rally, held in March 1932. For the rest of the decade the event followed the same basic format: long road sections from a variety of starting points, no great hazards due to the weather or the road surfaces, and an average speed originally of 22mph for the 1100cc cars, and 25mph for larger cars. The rallying point was always at an out-of-season seaside resort, and there were a few gentle driving tests on the sea front to produce a result. Naturally there was a *Concours*.

Because the 1932 event finished at Torquay, it was known as the Torquay Rally (the 'RAC' part of the title only evolved later). As the first of its kind, and as something of a domestic equivalent to the Monte Carlo Rally, it attracted a colossal entry – 367 cars, of which 342 actually started, and 311 reached Torquay. Some idea of the severity of the road section is suggested by the fact that only 47 of them were penalized. There was a choice of nine starting points, and the distance to Torquay in each case was about 1000 miles, via a circuitous main route involving no more than three or four intermediate check points.

The absurdity of current thinking among officials of the day is underlined by the nature of the tie-deciding test, consisting of a 100 yard *slow* driving test (in which the most marks were obtained by the car taking the *longest* time to complete a non-stop run *in top gear*!), followed by an acceleration and braking test, all in the same straight line. It was ridiculous not only because it was the exact antithesis of what real rallying stood for, but also because it virtually ensured victory for a car with fluid flywheel transmission.

The ultimate absurdity was that the winning car – a 15/18hp Lanchester saloon driven by Colonel A. H. Loughborough, equipped with the Daimler fluid flywheel and pre-selector gearbox – took a full 5min 7.8sec to complete the 100 yards, and barely appeared to be moving at all! The top ten cars in the over 1100cc category, and the winning Riley of Victor Leverett in the 1100cc group all had fluid drive of one sort or another. Donald Healey's familiar Invicta was fastest in the acceleration test, but could manage no slower than 2min 59.4sec for the slow-driving test, and finished fifth in his class. Second to Colonel Loughborough was Mercer's Daimler Double-Six saloon, driven for him in the driving tests by a young mechanic named Raymond England. Later to become known as 'Lofty' because of his great height, England eventually achieved fame as Jaguar's competition manager in the 1950s and became the company's chief executive in the 1970s.

In spite of the eulogies heaped on the event and on the town which hosted it (*The Autocar's* report covered no less than 12 pages), it was really much too easy to attain any international recognition. It was also clear, afterwards, that there had been a great deal of cheating in the *top-gear* slow-driving tests, in which the feathering of the clutch was strictly forbidden; even with RAC observers in the cars during the tests, some cars apparently had back-seat passengers operating hidden pedals under loose floorboards!

This controversial test was still retained for the 1933 rally, which finished at Hastings (2.6-litre Rover, 2-litre AC and Riley Nine taking class wins); but for the Bournemouth Rally of 1934, when no fewer than 384 cars started the event and only 14 of the 351 finishers lost time on the road, the whole thing was decided by two combined speed and manoeuvring tests. Singer claimed that a 9hp Sports model achieved the most marks of all, making it the outright winner, but the truth was that there was no outright winner in any prewar RAC Rally except the first one: Spikins's class win, therefore, was also matched by that of Spencer Wilks (managing director of Rover) in one of his own P1 12hp tourers, and by T. D. Wynn-Weston in a 20hp Rover Speed Twenty. Matters were even worse in 1935, when there

If only it could have been given a more powerful engine, the monocoque Lancia Aprilia could have been one of the most outstanding rally cars of the late 1930s

were not even any class results, with competitors merely being rewarded (MCC-style) with gold, silver or bronze awards. Thereafter, entries sagged, and did not truly recover until the postwar years.

In 1937 and 1938, although no general classification was ever declared, it was agreed that Jack Harrop (driving an SS100 open sports car on each occasion) was the unofficial winner. There was, at least, an attempt to make the 1939 event more competitive and less of a gentle tour. On this occasion it had only four starting points – London, Blackpool, Stratford-on-Avon and Torquay. All converged on Scarborough by devious routes (London starters, for instance, had to travel by way of intermediate controls at Llandrindod Wells and Southport, while Torquay starters first had to trek across to Kings Lynn), after which a choice of two routes, one more difficult than the other, could be taken to Buxton. After a night halt, the route then led

down to Brighton, where the usual driving and hill-climbing tests were scheduled. As the event was held at the end of April, there was no serious chance of bad weather on the way. Although there were well-known names in the list of 200 starters (among them racing driver Bert Hadley in a works-loaned Austin saloon, Kay Petre in a new 9hp Singer Roadster, Raymond Mays in a new car of his own manufacture, Fane, H. J. Aldington and Leslie Johnson in BMW 328s, George Hartwell in a big Humber, H. F. S. Morgan in one of his own sports cars, Tommy and 'Bill' Wisdom in identical SS100s, and Stanley Sears in a vast Phantom III Rolls-Royce), it was significant that some of the *real* competitors had still found time to compete in the Paris–Nice trials a week earlier.

The pity of it all was that the more difficult or 'colonial' section from Scarborough to Buxton, over roads and tracks in Yorkshire quite familiar to those of us who started rallying in the 1950s and 1960s, was cancelled just before the start, as it was thought to be too rough even for the trade-sponsored machines to tackle. As ever, therefore, the RAC Rally had to be settled by the

driving tests, in which the BMW 328s (called Frazer Nash-BMWs, of course, because of the Aldington family's links with the German concern) and the SS100s proved quite outstanding.

Leslie Johnson, in one of the BMW 328 team cars, should have been fastest of all, but partly spun in the last test and was overhauled by his team-mate A. F. P. Fane. Second best performance was by Sammy Newsome in a works-sponsored 3½-litre SS100. Class awards went to George Goodall (Morgan 4/4), H. F. S. Morgan (Morgan 4/4), Mike Lawson (HRG), G. S. Davison (Triumph Dolomite Roadster), H. J. Aldington (BMW 328) and to Fane. Naturally enough, the BMWs also won the team prize.

It was undoubtedly very British, great fun and extremely popular, but somehow it wasn't really serious rallying. Not that this stopped organizers in Wales and in Scotland from following suit. There had been no long-distance trialling or rallying in Scotland for some time, but the instant success of the 1932 RAC 'Torquay' led the RSAC to organize their own event. The time schedule of a Scottish rally was no more arduous than was that of an RAC, but the

No pre-war rally – except the Alpine Trial – was complete without a Concours d'Elegance *at the finish. A wide selection of cars, arranged on the terrace of the Casino, await the judges' attention at Monte Carlo in 1937*

Driving tests invariably settled the issue in RAC rallies held before and after the Second World War. Lord Waleran's V12 Lagonda is on its way to a ¼-mile sprint on the Blackpool promenade in 1938

scenery was magnificent, the weather in June was often splendid, and the road sections were much more interesting. The Scottish, like the RAC, never seemed to be run off at any great speed; on some occasions, for instance, the entire field was routed westwards over the Pass of the Cattle to Applecross village on the Atlantic coast of mainland Scotland, for a leisurely lunch halt, after which all the cars obediently trooped back again, to Loch Carron and civilization, for this was a dead-end road. The attraction was that it was one of the highest passes in the country – 2053ft at the summit – and therefore had quite a reputation. Both the Scottish and the Welsh rallies, however, were merely touring events, with driving tests thrown in to ensure a result; and the coachwork competition, as always, seemed to be as important as the actual motoring. Incidentally, crews on the RAC Rally might have expected some nights out of

bed, but never on the lesser British events. *That* would have taken all the social fun out of it.

By 1939 there were still few indications that British rallies were likely to be toughened up in the foreseeable future, but after the end of the summer it did not matter any more. For a couple of years the European political situation had been tense, and since mid-1938 it had seemed inevitable to most thinking people that another war was on its way. It came in September when Germany invaded Poland. One consequence, of course, was that almost all kinds of motor sport ceased immediately. It would be almost six years before the world was at peace again, and it would be nearly ten years before motoring in Europe returned to normality. By that time cars, roads and events were to be very difficult.

Leslie Johnson's BMW 328 spinning away its chances of victory in the 1939 RAC Rally

4 | Post-war Rallying – when is a Race not a Race?

For six harrowing years, from 1939 to 1945, the world was at war, and almost every organized form of motor sport was abandoned. Apart from the fact that it would have seemed morally wrong to continue any such self-indulgence, there were obviously no supplies to promote the sport. Among the combatant nations, all motoring necessities – petrol, tyres, spare parts *and* cars – were geared to the war effort.

Even after the war, it was very difficult to get motor sport under way again. In 1945 and 1946, most of Europe was in a state of disruption. In terms of material damage, Britain was less affected than most countries, but economic conditions were difficult.

For rallying, however, the war was more than a political watershed; it also marked the real transition from 'touring' rallies to rallies that bordered increasingly on open-road racing. In the 1930s, as already mentioned, almost every rally included a long road section merely to tire out the crews, obtaining its results from driving tests held on the way or at the finish. The honourable exceptions were the Alpine trials and the first of the Liège–Rome–Liège rallies. After the war, the change, though not abrupt, was immediately obvious and progressive. It meant that the days of the vast and luxurious *Concours* limousines were numbered, and that fast sporting cars like the BMW 328s, the SS100s, and their successors, would now come into their own. Only in the Monte Carlo Rally, that most prestigious and 'social' of all the big Internationals, would a *Concours d'Élégance* continue to be significant.

Another result was that the handful of British drivers such as Donald Healey and Tommy Wisdom, who had made their European reputations in the 1930s, would, for a while, be at the top. In the French and Italian Alps, against the schedules likely to be demanded by postwar organizers, there could be no immediate substitute for experience, and for the time being,

every postwar rallying standard would be set by the pattern, schedules and entries of the French Alpine Rally.

It was no lack of will that delayed the resumption of postwar rallying, simply problems of finance and petrol supplies. Rationing continued in most European countries for years, while war-shattered economies (and refining facilities) were rebuilt. In 1946, in spite of great enthusiasm, there was no practical solution; and even in 1947, the indefatigable Anthony Noghes, of the Monte Carlo Rally organizing team, could make no progress against French bureaucracy.

Probably the first notable postwar International event was the Lisbon Rally, Portugal having remained neutral, and prosperous, throughout the war. Because it was the first, it attracted a huge entry of 173 cars, which started the 1500-mile run from all over Europe. In May 1947 nobody seemed to mind the prewar format, least of all Godfrey Imhof, who won it outright in his new J-Type two-seater Allard sports car, despite his engine being damaged before the driving tests at the end of the event. To record this first postwar British win, incidentally, Imhof had enormous difficulty in obtaining fuel and arranging finance to indulge himself in what the British government considered to be a holiday.

Lisbon, however, was merely a prelude, and it was the French Alpine Rally, held in July, which really marked the beginning of postwar rallying. Even before the start, it had been nick-named 'The Great Race' by competitors, and the route, split into three long sections, included all the famous, formidable Alpine passes. It was not merely a question of maintaining the time schedule, but of scrambling to stay in the event at all. Surfaces, particularly of the minor roads at high altitude, were appallingly rough, and tyre wear was a real problem. Participating drivers who were to be even more notable in future years included Ian Appleyard, Maurice

Final test at Zandvoort in the Tulip Rally of 1955 – with 'works' cars from Triumph and Ford taking on an AC Ace in the circuit test

Gatsonides, Tom Wisdom, and Imhof, and among the cars were Jaguar, HRG, Sunbeam-Talbot, Lancia, Healey and Delahaye.

In setting the standard expected of serious rallying crews in future years, the Alpine organizers stipulated that cars had to be driven flat-out from start to finish. At the time, for example, it was considered remarkable that the most powerful cars were using more than two sets of tyres during the event. (If only the press could have foreseen the 1960s when, on some of the last great 'road races', works team cars were changing tyres every 30 or 40 miles!) Target averages for the over 3-litre cars was no less than 60kph (37.5mph), while even the 1.1-litre cars were asked to average 52kph (32.5mph).

Not surprisingly, therefore, the largest cars dominated the event if not the results (for in 1947, as in subsequent years, an outright winner was not always proclaimed), and it is interesting that it was Burgerhout's old-fashioned 3½-litre Delahaye which set the fastest times. Wisdom, as expected, won his class in the 'works' Healey

Westland tourer, and the youthful Appleyard opened his Alpine motoring with a class third in his own SS100 sports car.

The 'Alpine' had thus begun its postwar existence in the best possible way, setting the standards for all the *real* rallies of the late 1940s. In 1948, therefore, everyone who was anyone took part. For the British drivers, even reaching the start in Marseilles was difficult enough, because of restrictions on foreign currency; but for everyone concerned, the event was extremely tough, and the regulations highly exacting.

One great incentive of the Alpine Rally, as the most demanding of all high-speed road events, was not so much the dream of an outright victory as the chance of winning an Alpine *Coupe*. In postwar years, a *Coupe des Alpes* (like the *Coupe des Glaciers* of the 1930s Alpine Trials) was awarded to every driver who completed the road sections without penalty; this, because of the nature of the event, was no formality, and if more than a handful of *Coupes* were won on any Alpine it was thought to have been an 'easy' year.

For most of the 16 starters in 1948, therefore, winning the 1163-mile event was hardly a consideration; but the possible award of a *Coupe* was a real spur. All the expected tight road sections in the French and Swiss Alps had been included; and apart from being set at high average speeds, they were still open to all traffic – at the height of the Mediterranean holiday season. This format ensured that only 23 crews were unpenalized even at the end of the first day, while at the finish, in Nice, only eight of the coveted *Coupes* were actually awarded.

The Cols, already familiar to drivers, were later to become notorious. The rally traditionally reserved its most harum-scarum motoring for the last night, which included assaults on the Cols de l'Iseran, Galibier, Izoard, Vars and Allos, two of these being over 8000ft high.

In addition to the deciding ties on the road sections, the timed speed climb of the Izoard and the 'regularity' run up Mont Ventoux were merely extra demands on already exhausted crews. The cars driven by the eight unpenalized crews were Jaguar SS100, J-Type Allard, Sunbeam-Talbot 2-litre, HRG 1500, Citroën *traction*, Lancia and Simca. Ian Appleyard, Robin Richards (now of the BBC), Leslie Potter and George Murray Frame were the successful British drivers. There should have been another – Donald Healey in his Westland – but he stopped to assist an injured crew after an accident and lost his *Coupe* because of the delay: he had to be content with a mere class win which, in any other event but the Alpine, would have been satisfaction enough.

The Monte Carlo Rally returned in 1949 – a sign that things were getting back to normal – but it was not until 1950 that the first major British event (the *Daily Express* MCC National – *not* the RAC International) was promoted. The first of the postwar Montes admitted seven starting points – Glasgow, Lisbon, Oslo, Stockholm, Prague, Florence, and Monte Carlo itself – an average road mileage from each point of 1955 miles, with no competitive motoring of any nature until the cars reached the Principality. No fewer than 208 cars started, and 166 of them finished the course.

The whole event, for the majority of crews who were unpenalized on the long concentration runs, hinged on a regularity run comprising four laps of a six-kilometre circuit including the road from Mont des Mules to La Turbie. As *The Autocar* rather waspishly commented: 'It was as though the cars were asked to tackle Shelsley all-out 24 times, after coming 2,000 miles to do it. . . .' It was also rather typical of the pomp and

The most unlikely looking cars shone in European rallying in the 1950s. Here is an Alvis TC21/100 'Grey Lady' battling with a Mark VII Jaguar in a Tulip Rally test

Racing drivers occasionally found time to go rallying. Stirling Moss won three consecutive Coupes des Alpes *in Sunbeams. MKV 21 was the two-seater Alpine which he used in 1953 and 1954 for this remarkable achievement*

When a Jaguar Mk VII is sideways on sheet ice, it feels very large ... but Ronnie Adams recovered, and took this 'works' car to outright victory in the 1956 Monte

The only man who really tamed Jaguar's XK120 was Ian Appleyard, who used this self-same car for three complete seasons. He was the first of only three drivers to win a Coupe d'Or for three consecutive unpenalised runs in the French Alpine Rally

circumstance surrounding the Monte for so many years that the civic welcome in Boulogne for British crews took so long that cars were up to an hour late leaving the town, many being penalized at the next (Luxembourg) control!

The times, too, were changing, and while some British contestants thought it 'not quite cricket' that the French had clearly been practising the regularity run (benefiting accordingly), others decided that they, too, would have to be more organized in the future. It was not surprising that Trevoux's 1939-type Hotchkiss, which had started from Lisbon, won the event, but remarkable that Potter's Allard finished fourth and the redoubtable Ken Wharton (Ford Pilot) fifth. Class winners included Louis Rosier's 4CV Renault and Tommy Wise's Jowett Javelin; significantly, that man Gatsonides figured well in his Hillman Minx, and Mike Couper's vast Mark VI Bentley won the ensuing *Concours de Confort*.

Even though the Monte was neither the toughest nor the most 'professional' of the European rallies, it always seemed to gain the most press publicity and invariably attracted a huge entry. No matter that the organizers were so obviously pro-Gallic, and aggressively determined *not* to modernize their event; the glamour of the occasion, the celebrations at the finish, and the dramatic road conditions often encountered all made it a 'natural' for press and radio coverage. What really counted was its indefinable 'atmosphere'. Who could blame correspondents for wishing to be in Monte Carlo at that time of the year rather than anywhere else, and is it any wonder if this coloured their judgement? As Norman Garrad, the famous Rootes Group team manager, once said: 'Of course we do the Monte because of the glamour. If the best rally in the world finished at Wigan, do you think we'd be going?'

From 1949 to 1960, the Monte changed but little. Year after year it relied on the sheer grinding endurance (routine boredom in a mild year, heaving, digging and heroic driving in a bad winter) of long concentration runs from distant capitals; and year after year there were regularity runs, average-speed contests or driving tests near the finish to decide a winner. Even that might have been acceptable if conditions had been the same for everyone, but apart from the weather differences (drivers might encounter blizzards in Norway and Jugoslavia, and spring-like sunshine in France and Italy) there was the nagging suspicion of bias in the tie-deciders, of the secret checks on most crews not being so rigidly applied for the favoured French.

In the face of rallying developments such as the spine-tingling routes and schedules prescribed by the Liège–Rome–Liège organizers, and the high-pressure motoring drama provided by the Alpine, it was remarkable that the Monte Carlo Rally changed so slowly. Throughout the decade the emphasis, weather permitting, was on navigation and strict timekeeping rather than on high speeds, and no amount of criticism from the competitors seemed to get through to the organizers.

Only in exceptionally wintry years – such as 1950 (when only five cars made it to Monte Carlo without road penalty), 1952 (15 cars) and 1958 (nine cars) – did the event become a real *driver's* challenge. In 1952, for instance, Stirling Moss, in a Sunbeam-Talbot 90, battled his way from Monte Carlo into northern Europe, and back through the Massif Central, to take second place, very close behind Sydney Allard in a car of his own make; and in 1958, when much of the rally was decimated by the truly Arctic

The cars might look antique but the competition was just as fierce in the 1950s as it is today. In the 1957 Liège–Rome–Liège, a Peugeot 203 battles with a Ford Zephyr on the lower slopes of the Giau pass in Italy

Even though its space frame chassis looked fragile, the Mercedes-Benz 300SL was fast enough and strong enough to win events like the Liège-Rome-Liège rally of 1955, with Gendebien and Strasse driving

conditions, Peter Harper (Sunbeam Rapier) and Réné Cotton (Citroën DS19) were two of the three heroes who got through from Oslo on time.

The concept of individual routes joining up at a 'concentration' control north of Monte Carlo never varied, but this point was placed progressively farther from the Mediterranean. After that, and depending on the annual whim of the organizers, there might be a simple road section, long, strict regularity runs or merely a series of relatively energetic trips over the mountains.

Special stages were as yet unknown. Results were obtained either by driving tests, the use of the Monaco GP racing circuit or by the use of regularity runs in mountain circuits north and west of Monte Carlo. In fairness, I must admit that the mountain circuit became longer as the years passed. By 1954, when Louis Chiron's Lancia Aurelia GT won the event, it was 165 miles, by 1959 it was 270 miles, and for 1960, when the rally was completely dominated by

A massive power/weight ratio helped to win rallies in the 1950s, just as it does today. Imhof's Cadillac-engined Allard might have looked ungainly, but it was good enough to win the RAC Rally in 1952

Mercedes-Benz (who finished first, second, third and fifth), it had increased to 360 miles and occupied 12 hours.

None of this, however, deterred competitors. The British allocation (usually of 120 cars) was always over-subscribed, and in 1953 there were more than 400 starters. Most of them, admittedly, were wasting their time – or their money – but the same could be said even today about the majority of drivers in a Monte, Portuguese, Acropolis or RAC Rally; and where would rallying be if they did not trouble to compete?

Preparation, practice and professionalism were all-important, and 'works' teams from Ford, Standard-Triumph, BMC, Rootes, Citroën, Mercedes-Benz, Saab, DKW, Renault, and others all treated the event very seriously. It was not until 1960, however, that Mercedes-Benz set the sport by its collective ear, practising the mountain circuit for at least a month until they were corner- and gear-change-perfect, and proving that a simple reconnaissance was no longer good enough. Even in a tough year, the winning margin might be tiny: thus in 1952 Allard had beaten Moss by a mere 14 seconds, while in 1953 Maurice Gatsonides (Ford Zephyr) defeated Ian Appleyard (Jaguar Mk VII) by even

In the right hands, and in the right conditions, an Aston Martin DB2 was a rally winner – as Lyndon Sims (helped by Tony Ambrose) proved in the 1956 RAC Rally

Aston Martin themselves were always too involved in motor racing to take rallying seriously, yet their cars could have won all over the world. This is a 'works' DB2/4, driven by racing driver Peter Collins, on the Monaco GP circuit

less and his total penalty for the regularity run was *two seconds*. But it always depended on intricate navigation and timekeeping, a battery of instruments, excellent tyres and incredibly detailed local knowledge. Every year there were more complaints, and even the traditionalists on the organizing committee eventually saw that they would have to change their ways. For 1961 they bent so far as to introduce special stages – but hedged their bets with a complex 'formula'; that development, however, belongs to a later chapter.

In many respects, Britain's RAC International Rally followed the same path, though Britain's road system, weather, and legal restrictions over

The 'tiddlers' race at Zandvoort in a Tulip Rally of the 1950s, including Saabs, Austin A35s, Dyna-Panhards and Morris Minor 1000s

average speeds meant that the route could be even more pedestrian and boring to professional crews. Indeed, there is little good to say of the RAC Rally between 1951 and 1958, as it was usually settled by a handful of short driving tests, by regularity runs in mountainous areas of Wales or the Lake District, or by club-style navigation runs through the night.

That it seemed to suit a large number of British crews is beyond question, but it had no appeal to the Continentals who found better things to do. From time to time a concessionaire might be persuaded to bring a single 'works' entry from – say – DKW, but once was usually enough. On several occasions, the 'international' element in the RAC was missing completely.

The formula of the 1950s, like that of the Monte Carlo Rally, was rigid and familiar. From two or perhaps three start points, cars would converge, trek around a scenic, lengthy but usually rather easy route, and finish at an out-of-season seaside resort for some fairly desultory celebrations. There might be a driving test on some windswept moorside, a speed test at a racing circuit or a sprint at an airfield – but there was no concentrated high-speed motoring. Occasionally the event was held in balmy, even warm weather, but when the rally was held in March it was always likely to attract wintry conditions. In 1955, when the event almost collapsed under a welter of protests over procedure, and in 1958, when it became disrupted in Wales and the North, there was at least the challenge of battling through snow and floods instead of merely fighting fatigue and lassitude.

The driving test experts, who were often seasoned competitors in European events as well, lapped it up. Ian Appleyard put up best performance twice, in 1951 and 1953, in his well-known XK120 (NUB 120), 'Goff' Imhof won in 1952 in his J2 Allard, and Johnny Wallwork gave the Triumph TR2 a great debut by winning in 1954. It was only in 1958, when Peter Harper not only won the event in his works Sunbeam Rapier but also managed to complete the entire course, that true professionalism was rewarded.

It was the shambles of 1958, however, which caused outcry and finally triggered off some change. That year the regulations enabled crafty crews to cut out great chunks of the route, rejoin after a night's sleep, and still finish ahead of the stalwarts who had thrashed around the country according to the rules. For 1959 the RAC handed over to Jack Kemsley, who was a seasoned campaigner, and authorized him to make changes. It was Kemsley who transformed British rallying, and he should always get the credit for this.

Holland's Tulip Rally, first promoted in 1949, was as tedious as the RAC Rally in concept, but gradually toughened up, including more and more of the difficult sections in the mountains of France, West Germany and Switzerland, plus a series of long, full-blooded speed hill-climbs (effectively 'special stages') in these areas. Held in April or early May, the Tulip could usually rely on fine spring weather, and it was the sort of rally which team managers at least found predictable. They could not, however, rely on the organizers' quirks, for the Dutch club, led by Piet Nortier, was always likely to think up a strange and complex 'handicap' system to hold back the 300SLs and encourage the tiny British and European economy cars.

It was this and cunning, rather than high performance, which enabled cars such as Ken Wharton's works Ford Anglia and the Brookes's Austin A30 to win outright. There were famous occasions too, as in 1959, when the Morley twins, Donald and Erle, won their first major event, in their own Jaguar 3.4, or the 1953 rally, when several leading cars were disqualified at the end of the event for having non-standard equipment (including Maurice Becquart's Jowett Javelin for 'illegal' engine tuning), giving victory to a Dutchman in another Javelin. There was also that notable first event, in 1949, where everything depended on a driving test at Zandvoort, and on a 'handbrake turn' around a particular pylon. Ken Wharton's Ford Anglia performance was so outstanding that other competitors protested that his brakes had been 'modified'. Inspection showed nothing but a leaking brake union on one side, so his victory was confirmed; only much later was it revealed

One of the most formidable of all British rallying combinations was that of a Sunbeam Rapier driven by Peter Harper, who nevertheless won only one international rally – the 1958 RAC

that the leak had been caused deliberately, to make sure that only one rear brake (the important one) would be working for the test!

Other European events, varying in popularity depending on the year or route, now enlivened the scene. Apart from the Scandinavian rallies, so important to the developing history of rallying that they must be considered in a separate section, there were events such as the Lisbon, the Adriatic, the German and the Sestriere. After the Mille Miglia was hounded off the roads of Italy following the carnage of 1957, a rally was promoted in its place, but soon disappeared. Then, too, there was the prestigious Tour de France, which was something of a long-distance rally even if it required a racing driver in a sports-racing car to win it – not an event calculated to appeal to the average rally driver.

Nancy Mitchell, driving MGAs and other BMC products, was European Ladies' Champion twice – in 1956 and 1957. This was her Alpine rally MGA of 1956

The BMC 'works' team achieved respectability in 1956 with the introduction of MGAs to replace their saloons. Team captain John Gott took this example to the finish of the Liège–Rome–Liège

In the 1940s and the 1950s, however, two events stood head and shoulders above all others. Although for the press it was the Monte Carlo Rally alone that mattered, for the true professionals and 'works' teams, the really important events were the French Alpine and the Liège–Rome–Liège. For competitors, winning the Monte was great for reasons of publicity, and even winning the RAC was bound to keep the factory bosses happy, but achieving victory in a Liège or an Alpine was everything. Argument raged as to which of these toweringly demanding rallies was the better, but it was never truly resolved. Indisputably, the Liège was all endurance and reliability, while the Alpine was all speed. An Alpine could certainly be won with a fast, fragile car and a great deal of service and good fortune, but no delicate little piece of engineering ever scooped the pool in the Liège.

Given the choice (and I have heard several famous drivers venture an opinion), the crews usually plumped for the Alpine, probably because there was enough time for rest and relaxation during the event for it all to be enjoyable, whereas the Liège was one long, exhilarating but wholly exhausting marathon from start to finish.

Before analyzing the attractions of the Alpine, therefore, I must deal with the great Liège–Rome–Liège events of the 1950s. The rally – I nearly called it a race, for that is what it felt like to competitors – had a simple format. Cars started from Belgium and drove down over a combination (depending on the year) of French, Swiss, West German and Austrian roads into Italy; here they thrashed around the mountains, called briefly at Rome, and made a similar and no less demanding return journey. This route was regularly more than 3000 miles long and occupied up to four days of almost continuous hard driving. Rest stops or night halts? Don't be facetious – *this* was the Liège.

Maurice Garot, the Motor Union's architect of so many Lièges, once said that the event was never intended to be 'cleanable' – i.e. its schedules would always be quite impossible, and the rally, therefore, was really a race – a race against time. He must have been shattered to discover, in 1951, that Johnny Claes and Jacques Ickx (father of Jacky) had beaten his targets with Claes's ex-works lightweight Jaguar XK120. Garot swore that it would not happen again, and it never did. The Liège, indeed, was so arduous that instead of awarding cups for unpenalized runs, they were handed out just for finishing.

A year later, the 1952 marathon was won by Helmut Polensky in a 1.5-litre Porsche, who had large penalties and was one of only 24 competitors (from 100 starters) to complete the 3230-mile course. In 1953 it was Claes's turn again, this time with a very sick navigator, in a Lancia Aurelia GT; perhaps, with a healthy crew, his penalty might have been less than 16min 47sec, but even that was phenomenal for

One of the big battles, in rallies and in the circuit tests which usually ended them, of the late 1950s, was between Sunbeam Rapiers and Volvos. Two of each dispute the same corner at Crystal Palace in the 1959 RAC

an event which took 3 days 17 hours and 33 minutes to unwind, when every important section average was 60kph (37.5mph), and in which Claes drove the last 52 hours without respite.

In those days too, remember, neither radial-ply tyres nor disc brakes were available on European road cars, nor was there yet any support from an 'umbrella' of service cars. A mere glance at the cars which took the first five places in 1953 – three Lancia Aurelia coupés, a 2-litre Ferrari and an XK120 fixed head – indicates what kind of an event this was.

The Liège in the 1950s was apparently indestructible. In spite of the fact that the FIA were unhappy about the 'endurance' aspect of the event, that the French and Italian organizers became increasingly more jealous about the use of 'their' mountain roads, and even after the hue and cry following the Le Mans disaster of 1955, it never missed a year.

The format was always basically the same. Instead of cars starting singly, at minute intervals, three cars started, *line abreast*, at three-minute intervals. This was fine at the beginning of an easy section, but could be dramatic and potentially dangerous when a tight section was

You can almost see the shimmering heat of this control scene in a late 1950s Alpine Rally – cars in shot include 'works' Rapiers, TR3As, MGAs and Austin-Healey 100/6s, plus an Aston Martin DB2/4 and a Jaguar 3.4

in prospect. John Gott, when team captain of the BMC team, graded all sections by colours in his practice notes – from 'blue' for easy to 'red-plus' for impossible. As John Sprinzel commented in his book *Sleepless Knights*: '. . . with 'red' sections pandemonium breaks loose as cars attempt to drive up on both sides of the control table, for the first one into the next bend has achieved quite an advantage. When 'red-plus' is at stake, the control procedure is exactly the same, only crash helmets are worn!'

Almost all sections, except those close to Belgium, were difficult, and some were absolutely impossible to complete in the time (by John Gott's reckoning, these were 'red-plus' sections, and parts of the Liège's route seemed to be littered with them). Roads rejected by other clubs, because they were thought to be too slow, too rough or too dangerous, were usually

welcomed joyfully by the Liège committee. It was they who first used the horribly narrow, high, vertiginous, dangerous and loose-surfaced Gavia pass (in northern Italy), set it at 60kph, then waited calmly, and with complete justification, for the penalties to mount up. Linking this wicked sector with the Vivione (which was only 'better' because the Gavia was so awful) and the Stelvio made up the nastiest couple of hours' mountain racing that Europe could provide.

Every year the vast majority of competitors were forced to retire, if not with car problems or because of accidents, then due to sheer crew fatigue or excessive lateness. It used to be said that Maurice Garot's ultimate ambition was to achieve a Liège with only a single finisher. He came near to it in the 1960s when on one occasion only seven cars survived, but that story belongs to a later chapter.

To achieve this sort of retirement rate, the organizers made no bones about 'clipping' the official mileage of the more difficult sections. Well-known runs, from village to village over high passes, mysteriously became 'shorter' as

The penalties of trying too hard on ice without studded tyres . . . Pat Moss's Austin A40, and a Jaguar XK 150, do it in the approved manner

year followed year, and the time allowance was trimmed accordingly; no more than bland sympathy was offered to crews who did not spot this in time. The penalty for *any* lateness at some controls was on-the-spot exclusion, and there was no arguing; officials simply retained the road book when it was handed in for stamping, and were not to be moved.

Perhaps because it was so uncompromising, and because it was difficult to arrange time (and enough crews) for support cars, some works teams did not like the Liège. It was not the sort of rally where a given investment was sure to pay off. Especially after 1955, when the character of the event began to change (it became even rougher) success became more a question of individual driver's ability and experience, allied to the use of a rugged car, than to the support which could be guaranteed.

In 1955, for the last time, the Liège visited

When Erik Carlsson's Saab comes up behind to pass, it's usually wise to pull over – which is what this special-nosed Austin-Healey Sprite has just done . . .

In 1960, this counts as a big crowd to watch a rally. Tiny Lewis and a works-prepared Triumph Herald in the 1960 Monte

Rome on a 3200-mile route. The following year it retained its traditional title but went nowhere near Rome, striking deep into Jugoslavia and turning round at Zagreb. The first two or three events to use Jugoslavia's almost deserted roads were not as rough as they were to become in the 1960s, but they marked a definite watershed. Up to the late 1950s, the Liège was an extremely difficult challenge; after that, it became a true battle for survival!

Identifying the winners makes interesting reading, for following Claes's epic drive in 1953

came wins for Helmut Polensky (Porsche), Olivier Gendebien and Willie Mairesse (both in Mercedes-Benz 300SLs), Claude Storez's Porsche Carrera Speedster, and (in 1958) Bernard Consten's Alfa-Romeo Giulietta SZ, which had already won the Alpine that year. Sheer strength, it seemed, was not enough to win the Liège; flashing performance and years of hard rallying experience were also necessary. It may be no more than coincidence that the space-frame Mercedes 300SLs began to fade from prominence after the event took to Jugoslavia;

The cars may have changed, but the congestion in a service park hasn't eased. In 1960 a British rally usually attracted shoals of Rapiers, Minis, Sprites, Beetles, Minors, Anglias and TR3As. The author was actually co-driving Rapier no. 117 in this event

Mairesse's victory in 1956 therefore ranks as a masterpiece, both of endurance and car preservation.

A brief look at the route of that 1958 event reveals a lot about the strain placed on serious contenders for Liège success. After the start in Belgium, the first night and day was really no more than a high-speed cruise down German motorways, and the real motoring did not begin until the rally arrived in Italy, south of Austria. The agony began on the Jugoslavian border, at Predil, and continued in a long loop down the Adriatic coast, through the hot, dusty, uncivilized hinterland, and back again to Predil.

It was at this point that endurance really began

to count. Without even a token pause, the route then took in all the highest passes in the Italian Dolomites, including several timed speed climbs of the worst examples. The survivors then had to drag themselves across northern Italy to the French Alps, where they were faced with a final breakneck night of racing around passes also used on the Alpine Rally.

The hard motoring was over at Grenoble, where only 23 of the 98 starters were still running, and all that remained was the long trek back to Belgium. All this, mark you, had been run off at the end of August, over roads often busy with holiday traffic, and without a single halt for sleep or rest. To finish at all was praiseworthy, and for that reason Pat Moss's remarkable drive into fourth place (with an Abingdon-prepared Austin-Healey 100 Six) was truly memorable.

Yet despite the reputation of the Belgian marathon, during the 1950s the French Alpine Rally was even more popular. It seemed to have everything – a splendid selection of routes, a no-nonsense approach by the Marseilles organizers, a start and finish on the Mediterranean, and a slot in the calendar either in June or July. From year to year the details changed, but the basic format was unaltered; throughout the 1950s the route included southern France, a little of Switzerland and much of northern Italy. Indeed, it seems strange that although so many 'classic' rallies used the Italian Alps, there was no Italian event in the top flight of summer rallies. An average Alpine occupied more than 2000 miles, and at least two overnight rest halts, but in an extremely 'difficult' year that mileage was increased to 2500 miles.

On every event there were normal liaison sections, tight road sections and flat-out speed tests (mostly hill-climbs, but as rallying developed they took in what we might now call 'special stages' as well). That most important award, the *Coupe des Alpes*, could not be lost by a poor performance on a speed test, but even one minute's lateness at any time control was enough to make it impossible to win. The most prized of all awards, apart from that of outright victory, was the *Coupe d'Or* (Gold Cup), awarded to those who managed to win three normal *Coupes* in consecutive years. Only marginally less impressive was a *Coupe d'Argent* (Silver Cup), awarded for three non-consecutive unpenalized runs. A Gold Cup was almost impossible to win, and during the 1950s only two drivers – Ian Appleyard (1950–52) and Stirling Moss (1952–54) – ever achieved this.

By comparison with other glamorous (and rather easy) events, there was no encouragement for the amateurs or poseurs to enter the Alpine, which regularly had only 60 or 70 starters. Each of these, however, was usually a seasoned rally driver, fully familiar with the special challenge of this event. Every Alpine started from the harbour area in Marseilles, where the organizing club had its offices, and the finish was usually at Cannes, Nice or Monte Carlo. Overnight halts were normally at ski resorts or other holiday towns in the mountains, where the cars were invariably placed in *parc fermé*, but where the crews could rest before beginning the next headlong scramble.

Much of the route, by tradition, was always the same. The first speed climb was in the hills behind Marseilles, and it was customary for the event to tackle Mont Ventoux and the Col du Rousset at an early stage. This was followed by

One of the most familiar sights of the 1950s in European rallies was a 'works' team from Triumph. A regular team driver was Rob Slotemaker, and his co-driver on this occasion was Ron Crellin

the drive through northern Italy, which inevitably included timed climbs of the 39 hairpins of the Stelvio, a tight passage of the Gavia, and another speed climb of the Vivione; and after the second night halt (or final halt, depending on the length of a particular rally) came the last incredibly exciting night, taking in every one of the navigable high passes in the Alps between Briançon, Gap and the French coast. Rarely was there time to do more than draw the proverbial breath at controls. There might be a speed climb of the north face of the Allos, but crews could not relax at the summit for the descent of the south side often carried on as a tight road section as well; the Alpine was like that, and everyone loved it.

Even in the 1950s, before it became a real problem, there was the constant hazard of non-competing cars, and of livestock. The Alpine, after all, was one of the last examples of a really fast event being held on public roads. It is true that traffic was banned from the use of roads scheduled as speed hill-climbs and discouraged from using the tighter road sections, but for years the Appleyards, Harpers, Mosses and Buchets of the rallying business learned to expect encounters with the ubiquitous 2CV Citroën, a haycart, or an unruly flock of sheep.

Within reason, however, the Alpine was not

One of Triumph's great successes was in the 1956 Alpine Rally, when TR3s gained five Coupes for unpenalised runs. Three of them were with 'works' cars, driven by Tommy Wisdom, Paddy Hopkirk and Maurice Gatonides

a rough rally. Some of the minor roads were loose-surfaced and very dusty, but chassis-breaking was not the intention of the organizers. All the tight sections were held on tarmac surfaces. Many had their start lines in the middle of villages or small towns; the local populace and the *gendarmerie* appeared to love it, and the atmosphere was full of excitement. There was no question, on this event, of a rally driver being a hero only to himself and his co-driver; in the Alpine, he always seemed to be on display.

Target averages of 60kph, incidentally, may sound pedestrian by 1980s expectations, but were often extremely difficult in French Alpine conditions. There were sections, even until the end of the 1960s, which were so narrow, steep and twisty that a 60kph average was quite impossible to achieve, and drivers of Porsches, super-light Alfa-Romeos and Mercedes-Benz 300SLs were not ashamed to admit it. For the pilots of saloon cars, among which the Sunbeam-Talbots (later Sunbeams), the big Citroëns and

the Ford Zephyrs were always prominent, such averages were in the realms of fantasy. The organizers therefore applied differential average targets for various groups, ensuring that enough fast 'run-in' was always included to make these *Coupe*-stoppers just about feasible. But adrenalin is a marvellous thing; quite often, before the start of an Alpine, there would be gloomy forecasts (after practice had taken place) that such-and-such a section was 'not on', while on the event itself it always seemed to happen that several cars made it without penalty.

Certain teams consolidated their names on the Alpine Rally. The Rootes Group progressed from the dilettante use of 2-litre Sunbeam-Talbots, driven by 'friends of the management', through purpose-built two-seater Sunbeam Alpines piloted by such notables as Stirling Moss, Mike Hawthorn and Shiela van Damm, to the very professional Sunbeam Rapier teams, headed by Peter Harper. Ken Richardson's Triumph TRs – driven by the team manager himself, by Maurice Gatsonides, Paddy Hopkirk, Keith Ballisat, and Annie Soisbault – were so successful on this event that rivals must have been happy to see Triumph sidetracked into Le Mans racing at the end of the 1950s.

It was in the Alpine, too, that the BMC team,

formed under the direction of Marcus Chambers in 1955, began to gain in stature. Using MGAs at first, and (from 1958) Austin-Healey 100 Sixes, 3000s and Sprites, and with drivers like John Gott, Jack Sears and Pat Moss, they began to look more and more likely to take all the top honours: in the 1950s, however, they were still on the 'learning curve' and their domination of the Alpine would come in the 1960s.

Fast and rugged sports cars usually put up best performance in the Alpines of the period, even though no general classification was officially listed until 1956. Ian Appleyard set up best performance by anyone's standards in 1950, in his Jaguar XK120 repeated the dose in 1951 and finished fourth in 1952, all with unpenalized runs and all in the same car. The names (and the cars they drove) of other winners in the 1950s were equally familiar: the event was not held in 1955 (Le Mans disaster) and 1957 (petrol rationing crisis), but in other years winners included Alex von Falkenhausen (BMW 328), Helmut Polensky (Porsche), Wolfgang Denzel (Denzel), Collange (Alfa-Romeo Giulietta) and Bernard Consten (Alfa-Romeo Guilietta SZ). Even admitting that handling standards changed considerably in the postwar period, it was always clear that an Alpine 'winner' had to be both fast and nimble. If it was also a lightweight car, then so much the better.

Service and support became increasingly important, even though such activities were officially discouraged for many years. There is the story about the Rootes team manager taking photographs of Citroëns being serviced, in case he might need the evidence at after-rally discussions, and getting back to his team camp to find a Citroën manager returning the compliment!

The Alpine organizers soon abandoned the regulation limiting the number of tyres which could be used (on at least one event all spare tyres had to be carried in, or on, the rally car) when it became clear that such a requirement might lead to the use of dangerously worn covers. Instead, they merely notched up all the target averages and cut down on rest halts, so that there was precious little time available for repairs or rebuilds.

The 1954 event, the 17th of its type, was typical of the breed, notable for the winning of the second *Coupe d'Or* (by Stirling Moss) and for the performance of Denzel's own mid-engined (by Porsche) Denzel sports car. As so

All the strain of a 96 hour non-stop rally shows in the faces of BMC's John Gott and Ray Brookes, with their MGA Twin-Cam, after the 1958 Liège–Rome–Liège

often happened, some of the highest passes were still blocked with snow, which meant (to the universal relief of all drivers) that the Gavia had to be bypassed, and even the Izoard (a main road, by comparison) proved impassable. There were 79 starters, factory-backed teams from Sunbeam, Triumph, Healey, Ford, Renault, Daimler, DKW and others, and the usual high average speeds. The first halt was at St Moritz, the second at Cortina d'Ampezzo, and the finish back in Cannes. It was the year when many cars lost their *Coupe* by failing to achieve target speeds on a German autobahn, when the delights of the Vivione Pass were introduced for the first time, when the celebrated 188-mile 'Circuit of the Dolomites' took place, and when Triumph's TR2s made a remarkable debut by winning the team prize. Eleven crews won *Coupes*, making it something of an easy year by Alpine standards.

Each rally, of course, was notable for a different reason. The 1956 event, for instance, crossed into Jugoslavia, exactly as the Liège did a few weeks later (and was another triumph for Triumph, who won five *Coupes*), while the 1958 event saw the debut of the 2.2-litre TR3As, the six-cylinder BMC Abingdon Austin-Healey team, and timing which proved to be impossible for everyone (and had to be retrospectively modified so that seven cars could be awarded

The big DS19 Citroëns could continue rallying when seemingly battered to death by the terrible rally roads of the world. The driver is Lucien Bianchi, and the country is Jugoslavia

It may look like a road race, and many competitors treated it like one, but this was merely a massed-restart from Sofia in the 1961 Liège–Sofia–Liège Rally. Cars prominent 'on the grid' are Citroën DS19s, Porsches, and an Austin-Healey 3000

with *Coupes*). This was also the rally in which Paddy Hopkirk climbed most of he Stelvio pass with a punctured tyre on his works TR3A, cooked the engine, and was sacked for his pains.

Throughout this period, naturally, there were a few other events which tried to emulate the Alpine, but the magic always seemed to be missing. One such example was the Geneva Rally, which, to reapply Winston Churchill's famous remark, was 'a modest little rally with much to be modest about'. The Lisbon was still held, still counted for the European Championship (although its organizers ofter insisted on strange and nit-picking rules, as on one occasion when a works car was disqualified for having black numbers on a white patch, instead of white numbers on the black patch), and still relied to some extent on driving tests to arrive at a result. There was also the Adriatic Rally, held in high summer in Jugoslavia, which usually favoured the stronger and more durable type of saloon cars.

In the meantime, great changes to the rallying scene were developing, in southern Europe, Africa and other far-flung places. There was evidently a strong demand for events in which strength and reliability (in both cars and drivers) mattered more than being able to rustle up the fastest and most exotic sporting coupé; and such events had now begun to appear. A shorter type of motoring marathon was on the way.

5 | Who needs Real Roads?

Although the great sport of rallying was invented and developed in Europe, this certainly did not mean that it was a sport ideally suited for adoption all around the world. Initially, the superior state of European road systems and surfaces, kept it fairly local. Indeed, it took some time for it to become established in other continents. As we have seen, up to the end of the 1930s most of the important rallies, and nearly all the top-class drivers, were to be found in Europe.

With the exception of North America (and then only in parts), other countries and continents, at the beginning of the 20th century, were neither sufficiently developed or prosperous to make rallying feasible. Terrible roads, especially in remote regions, made long-distance motoring difficult for all but the most adventurous drivers. The New York to Paris marathon of 1908 showed that even the North American countryside could be impassable at times, particularly in winter.

It would, for example, have been no more possible to run a 'Prince Henry' type of trial in Australia before the First World War than to promote one in Africa or South America, not merely because there were so few cars available (and, therefore, by definition, so few potential rally drivers), but also because tracks outside the main towns and cities were so appalling. Furthermore, social conditions and habits were not yet appropriate for the *Concours* type of event.

In such countries, therefore, a special form of rallying eventually began to develop. Since the roads were not good enough for European motor sport, it had to be tailored to the existing roads, tracks or, sometimes, passable wastelands. Open-road racing, or rallying 'against the clock', had to take account of the poor conditions and come to terms with them.

Outside Europe, therefore, organizers directed their efforts towards rough-road motoring, which required different types of cars and drivers. At a time when European rallying stars were still swivelling round pylons, sprinting up and down seafront promenades or polishing their immaculate limousines, drivers in other parts of the world were learning to handle big, rugged cars, building up their own strength and fitness, and hurling their much-modified machines across whatever terrain was available. Nobody seemed to care whether the result was rallying or racing.

One of the very first long-distance rough-road events, which set a trend later copied by several other developing nations, was the Gran Premio Nacional, promoted by the Automobile Club Argentino in 1910. Although there was certainly an element of rallying involved, especially where the tracks only approximated to a civilized road, the Gran Premio was a genuine race. The first event covered 465 miles and attracted only seven starters. Although its popularity grew steadily, the Gran Premio remained a national event for many years, and it was not until 1933 that the route was altered, and lengthened, to more than 1000 miles. By the end of the 1930s, and in the early 1940s, it became a fertile nursery for a series of racing drivers – among them Juan-Manuel Fangio and Froilan Gonzales – to learn and prove their craft. Rallying of the recognized modern type did not arrive in South America for several more years.

The great off-road or rough-road trials and rallies blossomed in several continents after the Second World War. There had to be an interval while nations recovered from the ravages of battle, while civilian life returned to something like normal, and until petrol rationing had been swept away. In the Commonwealth countries, the great surge forward was mainly due to the efforts of British expatriates with some experience of European motor sport.

The most famous of all the rough-road events, though not the longest nor even the first, was, without doubt, the Safari, and it deserves a descriptive section to itself. I use the shortest version of its title for two reasons, firstly because that is the name by which the event has always been known, and secondly because (like other famous events) it has changed its official title more than once in the last two decades. What-

Mercedes-Benz produced the ideal Safari-type car in the 1950s – rugged, reliable, and fast enough. In these 1959 conditions, however, every car was struggling for grip

In the 1950s, if rallying was rough, and if traction was hard to find, a VW Beetle was often among the leaders. This one, driven by J. Townsend and D. Shepherd, won its price category in the 1958 Coronation Safari

ever its name, the Safari is arguably *the* most famous and, commercially, *the* most important rally in the world today. Its reputation, incidentally, was established in the days when to enter the Safari one had to have a standard saloon car in Group 1 tune.

There had been a Nairobi-to-Johannesburg cross-country race in the 1930s, and this was succeeded by the Nairobi–Cape Town–Nairobi run in the 1940s. East Africans who had competed in these pioneering events then began discussing the prospects of a long-distance event confined to their own part of the continent. As the drivers and organizers were all amateurs, they had to build their event around leisure time; and in 1953 they found an ideal opportunity in the national holiday to celebrate the Coronation of Queen Elizabeth II.

The Coronation Safari, as it was aptly named, was at first something of a jaunt for local drivers from Kenya, Uganda and Tanganyika. Organized under the auspices of the Royal East African AA, in May and June, the original plan had been for a 1500 mile clockwise circuit around Lake Victoria, but poor ferry connections caused that idea to be scrapped. Instead, there was a starting point in each of the three countries involved, and the finish was to be in Nairobi. Although many well-known East African 'main' roads were in the route, conditions were often quite

awful, for this was the equatorial 'winter', which meant that a great deal of rain had been falling.

In several respects, the first Coronation Safari was certainly 'strange'. Not only was the entry restricted to what we now understand as Group 1 touring cars, but the cars were grouped into categories by price rather than engine size. Even more remarkable was the fact that the cars were not started at intervals, but *en masse*; from Nairobi, where 42 of the 57 entries set out, they all followed the mayor to the city outskirts, and when he pulled aside, the race was on!

Average speeds were set at between 43mph for the cheapest cars to 52mph for the most expensive, but even though the 'best' roads in the three countries were used, there were mass delays in Tanganyika. At one point, the whole event halted, and although only 16 cars made it back to Nairobi, 27 crews were classified as finishers because they had still been running at the end of the last uninterrupted section. For the record, it was a VW Beetle driven by Alan Dix which won that first event, with a time penalty of only 17 minutes.

The next three Safaris were still strictly local affairs, two of them being far too easy because slower time schedules coincided with dry weather conditions. In those early years, Vic Preston was a member of the winning crew in

1954 (VW Beetle) and 1955 (Ford Zephyr), while in 1956 Eric Cecil's Auto Union 1000 victory was only achieved by a race-circuit tie-breaker after no fewer than 78 cars had finished, 13 of them unpenalized.

Even so, Maurice Gatsonides had competed in the 1956 event, in a works Standard Vanguard, and it was his report to the FIA in Paris which led to the Safari getting its full International permit for 1957. Since the event, still called the Coronation Safari (a title it kept until 1960), was also moved to its now-traditional Easter weekend date, it is worth looking in a little more detail at its format, and at the fortunes of the crews.

The 1957 Safari had a route of over 3000 miles; but because of the impossibly wild bush conditions, the course had to be shortened by more than 200 miles during the actual event. Nearly three-quarters of the route was over unmade or even non-existent roads, many of which were turned into swamps, mud-baths, or deep flood zones by the heavy rain which tends to fall in East Africa at about this time of year.

The International permit in 1957 was good for prestige but did nothing for the entry, which still consisted entirely of local East African drivers. There were 64 starters but only 19 finishers, many of those who retired being forced out by the weather (and road conditions) rather than by mechanical failures. This time it was Englishman Arthur Burton's turn to win in a VW Beetle (partnered by Gus Hofmann), and a VW team also took the team prize. The other class winners were Mike Armstrong/Morris

In the late 1950s, the sturdy Alfa Romeo Giulietta chassis was mated to a stubby and attractive little Zagato coupe style, and – even with only a 1,290cc engine – was an outright winner on several occasions. In 1958, this particular car, driven by Bernard Consten, won the Alpine Rally in July

Temple-Boreham (Fiat 1100TV) and Jim Feeney/'Nick' Nowicki (Peugeot 403).

A year later the Safari attracted eight overseas drivers, but they were disappointed by a 'dry' event spoilt by controversy, scrutineering penalties and protests, not to mention the fact that the rules did not provide for the nomination of an outright winner. None of the Europeans (who included Ronnie Adams in a Mercedes-Benz 220 and Per Malling in a Volvo PV444) won awards.

The real build-up of the Safari 'legend' came in the next few years, with an assault by works teams and drivers. For the first time, East African tracks were sampled by drivers who had to become familiar with 'murram', 'black cotton', 'washaways' and 'flash floods'. Newcomers found it all too easy to misread road conditions and break their cars in the process; it took years for some drivers to come to terms with the bushcraft and outback-mechanic methods needed on an event where the rally car might be without service support for hours on end. It was in these years that the Safari's most lasting (and erroneous) legend grew up – that the event could never be won by an overseas driver; nobody argued that the overseas professionals were not fast enough, merely that they would

Condrillier's 'works' Renault Dauphine – seen behind one of its team mates at the Monza test – won the 1959 Alpine rally outright, helped along by favourable target times

never learn enough about the special hazards involved.

The first truly 'international' Safari, therefore, was in 1959, when factory teams from Ford and Rootes were entered. Ford sent no fewer than three Zephyrs and three Anglias, while Rootes entered three Hillman Husky utility vehicles and a Humber Super Snipe instead of their more familiar Sunbeam Rapiers; as the Huskys shared the same chassis engineering with the Rapiers, the cars were expected to be competitive. It was a typical 'classic' Safari route, centred on Nairobi, but stretching as far south as Dar-es-Salaam in Tanganyika and as far north as Kampala in Uganda. Torrential rain fell before the start, but during the event itself many of the roads became dry and dusty again.

With 'names' in the factory teams like Peter Harper, Peter Jopp, Paddy Hopkirk, Ronnie Adams, Edward Harrison and Denis Scott, a win for a European might have been expected, but – as was to happen so often in the next few

years – it was an East African resident, Bill Fritschy (Mercedes-Benz 219) who beat the lot, though the British-driven Zephyrs finished second and third. None of the Huskys survived (Peter Harper broke his arm in an accident) and the Anglias were outclassed. In that year, incidentally, two other names crept into the list of starters – Bert Shankland and Joginder Singh – not then famous, but destined to play a significant role in future Safaris.

A year later the rally was renamed the East African Safari, gaining a considerable boost as hordes of Fords and Rootes cars (Rapiers this time) were joined by an optimistically entered trio of BMC Minis, all offering a formidable challenge to local drivers of Mercedes-Benz, VW and Citroën cars. Once again it was a case of local knowledge beating star driving talent, for Fritschy won his second Safari from Temple-Boreham's Citroën ID19 and Vic Preston's works Zephyr. Rootes's Rapiers made no impression, but Ford's new 105E Anglias won their class, and Zephyrs once again took the team prize; the Minis, predictably because of their minimal ground clearance, were soon annihilated.

Before long, however, there were more concerted works attacks from Europe, as well as increasing under-the-counter assistance to East African Peugeot, Mercedes-Benz and VW drivers. Renaults entered for the first time in 1961, and Rovers in 1962, but more significant was the appearance of two Saabs in 1962, followed by the first official Nissan-Datsun entries in 1963. At the time, most people thought the Japanese cars were a bit of a joke, but smiles faded in 1966 when a Datsun first won its class, and there was no more banter after 1970 when they won outright.

While all this was going on, however, an unimportant little European Championship event in Greece – the Acropolis Rally – had begun to make its own rough-road reputation. Though never as prestigious as the Safari (it was neither as remote, nor as hazardous or long), the Acropolis nevertheless combined heat, rough roads and endurance. Before the rustic delights of Greece were eroded by modern civilization (bringing a wholesale improvement in driving conditions), the Acropolis made almost as many demands on a car as did the last generation of Liège–Sofia–Liège rallies. It was not without significance that a potential winner of the Acropolis often had to be built almost to Safari specifications; on some occasions, cars that had completed the Safari without structural failures were rushed back to Europe, refettled, and given another run in Greece.

Yet the Acropolis had not initially been a very demanding rally. During the first three years (1956 to 1958) that the event was included in the Championship, it was won by fast GT cars like a 'gullwing' Mercedes-Benz 300SL (driven by Walter Schock), by a Ferrari 250GT (Estager), and by a Lancia Aurelia GT (Villoresi). Something of a change occurred in 1959 when Wolfgang Levy's Auto Union 1000 beat Hans Walter's Porsche Carrera, and in 1960 when a *real* rough-road car (Schock's Mercedes-Benz 220SE) won the event outright from Erik Carlsson's two-stroke Saab and Peter Harper's rugged Sunbeam Rapier. There was an outright win for Carlsson in 1961, and for that remarkable little German, Eugen Bohringer (Mercedes-Benz 220SE) in 1962. Bohringer won again, as expected, in 1963, using the similar but larger-engined 300SE, while in 1964 it was Volvo's turn to gain the laurels, with Tom Trana using a PV544 to beat Ogier's Citroën DS19 and Pat Moss's Saab; indicative, however, of the steady improvement of Stuart Turner's Minis was the

If one mastered the handling, a rear-engined Porsche Type 356 was often strong enough and fast enough to win major international rallies. Hans-Joachim Walter won the European rally championship in such a car in 1961, and was second overall in this event, the 1962 Alpine, behind the Austin-Healey 3000 of the Morley Twins. This car had a 2-litre four-cam Carrera engine

fact that in the latter year Paddy Hopkirk's 1275S led outright until hours from the finish.

As the 1960s progressed, it was interesting to see the type of cars which emerged as 'rough-road' champions. The big Mercedes-Benz and Volvo saloons were, predictably, usually among the awards; and it was not surprising to see the ubiquitous VW Beetles disappear from the lists because of their limited performance. The Beetles, in fact, were by now in a tight corner. In standard form, they were very strong but very slow; they could be made to go considerably faster, but this was always at the expense of reliability. Private owners previously faithful to Wolfsburg found that they had to buy a Porsche to redress the balance, which was very costly and still not a guarantee of success.

One astonishingly competent car (although

In the mid-1960s rugged cars like the Peugeot 404 confirmed their reputation in events like the East African Safari. Bert Shankland from Tanzania, an ex-patriate Scot, won the event twice in cars like this

Years after the Austin-Healey 3000 was retired, the Datsun 240Z grew up to replace it. In 1971, Edgar Hermann won the event in this factory-prepared example; the previous year he had used a Datsun 1600 SSS to win his first Safari

to be outpaced as rally speeds increased) was the big Rover 3-litre. Once thought to be no more than a stodgy, heavy middle-class saloon, the 3-litre was thrust into major international rallying in 1962 by the Rover factory, who were out to prove the exact opposite. The 3-litre had a short rallying career, for Rover's long term aim was to publicize the Rover 2000 which followed, but in two short years it built up quite a reputation. The trouble was that Rover insisted on keeping the cars very standard, so that to enter them ostentatiously in the 1963 RAC Rally without any service support was rather a meaningless gesture.

It was a pity that company politics and a limited budget prevented Rover's great rivals at Triumph doing more with the Triumph 2000, for this was also a promising cross-country 'tank'. We all had to wait until 1970 and the *Daily Mirror* World Cup Rally to see the point proved.

I thought long and hard before deciding *not* to include the last spine-tingling Liège–Rome–Liège and Liège–Sofia–Liège rallies in this chapter. Undoubtedly the events were rough enough to qualify for inclusion, and they certainly attracted a more professional standard of entry than that of the Safari or the Acropolis. But the chassis-breaking sections of the Liège formed only a part of the events, because these roads, no matter how bad, were used regularly for traffic, and because there was much more opportunity for a determined factory team to arrange for regular service and support. Liège weather, like that of the Acropolis, tended to be hot and dusty, so there was never any risk of floods or impassable bogs preventing a fair result. For these reasons, therefore, I merely mention the Liège at this point, and defer a detailed description until Chapter 7, where it rightfully appears as the last of the 'great road races'.

Even by the end of the 1960s, too, the Acropolis had really ceased to be a rough-road event, as shown by victories in 1967 by BMC Mini (Hopkirk), in 1968 by Ford Escort TC (Clark) and 1969 by Porsche (Toivonen). Thereafter, the Greek event was merely one of the world-class gravel-rallies which became so important to the developing World Championship series in the 1970s.

As the years passed, therefore, rough-road rallying tended to become confined to Africa. The Safari, no matter what it was called or how

If only BL had developed the commitment, or found the money, at the right time, their Triumph 2000s could have been Safari winners. Brian Culcheth tried hard on this occasion, but was let down by a lack of experience in preparation

it was restricted for political reasons, remained the standard at which similar events had to aim. Other African countries organized their own events, usually following the Safari format slavishly, and occasionally a peripatetic driver might turn up to enhance his reputation. Safari 'superstars' like Bert Shankland from Tanzania, Joginder 'Raghead' Singh from Kenya and Shekhar Mehta of Uganda were never fast enough to come to Europe and win a pace-notes event, or be competitive through forests, but put down in a wilderness anywhere in the world they could be expected to figure in the results. They scored by virtue of their experience and cunning, their ability to read a strange and un-

predictable route, and their capacity to 'pace' a car over the most inhospitable terrain.

There has never yet been another African event to match the Safari, though this opinion may have to be revised during the 1980s. A splendid semi-desert event was promoted in Morocco in the 1960s, and took on World Championship status from 1971; at the peak of its popularity in the mid-1970s, it was virtually forgotten by the end of the decade. Bandama, that splendid Safari 'look-alike' promoted towards the end of every year in the Ivory Coast (West Africa), came to prominence in 1971 and was included in the World Championship for the first time in 1978. In Australia, of course, there is the Southern Cross Rally, won so many times by Andrew Cowan in Japanese cars; this event lacks the speed and prestige of the African events, but has most of the other virtues. The Safari and Bandama, after all, achieve results simply by the means of long road sections and

By 1972 the Safari cars were so fast that photographers needed light aeroplanes to keep up with them. This was Hannu Mikkola's winning Escort RS1600 on its way to an historic victory – he was the first non-African to win the Safari

Side view of Vic Preston's 1974 Escort RS1600 shows that they were being used as veritable advertising billboards. In that year 'Junior' took ninth place

high target average speeds; in Australia, for all the usual reasons, special stages are needed. As for other venues, because of rapid industrialization and social advances, it is highly unlikely that new contenders will appear. For that reason alone, no event held in the Middle East, for example, can ever become a latter-day Safari; ten years ago it might still have been possible, but not any more.

In Nick Brittan's book *Safari Fever* about Ford's successful onslaught on the 1972 Safari, there is a useful historical section on the event by John Davenport. That section describes the Safaris of the 1960s as the 'Golden Years', and I would not argue with that. It was the period when the Safari was transformed from an adventure for venturesome amateurs to a challenge for the factories: developing from an event for 'standard' saloon cars into one for the more exotic type, and finally emerging as a showcase for the best rally cars, teams and drivers in the world.

Until 1966 the Safari was strictly 'Group 1' (an experiment permitting Group 3 Grand Tourers, in the 1960 event, was not repeated), although enterprising homologation of parts by some manufacturers had enabled fast cars to be developed, even for this event. The records show that from 1961 to 1966 every winner was an East African, but that the cars were all European (two wins for Peugeot, one each for Mercedes-Benz, VW, Volvo and Ford). The most remarkable win was in 1965 by Joginder Singh, whose Volvo PV544 was well and truly secondhand before the event began; and the luckiest was probably by 'Nick' Nowicki in 1963, when there were a mere seven finishers from 84 starters. The most determined (and, as it happens, successful) assault was by Ford in 1964, who entered no fewer than six Cortina GTs, won outright (with Peter Hughes driving) *and* took the team prize into the bargain.

In the same period, however, the biggest publicity was gained by one team – and one man – who never quite managed to win. The team was Saab, and the man – as if you hadn't guessed – was Erik Carlsson. On the face of it, a tiny high-revving two-stroke 850cc engine was unlikely to be competitive, but the giant Swedish driver made up for that. There were works Saabs in every Safari from 1962 to 1966, yet the best they ever achieved was second in 1964.

On the first occasion, Carlsson and Pat Moss both led for a while, but Pat's car hit an animal and Carlsson's rear suspension later collapsed; Pat ended up third, having finished equal second with Nowicki's Peugeot before a scrutineering penalty was applied, and Erik took sixth place. A year later Carlsson (partnered by Gunnar Palm) was entered again, leading for much of the event before his car collided with a wild animal and was subsequently forced to retire with broken front suspension.

In 1964 it was an even more closely knit team, for Erik and Pat had married, and both were entered in their own team cars. 1964, of course, was eventually Ford's year, and an extremely 'wet' one by many Safari standards, yet Carlsson finished second overall, just 15 minutes behind Peter Hughes's Cortina GT, and Pat managed ninth place. In that year Carlsson established a Safari legend: on finding his Saab stuck in ruts, he managed – with the help of co-driver Gunnar Palm – literally to roll the car sideways out of trouble by sheer manpower.

There were still two more attempts to go. In 1965 the family commitment was even greater when Erik took along Pat's famous brother

The Escort's second Safari victory came in 1977, when Bjorn Waldegard took his Boreham-prepared RS1800 through mile after mile of swamp like this

Stirling as his co-driver. Erik did not get far, and although Pat led the event for some time, she later had an accident with a renegade lorry and had to retire. Victory in a very wet and sticky event went to Joginder's old Volvo. In 1966, as in 1965, mud was the main reason for many retirements, and the only factory Saab entry (for Pat Moss and Elizabeth Nystrom) was forced to give up with front suspension derangements caused by helping to pull Bert Shankland's Peugeot 404 out of one such mud hole. Ironically enough, Shankland then went on to win the event himself!

A year later Shankland and his Peugeot won again, in the first Safari that allowed in Group 2 cars. Ford had hoped to win with their Mk II Cortina GTs, and indeed Bengt Soderstrom led for much of the event. In the end they had to settle for second and third overall placings (Vic Preston's old-style Lotus-Cortina being second), and took the team prize yet again. Even in this, the first Safari to allow modified touring cars to compete, target average speeds were often higher than 60mph, yet some of the best teams were able to 'clean' most of them. In the entire event, Shankland's total penalty (using a Group 1 Peugeot) was only 59 minutes.

In the next few years the Safari changed con-

After the Peugeot 404 came the 504, then the 504 Coupé, then the V6-engined Coupé. It was the latter model which was ideal for Jean-Pierre ('Jumbo') Nicolas to use to win the 1978 Safari

siderably, becoming less of an East African spectacular and more of a modern world-class rally. The reason, without doubt, was that more and more factory teams became involved, and that in order to cater for them, target averages and the general layout of the event had to be altered accordingly.

There were really two reasons for the factory invasion – one practical and one emotional. Nobody, by that time, disputed the commercial importance of the Safari – it seemed to be agreed that an outright victory was as important to sales, particularly in developing countries, as a Monte Carlo success would be. The emotional reason was (and to a certain extent, still is) tied up with the old saying that 'Only an East African driver can win the Safari'. Some drivers and teams were, without exaggeration, obsessed by this, regarding it as a myth that ought to be demolished as soon as possible.

The records show that it took time – and a great deal of money and frustration. In 1968, an extremely difficult year in which only seven crews managed to finish, Nowicki repeated his 1963 success, using a Peugeot 404; there were works cars from Ford, Datsun and BMC (in 1800s), along with a factory-prepared Porsche for Edgar Hermann, all of which failed. A year later, the whole concept of the Safari was upset because of a political tiff between Tanzania and the other East African countries, so that the route had to be switched through Uganda instead. Factory teams on that occasion included Ford Germany (Taunus 20MRS), Lancia (Fulvia 1300), Porsche (911), Saab (96V4) and Datsun (1600SSS). The overall target average was above 60mph, with some sections set at more than 85mph. Once again, European drivers dominated at first (Soderstrom's Taunus led until 500 miles from the finish), but it was Robin Hillyar's Taunus which finally won.

1970 heralded Japanese domination of the Safari, for Edgar Hermann won in a factory-prepared Datsun 1600SSS, and triumphed again a year later in a rorty two-seater Datsun 240Z coupé. The list of results in 1970, incidentally, was significant, for there were no fewer than six Datsuns in the top dozen. In 1971, the first 'Group 4' Safari, Ford of Britain, returning to Africa after taking a two-year sabbatical in favour of Ford Germany, were astonished to see how the event had meanwhile speeded up; and their Escort Twin-Cams were beaten not only by the conditions but by the pace. Next year, however, they were back with 205bhp Escort RS1600s, and this time they made no mistake.

It was in 1972 that the Safari myth was finally broken, for the event was won by a non-African driver. Without undue luck, and without any undue effort, Ford not only won a mainly dry rally, but did it thanks to Hannu Mikkola. Mikkola's winning margin over Zasada's Porsche 911S was 28 minutes, and two other RS1600s were third and fourth. What was so very satisfying after the debacle of 1971 was that the best two surviving Datsuns (of Hermann and Aaltonen) were down in fifth and sixth positions.

The cosmopolitan invaders nearly did it again in 1973, but in a fantastic dead-heat, in which the 'furthest without penalty' tie-decider had to be invoked, Harry Kallstrom's Datsun 1800SSS was beaten by Ugandan Shekhar Mehta's Datsun 240Z. Ford, hot favourites to repeat their 1972 performance, lost their competitive RS1600s after the cars had led the event for a considerable time, and the factory-prepared Porsches all retired. There were four more Japanese successes in the next seven years – two for Colt (both driven by Joginder Singh) and two for Datsun (160Js driven by Shekhar Mehta) – but each of the other three events were won by Europeans in European cars. Ove Andersson (Peugeot 504) scooped the pool in 1975, Bjorn Waldegard splashed his way through one of the wettest Safaris on record to win in an Escort RS1800 in 1977, and Jean-Pierre Nicolas (popularly known as 'Jumbo') used a Peugeot 504 V6 Coupé to win the 1978 event.

Meanwhile, a string of visiting teams had discovered that the Safari could not merely be conquered by time, effort and money. They included Alpine-Renault, really too fragile in spite of their success in Morocco, Citroën (too complicated), Porsche (not sufficiently serious, although they tried often enough, with Waldegard so nearly winning in 1978), Fiat (lack of experience), Mercedes-Benz (dare we say, too cocky?), and – unhappiest of all – Lancia.

The all-purpose rallying 'supercar' which so-nearly won the roughest of rallies so often was the Lancia Stratos. In Safari form, driven here by Sandro Munari, it was by no means the sleek and purposeful-looking 'racer' we knew in Europe

Bjorn Waldegard's Martini-sponsored Porsche 911 led the 1978 Safari for many hours, then suffered a rear suspension collapse, and eventually finished fourth

In the 1970s, Datsun won the Safari four times, in every case with standard-looking (and sounding) quantity-production cars. In 1979 Shekhar Mehta used a 160J, with single-cam 2-litre engine, for his second personal Safari win

I leave mention of Lancia to the last, because there were few more thrilling sights than that of a brightly-liveried Stratos, sometimes with body panels missing, surging through deep floods or powering its way helter-skelter across the limitless African plains. Factory Stratos entered in 1975, 1976 and 1977, and on each occasion they might have won. Sandro Munari was second to Andersson's Peugeot in 1975 (Waldegard's Stratos was third), the team failed completely in 1976 after many mechanical failures, and Munari was third in 1977 behind Waldegard's Escort and Aaltonen's Datsun. Aaltonen, incidentally, is probably the most determined (and the most unlucky) European never to have won the Safari; he had competed since the early 1960s, chalked up a record number of excursions and accidents, taken second place several times but never quite attained his ambition.

In all this time, the reputation of the Safari, as the world's fastest, toughest and most prestigious rough-road rally has never wavered. The pace of modern rally cars is such that average speeds nowadays regularly have to be set at more than 100mph (especially on sections where the once impassable East African roads have been graded or even – horror of horrors – given a coating of tarmac), with team service support consisting of an army of cars, super-

visory 'spotter' aircraft and even the occasional helicopter.

The cost of such operations, obviously, is enormous. Ford admitted to spending more than £50,000 to win in 1972 (and the real figure was probably nearer to twice that), while Mercedes-Benz certainly spent well over £250,000 in 1980 *and* failed to win the event. It is this scale of cost, of course, which eventually deters many teams. Even Ford, with every chance of being competitive, ducked out in 1976, and the list of unsuccessful teams who made the trip once, or at the most twice, is lengthy.

Cheaper, if not more predictable, competition for the Safari came in the 1960s and 1970s from Morocco and the Ivory Coast. Both were countries having strong historical connections with France and active interests selling French cars, so it was not surprising that both the Rallye du Maroc and the Rallye Bandama attracted factory teams from France, with the rest of the rallying world following later. It was probably French experience and expertise, rather than any other consideration, that enabled their cars to dominate both events throughout the 1970s.

The Moroccan Rally developed from a local effort in the late 1950s into a more prominent International at the end of the 1960s. By that time it was something of a Citroën monopoly (the DS being ideally suited to the appalling cross-desert route); in 1970, for instance, Citroën were so committed to success that they pulled out their team drivers from the *Daily Mirror* World Cup Rally (while the marathon cars were taking an enforced rest on board ship to South America), supplied a new set of DS21s for the Moroccan event, and duly achieved a remarkable success, with Bob Neyret driving the winning car. A year later Citroën won again, this time with the Maserati-engined SM coupé, driven by local-man Jean Deschazeaux, but by this time the opposition was increasing rapidly. A year later Lancia had the temerity to beat the French on their 'own' ground (and it was a Finn, Simo Lampinen, who drove the winning Fulvia HF coupé), but from then until 1976 (after which the Moroccan event disappeared from the calendar) the event was once again a French monopoly, with two wins each for Peugeot and Alpine-Renault.

It was no surprise, of course, for Morocco to be won by Peugeot 504s, which had already made their name in Africa and many other rough-road events, but in 1973 it was a real shock to see the little rear-engined, plastic-bodied Alpine-Renault coupés beat the might of Citroën, Peugeot and Fiat. In many ways it was a masterpiece of preparation, development and servicing over design, for the once-fragile little cars (which had also started winning events such as the Acropolis) were now built like tanks, were thoroughly skidded underneath, and were massively rebuilt at every opportunity. At this stage in the event, seasoned drivers such as Rauno Aaltonen were quoted as saying that Moroccan stages were 'much more severe than the Safari', even though there was usually the luxury of an occasional night in bed. That the 1973 win was no fluke was proved a year later, when Jean-Pierre Nicolas beat the Renault team in his Alpine-Renault; but in 1975 and 1976 it was Hannu Mikkola and Nicolas (again) who drove the marvellously strong Peugeot 504s to victory.

In 1976, indeed, there was more than usual worldwide interest, with factory teams from Fiat, Lancia and Ford. The entries from Bore-ham were of cars previously prepared (but not used) for the Safari, while Fiat sent strengthened 131s, and Munari had a single Stratos. The Fiats and the Fords both wilted under the strain (proving that Morocco could be as demanding as the Safari) while the Stratos finished third, 78 minutes behind Nicolas's Peugeot. That year, if for no other reason, Morocco distinguished itself by including the longest special stage of all time – an 800-kilometre section across the rocky desert towards the Spanish Sahara.

As the 1970s wore on, however, it was un-doubtedly the Bandama Rally that became more glamorous every time it was held. When Bob Neyret (Peugeot 504) won the first event in 1971, it made little impression; but it achieved instant notoriety in 1972 when the last two drivers left in the event – Tony Fall and Shekhar Mehta – ran out of time in face of a very fast schedule, the organizers refusing to modify their targets, and the event becoming one of the very first rallies ever known in which there were no finishers at all!

Bandama, however, still had a limited follow-ing, mainly for French or European drivers in French cars, and there was really so little interest from other nations that after the 1974 event Henry Liddon's *Autocar* report was headlined 'What's Bandama?' On that occasion it was Timo Makinen and Liddon (doubling his re-

One of Daimler-Benz's first serious attempts to win the Safari came in 1979, but most of their cars suffered mechanical misfortune. This was Andrew Cowan's 280E saloon, on its way to fourth place

porting function with a co-driver's job) who won in a works-prepared Peugeot 504. The event actually started on Christmas Day, which seemed a bit hard, and attracted 52 entries, though only six made it back to the finish in Abidjan. Makinen's penalty was 110 minutes, and his winning margin over Chausseuil's Datsun 180B was 51 minutes; nothing as precise as seconds have ever been needed on *this* event.

In the next few years French and Japanese cars dominated the results, Peugeot winning in 1975 and 1976 (Bernard Consten and Timo Makinen again, this time in a 504 V6 Coupé), and Andrew Cowan's Mitsubishi Colt Lancer in 1977. For 1978 Bandama became a World Championship event, but entries were still limited to 51 and there were only nine finishers. There were Peugeot's, Mitsubishis and Datsuns on some numbers, but Fiat did not appear, the single (Group 2) Opel Ascona retired with engine trouble, and the cheeky little Renault 5 Alpines were not really suitable for this sort of going.

As Martin Holmes commented in the first of his rallying annuals, Peugeot eventually won and nobody had really expected otherwise. The 504 Coupés, complete with V6 engines, were too strong *and* too fast for the opposition, which was no surprise. Unpredictably, however, Jean-Pierre Nicolas repeated his Safari performance and won the event for Peugeot, beating Timo Makinen (who had an identical car) by 15 minutes, and Ragnotti's remarkable Renault 5 Alpine by 82 minutes. By 1979, however, other teams had decided that Bandama was not only worth doing (can you think of a nicer place to be in December, when the sun is shining?), but that Peugeot could be beaten. Works cars from Toyota and Mercedes-Benz backed their opinions with action – Toyota entering only two but Mercedes-Benz sending no fewer than four of the 450SLCs complete with 300bhp 5.0-litre engines.

The last Bandama Rally of the 1970s, therefore, was not only long and very fast (5622 kilometres in a scheduled 55hr 30min – an overall target average of 101kph, or 63mph), but also worth including in the World Championship. As it turned out, Mercedes-Benz had spent so much money on preparation, practice and service coverage, that all four cars finished in the top four positions. Hannu Mikkola won the event, with a penalty of 203 minutes, but Bjorn Waldegard's car finished second, 35 minutes behind, and Waldegard secured the driver's Championship by that drive. For the first time in the 1970s Bandama was something of a humiliation for Peugeot, who lost three of their

four factory-prepared cars with mechanical breakdowns, though Ove Andersson's Toyota Celica Liftback was the best 'non-Mercedes-Benz' finisher. The 1979 event was historic in two respects – it was the first-ever World Championship event to be won by a car with an eight-cylinder engine, and the first to be won by a car with an automatic gearbox.

Even in such a large, sparsely populated country, however, there were several ominous signs which the more sensitive observers noted with alarm. Although there were no serious accidents involving non-competing cars or stray animals, many drivers were obviously and very vocally worried about their 'near-misses'. There are no special stages in this type of rallying, even though speeds are very high and the roads always open to other traffic. Those most exposed to danger are the 'top seeds' who are running at the front of the field and who often arrive at high speed in places where they are not expected by the local populace; and when people are alerted, foolhardy and uncontrolled crowds of spectators are likely to pose an additional hazard.

As mentioned at the beginning of this chapter, this type of rough-road rallying is only truly justified in zones that are undeveloped and almost unpopulated. The problem now is that few such areas still exist, and I see absolutely no likelihood of successors to the Safari, Morocco or Bandama appearing in the 1980s. It was precisely these problems – of mounting congestion and of hostile public opinion – which caused great changes in European rallying in the 1950s, and this revolution deserves a chapter to itself.

Daimler-Benz started entering official 'works' teams in World Championship rallying in 1978. In 1979 they had a remarkable 1-2-3-4-victory in the Bandama Rally, which ended the season. Hannu Mikkola, in car number 6, was the overall victor

6 | To the Woods!

It was rally cars themselves, and their improving performance, which brought about great changes in European rallying during the 1950s. In some countries, indeed, their antics could no longer be tolerated on the public highways. This was not a sudden development, but one which had been brewing for some years.

As early as the 1930s, it was the sparkling performance of the big Delahaye and Hotchkiss 'Grand Touring' cars, the purposeful ability of the two-seater SS100s and BMW 328s, and even the surprisingly fast V8-engined Fords, which transformed rallying from a rather leisurely sport for gentlemen into an exciting high-speed business. After the Second World War, their place was gradually taken over by Jaguar XK120s, rear-engined Porsches, twin-cam engined Alfa-Romeos, and Mercedes-Benz 300SL 'gullwings'.

The pace of the cars and the increasingly crowded roads over which they were asked to drive at breakneck speeds, faced the sport with a dilemma in the 1950s. In some countries of Western Europe it became politically difficult to organize what were in effect 'speed events' on open roads. Not only did ordinary people begin to object, but the police, too, became most unhappy, so that government authorities began to take notice. Alternative types of competition had to be found.

Open-road rallying, therefore, began to be concentrated on the more sporting countries such as France, Italy, Austria and their immediate neighbours. Other nations, including the Scandinavians, the Benelux countries and the British Isles, all of which tended to take more heed of public protests, had to enforce changes. In every case, their solution, achieved in different ways, was to get high-speed rally motoring off public roads.

In Britain, the authorities ensured that there would be virtually no high-speed motoring at all, so that the most important British events became little more than lengthy, boring processions between driving tests or regularity sections. The RAC International Rally even proudly announced itself as the 'Rally of the Tests', which cut no ice with the European professionals, who dismissed it as irrelevant.

European nations such as Holland, Belgium and Switzerland did not ban fast rallying but merely shifted the problem on to someone else's door step. This was done, very simply, by directing the routes of their rallies into neighbouring France or Italy, where people were much more enthusiastic about that sort of thing!

The Scandinavian solution, however, was completely different. In the beginning it was influenced by local geographical and road conditions, but eventually it set a standard that the rest of the world was to follow. Organizers in Scandinavia found that there were thousands of tracks (it would be exaggerating to call them roads) which were privately owned but could be used for performance tests on rallies. Although there would still be a lot of public-road motoring, it need not be at high speeds; all the

The most unexpected cars sometimes found 'works' support in rallying. This was Raymond Baxter's factory-prepared Rover 3-litre, racing at Oulton Park, in the 1962 RAC

speed tests could be concentrated on sections from which the public was excluded.

By their nature and surface – such tracks were often twisting, and usually lined with trees, with either a loose gravel surface in summer or completely covered by snow and ice during winter – they made different demands on the team. More than ever before, a skilled driver and a car which handled really well were just as important as sheer straight-line performance.

Sometimes, to keep politicians and law-makers happy, a target time was set for each of these sections, but this was usually calculated at such a high average speed that the whole thing was a race against the clock anyway. Often, however, there was no target, and a car's time over these long sections was its penalty. In this way, therefore, the 'special stage' was born.

All this was significant enough, but it was also interesting to note that the first Scandinavian 'special-stage' rallies were being dominated by smaller and altogether more agile machines than the fast sports cars which were winning the traditional tarmac 'road races'. It did not take long for the braver, more versatile and more analytical drivers to work out a new technique for special-stage motoring; they soon realized

In the early 1960s, Volvo's PV544 was strong enough, and fast enough, in Tom Trana's hands, to be a 'winner' on loose-road events – which is precisely what he did in the 1963 RAC Rally. He repeated the dose in 1964

that loose surfaces were best tackled in a car with its weight concentrated over the driven wheels. Rear-engined cars like the Porsche, whose performance and handling were improving every year, had a great deal of traction. Cars with front-engine/front-wheel-drive layouts could often make up for power deficiencies with really spectacular handling. At the beginning of the 1950s, however, such cars were in surprisingly short supply. A two-stroke DKW was obviously a good tool for the job, but it must also have been a great source of joy to Saab to realize that their own products were potentially ideal for the new rallies at home.

The Scandinavian rallies not only saw the rise to success of new types of cars but also encouraged the development of different driving techniques, which were quickly exploited by bold and hitherto unknown drivers. It was no longer enough to treat every section merely as a racing exercise on open roads, against the clock rather than against other cars. In Scandinavia, the 'classic' line into and through every corner, and the 'classic' sequence of braking, gear-changing and car positioning, simply did not work effectively in situations where the stages were secret, the surfaces loose and the frictional grip low.

Initially it was the Swedes, and then the Finns, who won renown for their driving in these special-stage events – understandably because they were so thoroughly familiar, most of the time, with the conditions. Elsewhere in Europe,

If Leyland-Triumph had not been ruled by Donald Stokes, they might have been allowed to develop their Triumph 2000s further than this. The 1964 cars, still quite unproven, had triple Weber carburettors and 150bhp!

What goes up must come down, but in the case of the Mini-Cooper S there was only a very light thump. Rauno Aaltonen hurdling a Scottish bridge on his way to winning the 1965 RAC Rally, and taking the European Championship for that year

motorists in town and country, journeying either for business or pleasure, were accustomed to sealed tarmac surfaces. In Scandinavia, however, many public highways (except for the main highways) still had loose surfaces in the 1950s. During the long winter period (which lasted for four to five months) there was snow and ice on all roads. The hazards of low-friction driving were familiar to all drivers, sports-lovers or not, and it soon became second nature to them to swing their cars around even in normal, non-competitive situations.

This type of ingrained experience enabled the Swedes and Finns to become phenomenally fast on the loose or icy special stages. The techniques entailed, often at one and the same time, swinging the car virtually 'sideways' before, during and after negotiating a corner, braking and accelerating in the most unexpected places (sometimes at the same time) and generally

A big man in a great-hearted car – Erik Carlsson in his 2-stroke Saab in the 1963 Midnight Sun Rally

keeping the car much more 'unbalanced' at high speeds.

By 1952, the Swedish 'Midnight Sun' rally (so named because it was held in high summer, when, in northern Sweden, the sun never sets) had a few special stages in its itinerary, though these were by no means as concentrated as they would later become. In 1953, for instance, when John Gott's rallying review in *Autosport* talked of 'the practised technique of the Swedish drivers' coming into prominence', there were only five such stages. Three years later the same renowned commentator was suggesting that the Scandinavian events were really 'best suited for home consumption only', as the driving techniques required were so specialized. The number of stages, however, continued to mount, and the target averages (which were in excess of 80kph, or 50mph, even in 1953) continued to rise.

In 1952 Olaf Persson's 1.5-litre rear-engined

Porsche won the Midnight Sun rally, and Bergan's front-wheel-drive Citroën won the Norwegian 'Viking'. In the Midnight Sun, which always had a more international appeal, there were three Porsches in the top five, and an Aston Martin DB2 (driven by a Swede, A. Hemmingsson) was fifth. Fourth, incidentally, was that genial German, Huschke von Hanstein, in a Porsche supplied by the factory for which he worked. A year later, two of the top five from 1952 finished in the first five positions again, though this time it was Store Nottorp's Porsche which won the event from, of all things, Kvastrom's vast Ford Custom saloon.

Certainly, for this type of event, the engine-over-driving-wheels formula seemed essential. It had, in any case, already proved highly desirable all over Europe for competitors tackling many events. The European Rally Championship for drivers had been inaugurated in 1953, when Helmuth Polensky won in a Porsche. A year later, his erstwhile co-driver, Walter Schluter, took the championship in a front-drive two-stroke DKW. The fact that the next two

European championships fell to Mercedes-Benz (Werner Engel in 1955, and Walter Schock in 1956) had little effect on the Midnight Sun. Hammerlund's Porsche won in 1954, Borgetfors also used a Porsche to win in 1955, and there was a major upset in 1956 when outright victory went to Bengtsson's VW Beetle.

Even more significant, however, was the inexorable rise of Saab. There were three Saabs in the top five in 1956, driven by Carl-Magnus Skogh, by Kronegard, and by a cheerful and burly young man named Erik Carlsson. In 1959, after three years in which his *Pa Taket* ('On the Roof') reputation had become firmly established in other European events, Carlsson duly won the Midnight Sun event outright, beating his old rival Skogh into second place. This is not to belittle the two Volvo PV444 wins of 1957 (by Jansson in 1957, and by Gunnar Andersson in 1958), but it truly signalled the impact of Saab, Carlsson and the whole special stage/front-drive phenomenon. In Norway, incidentally, Skogh and Carlsson had already cleaned up in 1956, while Skogh was third a year later. By 1960, however (and this is to run ahead of our story slightly) there was no doubt that Saab had a very suitable car for their purpose. The Thousand Lakes rally of Finland had by then come to prominence, and in that year was dominated by Messrs Bremer, Carlsson and Skogh, while it was Skogh who won the Swedish Midnight Sun and Norwegian Viking Rallies outright.

By the end of the 1950s, therefore, special-stage events were ready to spread to other countries. One reason was that Scandinavian drivers had competed, and won, elsewhere in Europe, and another that European works teams had gone to Sweden, been thrashed, and returned full of praise for the new rallying format. Even before Carlsson burst on the European scene, two of his compatriots had won the European Rally Championship, Ruprecht Hopfen (Saab) in 1957, and Gunnar Andersson (Volvo) in 1958.

When works teams from outside Scandinavia had visited the Midnight Sun event in the 1950s, they had not only been unable to match the pace of the Swedes and Finns, but had soon discovered that rugged preparation and good underbody protection were as important as sheer straight-line performance from their cars.

Rootes sent three Sunbeam Mk IIIs to Norway in 1955 without success (though Shiela van Damm and Anne Hall picked up enough points to clinch the European Ladies' title for that year). In 1956 Ford, Rootes and Triumph all sent cars to Sweden, but the best British performance was by Peter Harper/David Humphrey, who were fifth in their class and 24th overall in a Sunbeam Rapier Mk I. As John Gott again commented in *Autosport*; 'Even Nancy Mitchell, currently Britain's leading lady driver, and certainly amongst Europe's best five . . . finished behind ladies unheard of outside Scandinavia.' Walter Schock (Mercedes-Benz 220), who was on his way to the 1956 European Championship, could finish no higher than 55th, and Strahle (second in the Championship that year) fared little better.

Because of the aftermath of the Suez war, 1957 was a thinly supported year. In 1958, however, Peter Harper (who was trying hard for the European Championship) was well beaten in the Midnight Sun event by Gunnar Andersson, who then went on to take the title himself. No other British crew was even competitive.

It was at this point that the Scandinavian approach to rallying began to affect Britain. In 1958, as already mentioned, the format and organization of the RAC rally had become very unpopular; even though all the British works teams were honour-bound to compete, they made it quite clear that the event was not up to modern European standards. In that year, severe wintry weather in Wales, the Lake District and southern Scotland decimated the field, and although Peter Harper won the event and managed to complete the entire course in his Sunbeam Rapier Mk II, it was something of a hollow victory.

There was such an outcry following the 1958 rally that the RAC was handed over to Jack Kemsley. His first job was to restore the 'image' of the RAC Rally, making it a credible event that would attract foreign competitors, while his long-term task was to turn it into a world-class event.

For 1959, he could do no more than banish some of the obvious anomalies in the regulations, cut down on the specialized manoeuvring tests, and increase the sheer endurance aspect of the event. To avoid the worst of the winter weather, too, it was decided to move the rally from its traditional date in March to one in November, in the hope that snow and ice would not intervene. It was doubly unfortunate, there-

Britain's first-ever 'special stage' was over Monument Hill, near Dalmally in Scotland, on the 1960 RAC Rally. It all looked very 'amateur' at the start line of that epoch-making test as Mrs B. Neate (Volvo 122S) prepares to launch herself into the unknown

fore, that unseasonal weather again brought the event to a halt in the mountains of Scotland in 1959; but it also has to be said that no modern RAC Rally ever seems to take place without encountering *some* snow!

In 1959 the event started from Blackpool on a Tuesday afternoon, and finally reached London three days later, with no intermediate overnight halt, and with only three breakfast halts by way of rest. Jack Kemsley's name, and his avowed intentions, were sufficient to attract competitors from Europe, including Erik Carlsson (Saab 93), Wolfgang Levy (Auto Union), Paul Coltelloni (Citroën ID19), and others slightly less famous. Levy, co-driven by Stuart Turner, would certainly have won if he had not been held up in the snowdrifts north of Braemar, but as it was victory went to Gerry Burgess in a battered works Zephyr.

A year later, the RAC Rally went a stage further. Kemsley had talked – *and* listened – to the topmost crews, and had simplified the format. The continued skid-pan test at Wolvey near the end of the event was an irrelevance, but all other driving tests, along with any pretence at regularity, had been swept away. There were

sprints, speed hill-climbs or circuit tests along the way, but by far the most significant feature was the inclusion in the Scottish section of four special stages, three of which were held on public highways, thus explaining the 30mph target speeds and the fact that they were 'cleaned' by a number of competitors. The first of the four, which (in retrospect) was a landmark for the rally, was a mere two miles of rough, twisting track over Monument Hill, north of Inverary, set at 40mph.

This new format was enough to attract a clutch of foreign crews, including two cars from Mercedes-Benz, two Volvos, six Citroëns, and Erik Carlsson's Saab 96, who were faced by a battery of British factory cars. In the event, the Monument Hill section was decisive. Carlsson hurled his red Saab across the rocks and ruts of the Scottish hillside in 2min 58sec – and no other car beat the bogey. For the rest of the event, Carlsson's co-driver (Stuart Turner) kept him on course, and victory was assured.

Carlsson, therefore, won his first RAC Rally, with an unpenalized run (something previously unheard of), but this did not mean that the event had been easy. There was enough fast motoring in between times, and almost all the foreign crews went home happy. René Trautmann (Citroën DS19), however, lost his chances of the European title by crashing through a wall on an innocuous road section, causing the Mercedes-Benz team to withdraw as their title win was already assured; Walter Schock was not popular with the organizers *or* with his team manager for his early withdrawal.

A year later, in 1961, the RAC Rally truly came to maturity. Building on the experience of previous years, Jack Kemsley concluded months of patient negotiation with the Forestry Commission, and was able to announce that the event would have a whole series of special stages, on private ground, and set at high average speeds. At first, 16 stages were promised, but by November no fewer than 24 stages had been found, comprising more than 200 miles, or one-tenth of the events' total mileage. The longest of all (in Yorkshire) was 21 miles, which by British standards was quite a distance, and all were set at between 40mph and 50mph average speeds. That, to the enthusiast more accustomed to the 70mph and 80mph averages set by the cars of the late 1970s and early 1980s, might sound laughable; in 1961 it was quite enough.

To all but those previously battle-hardened in Scandinavia, the rough and loose forestry roads were a really unknown challenge, and many crews ran into trouble because their cars lacked underbody protection. There were even more overseas competitors than in 1960, and it fell to Erik Carlsson (who was running as No. 1 because of his 1960 victory) to be the first-ever competitor to tackle a forestry stage in Britain. That stage, appropriately enough in view of the permanent place it now has in the British rallying scene, was in Keilder Forest, north-west of Hexham.

On this event, however, British factory drivers were certainly not disgraced. Although there was simply no catching the ebullient Carlsson (whose Saab must have been one of the least powerful cars in the event, and he certainly one of the heaviest drivers), British drivers took the next four places, and Rootes won the team prize with their rugged and surprisingly fast Rapier Mk IIIs. It was the remarkable Pat Moss who took second place behind Erik, in her Austin-Healey 3000, while Peter Harper and Paddy Hopkirk were third and fourth in works Rapiers.

Once the event had achieved respectability, however, there was no stopping its development. In 1962 the number of stages rose to 38 and the total stage mileage to more than 300, and on this occasion the target average speed was raised to 50mph every time; several stages

It looks lonely in the hills of Culbin Forest, in the North of Scotland, but Erik Carlsson is giving the rest of the rallying world an object lesson in loose surface driving in the first RAC Rally (1961) to use forestry territory. He won – one almost says 'of course'

The Saab 96 was equally at home on tarmac, where the drivers – like Erik Carlsson in 1961 – rarely seem to lift their feet from the throttle. This was Mallory Park in 1961

Ford's only outright victory with the Mk II Zephyr was in the 1959 RAC Rally, when freak weather conditions and resourceful route finding allowed Gerry Burgess to take this car through all controls ahead of 180 others.

Several years of development allowed Auto-Union-DKW to turn their two-stroke front-wheel-drive design into a rally winner. This was the Auto-Union 1000 coupe with which Wolfgang Levy and Stuart Turner so nearly won the 1959 RAC Rally, but were outwitted by the weather

had been 'cleaned' embarrassingly often in 1961, and Jack Kemsley was determined that this should not happen again. None of this perturbed Carlsson, who won his third consecutive RAC Rally quite comfortably, though on this occasion Austin-Healeys driven by Paddy Hopkirk and Pat Moss were second and third, and it was 'Tiny' Lewis's turn to urge a factory Rapier into fourth place. Eric and Pat stuck so closely together throughout the event that someone suggested that they must be in love. He was right – the engagement was announced during 1963, and the marriage followed shortly afterwards.

In 1961–2, however, three extremely important developments coincided to revolutionize European rallying, and the effects were to be felt all over the world for the next decade. In Britain, Stuart Turner took over from Marcus Chambers, as competition manager of BMC, and almost at the same time the Mini-Coopers went into production. At about the same time, Rauno Aaltonen emerged as the first of the fast, remarkably skilful Finnish drivers, and was almost immediately asked to drive a Mini. The combination of Mini-Coopers, Finnish drivers, and the management of Stuart Turner was soon to prove irresistible.

As a rally car, the Mini had started slowly, for it had been much too slow in single-carburettor 848cc form. From the autumn of 1961, however, the 997cc twin-carburettor Mini-Cooper (complete with tiny front-wheel disc brakes) went on sale, and rallying prospects were transformed.

Already, in 1962, Aaltonen had electrified the rallying 'circus' by his performance on the Monte Carlo Rally (before a crash put him out of the event), and Pat Moss had won the Tulip outright on handicap. However, in Sweden, after years of domination by Saabs or Volvos, a BMC-Sweden Mini-Cooper, driven by Bengt Soderstrom, shattered everyone with an outright win in the Midnight Sun Rally, and Carlsson could do no better than third place.

In the RAC Rally at the end of the year, however, not only did Rauno Aaltonen's Mini-Cooper finish fifth, but a rather headstrong young man called Timo Makinen took seventh place, and (along with Logan Morrison in the third car) the Mini-Coopers also won the manufacturers' team prize. Almost at a stroke, it seemed, BMC gave notice that it was not only Saab who could win rallies with front-wheel-drive cars, and that they had discovered a new

Anne Hall and Ford were names closely linked in the 1950s and early 1960s. Here is Anne in a new Anglia Type 105E, tackling a driving test in the 1961 RAC Rally on her way to third in class, and second (to Pat Moss) in the Ladies' contest

breed of driver to help them. In the meantime, however, Pat Moss won the German Rally outright (again on handicap), and she also finished third on the Geneva Rally later in the year.

From this time, the legend of the 'Flying Finns' evolved rapidly. Indeed, within a year or so, team managers seemed to consider it the done thing to sign a Finn. Traditional teams like Rootes held off, and suffered accordingly, and it was Triumph (and Simo Lampinen) who were the next British team to forge an Anglo-Finnish partnership. Ford, for their part, tried (and nearly succeeded) to sign Erik Carlsson, and did not persuade a Finn to join them until Hannu Mikkola was given his first works drives in 1968.

The Finns are probably no better as rally drivers, over 'unseen' roads, than are the Swedes; it was merely that several brave young men all seemed to mature in Finland at about the same time. Before the 1960s, certainly, no Finn

had ventured abroad to make his name in important European events. There was no Finnish 'Thousand Lakes' event until the late 1950s, but in 1961 Rauno Aaltonen electrified everyone with the pace of his driving in a bulky Mercedes-Benz 220SE, and it was enough for Eugen Bohringer to invite him to co-crive in the German rally later that year (when their works 220SE took second place to Hans Walter's Porsche Carrera), and for the astute Stuart Turner to offer a BMC contract in 1962.

Stuart Turner, however, was not only famous for his vision in signing Rauno Aaltonen and Timo Makinen for BMC, but for the way in which he changed every aspect of rallying. Where many other team managers had been amateurs or mere administrators, Turner was a battle-hardened rallying veteran. Nothing, from pre-event practice to rally car equipment or to service and support on the rallies themselves, was too trivial to be ignored. Turner, like Stirling Moss in the motor-racing business, was a firm believer that 'the event begins when the regulations arrive'.

As far as rough-road rallying and special stages were concerned, for example, it was

Turner who first thought of using winter-treaded tyres for better grip in loose, boggy conditions, and he was the first team manager to nag his supplier into developing these tyres with radial-ply carcases, which had previously not been thought necessary. With respect to the cars, it was also Turner who first refined the whole idea of an ideally specified 'homologation special'; the Austin-Healeys were a case in point, but it was the Mini-Cooper Ss, which Abingdon were able to use in 1965–7, that were so special, and by no means the same as those first sold to the public in 1963–4.

Like Stirling Moss, Turner was a great one for leaning hard on the limit of the regulations, or even for driving a coach-and-horses through any particular rules which had been badly drafted. There was considerably more than wishful thinking in the stories one heard of unemployed works co-drivers being directed to drive through British special stages just before the roads were officially closed, so that they could assess the conditions and advise team members of what they were up against!

As far as loose-surface rallying was concerned, however, it was BMC's Minis, and their progressive development, which made such an impact in the early and mid-1960s; between them, Saab and BMC dominated the scene for some years, with dissimilar cars but with very similar results and performance. From BMC, the 848cc Mini became the 997cc Mini-Cooper in 1961, and evolved into the more powerful 1071cc Mini-Cooper S of 1963. A year later BMC were also able to offer the 970cc (short-stroke) and 1275cc (long-stroke) derivatives. Although the 970S was a useful car for the 1000cc class, it was the deep-chested 1275S which was so outstanding. Not only class and category wins, but outright victories, were within its scope.

Saab followed the same sort of development path, although they were not so assiduous in their approach to homologation. Whereas the Cooper S was at its peak between 1964 and 1968, it speedily became obsolete thereafter. Saab, on the other hand, had been winning in the 1950s, and carried on successfully into the 1970s before the 93/96 family was displaced by the larger and more powerful 99 range.

The winning Saabs of the 1950s were three-cylinder two-stroke 93s, but Erik Carlsson, Carl-Magnus Skogh and a host of Scandinavian private owners began using 841cc 96 models in 1960. Even in this form the engines were remarkably tuneable, though the four-wheel-drum brakes were a distinct handicap (but, as Carlsson once said, with a big grin: 'Brakes only slow you down, anyway!'). In 1964 the 40bhp 96 evolved into the 55bhp 96 Sport which, apart from its extra performance, also had front wheel disc brakes. However, even in the most highly tuned form, the 841cc engine rarely gave more than 80bhp (at a time when a Mini-Cooper 1275S was producing more than 100bhp in Group 2 guise). From the autumn of 1966 the first-ever four-stroke Saab – the V4 – appeared, which allowed more than 100bhp to be developed, and this was steadily improved and increased over the years.

Victory for these front-wheel-drive cars was not, however, guaranteed. Jansson's rear-engined 2-litre Porsche Carrera won the 1963 Midnight Sun Rally from Carlsson's Saab (an event, incidentally, in which one of the stages was a three-dimensional dash through the tunnels of an iron-ore mine at Kiruna); and Tom Trana's Volvo PV544 beat Kallstrom's Cooper 1275S into second place in the 1964 event, after which the rally was moved to a February date and renamed simply the 'Swedish'.

In the early 1960s, indeed, the rugged but distinctly oldfashioned Volvos won events all around the world. Volvo used these, the original postwar type of cars, in preference to the current type 120 'Amazon' because they were lighter and more nimble. Not only could a Volvo, which had a conventional front-engine/rear-drive layout, win in the rough mud-plugging terrain of Africa and among the rocks of Greece, but it was also sufficiently speedy and versatile for heroes like Trana and Gunnar Andersson to be competitive in special-stage rallies.

In the RAC Rallies of 1961 and 1962 there were no competitive Volvos, but in 1963 and again in 1964 victory went to Tom Trana's factory-entered PV544. On both occasions it looked easy enough for the young Swede, but it was significant that no other Volvo driver ever came close to winning this high-speed event. Trana was one of those men who only really excelled in one car; his career was badly affected by an open-road crash on the British Gulf London Rally in 1965, when his co-driver was killed.

The first few 'special stage' RAC Rallies were memorable, too, for the performance of the BMC-prepared 'Big' Healeys – the 3000s which became increasingly competitive as the 1960s progressed. Without the snow blockage, a Healey might have performed really well in the 'endurance' RAC of 1959. In 1960 Donald Morley's car was third, in 1961 Pat Moss took second place, and in 1962 Paddy Hopkirk also took second. Timo Makinen could do no better than fifth in 1963, but was second in 1964 and second again in 1965. All this, mark you, was with a car which in 100/4 state had been dismissed as unsuitable for rallying, which had very limited ground clearance, and which had a weight distribution not at all ideal for loose-surface rallying.

The Big Healey, however, had three features in its favour – it was enormously strong in works form, it was always driven by the bravest and most resourceful men *and* women, and it was built and serviced by the BMC factory team. It is not overstating the case to suggest that the Healey 3000 was the best car never to win an RAC Rally, for it was always fast enough – and it was so near, so often.

One of Ford's important signings in the 1960s was Ove Andersson, a classy driver of Lotus-Cortina and Escort Twin-Cams. On this event, the 1968 1000 Lakes, his team-mate Hannu Mikkola won his first major event in a similar car

From 1963, however, it was always likely that a Mini-Cooper S would start to dominate the 'classic' loose-surface special-stage events. In that year Paddy Hopkirk's 1071S took fourth place, in 1964 the team encountered all types of mechanical disaster, but in 1965 Rauno Aaltonen took a 1275S to a narrow victory over team-mate Timo Makinen's Austin-Healey 3000. A year later BMC might have won again if they had enjoyed mechanical reliability, but Kallstrom's second place (with Aaltonen fourth and Tony Fall fifth) was the best they could achieve.

Similarly, a Mini-Cooper did not win the Finnish Thousand Lakes Rally until 1965, when Timo Makinen led Rauno Aaltonen home in a 1–2. The astonishing Makinen repeated his Thousand Lakes performance in 1966, and completed a hat-trick in 1967, after which the phenomenon of the Mikkola–Escort combination took over.

Even by the mid-1960s, however, the concept of special-stage rallying on loose surfaces, on private ground, had not spread very far. In 1965, for example, there were 12 European Championship rallies, of which three were classic 'winter' events on snow-covered roads and six were public-road events. One – the Acropolis – stood alone, while only two, the Thousand Lakes and the RAC, followed the 'forest'

Bjorn Waldegard has been a winner on every conceivable surface. So, too, has the Porsche 911, which does not even have its wheels on the ground in this Swedish Rally shot

formula. The Swedish, by this time, was a winter event, using forestry stages well covered by snow and ice.

Nevertheless, it was becoming clear that other nations would soon be losing the privilege of rallying on public roads. By the end of the decade the French Alpine was the last of these spectacular road races. Other events such as the Tulip and the Geneva would be in eclipse, and new events using private ground would be added.

It was in Britain that what we now jokingly call 'forest-racing' took complete control. Immediately after the RAC Rally of 1961 took 'to the woods', the Scottish Rally adopted the same formula, along with the Welsh and (from 1964) the Gulf London. Almost every little motor club, it seemed, found ways of using forest stages, and for a time there was a real danger of the Forestry Commission territory becoming over-used. It was only top-level diplomacy, and a rigidly applied rationing system, that saved the day.

Ford, having scratched around on the fringe of full-time professional works rallying for years, finally took on a proper team organization in 1962, developed (with Colin Chapman) the Lotus-Cortinas in 1965 and 1966, and emerged as a major force in the sport. With the earlier Cortina GTs they had been able to use simple, reliable and adequately fast rally cars (which were good enough to win the East African Safari in 1964), but once the Lotus-Cortinas had been made to stick together (the early examples were almost hilariously fragile), they had potential winners.

Even in 1963, Henry Taylor had virtually carried an early Lotus-Cortina to sixth place in the RAC. There were no Lotus-Cortina entries in 1964 (though Cortina GTs won the team prize and Vic Elford's car took third place), and in 1965 the team was thwarted by the wintry weather and mechanical disaster. In 1966 Bengt Soderstrom made it all up by winning the event outright, by more than 13 minutes. Ford never had another opportunity to win the RAC in a Lotus-Cortina, for the 1967 event was cancelled at 24 hours' notice due to the widespread outbreak of foot-and-mouth disease: in 1968 they preferred to send Lotus-Cortinas from London to Sydney instead of around Britain, and after that the Escort had taken over at Boreham.

No sane rallying enthusiast would have wanted to push an unwelcome rally through areas affected by the deadly animal disease in 1967, but even the most public-spirited among us were sorry to miss the opportunity of seeing Group 6 prototypes, including a lightweight Austin-Healey 3000 for Rauno Aaltonen, a fuel-injected Cooper S for Timo Makinen, Vic Elford in a Porsche 911R and Erik Carlsson in a 1.7-litre Saab 96 V4. It was also worth noting that world-champion Grand Prix driver Denny Hulme was entered in a prototype Triumph 2.5PI (with the author in the hot seat alongside him) and Graham Hill was down to drive a Lotus-Cortina. A year earlier, incidentally, Jim Clark had also electrified the crowds with his handling of a Lotus-Cortina (and had been on the leader board before leaving the event in a spectacular crash), while Graham Hill had driven a works Mini-Cooper S.

By the end of the 1960s, without question, the RAC Rally had taken its rightful place among the world's most popular and important motorsporting events. It now had a fine organizational reputation, a very popular format, the guarantee

Even if your excuse is that the surface is that of a frozen lake, it helps if you are roughly pointing in the direction of travel. In this Swedish rally shot, Daniellson's Opel Kadett Coupé is in mid-spin. Incidentally, the time of day is about 3 pm, but nightfall is very early in a Scandinavian winter

of huge entries, and, invariably, news-making potential. In retrospect, therefore, it is surprising to recall that the event was almost completely overshadowed (in Britain) by the London–Sydney Marathon in 1968, and that sponsorship was not allowed on the cars until a year later.

Further change, however, was on the way, and from 1972 the RAC Rally was to take on a new look, with the start of what I propose calling the 'Escort years'. Meanwhile, between 1968 and 1971, the event reverted to type, and a front-wheel-drive car won on every occasion. Twice the victory went to Saab (to Simo Lampinen in 1968 and to Stig Blomqvist in 1971, both in V4s), but in 1969 and 1970 the honours went to Lancia.

There will be much more about Lancia in later chapters, for the rise of the works-blessed Jolly Club cars began in Italy and France in the early 1960s, and fully works-prepared cars were winning events outright by the mid-1960s. This,

however, was in the Flavias, which were too bulky for special-stage events. Everything changed in 1965 when the gorgeous Fulvia coupé was revealed, and from the moment that the light and starkly equipped 'HF' model appeared in 1966 it was clear that Lancia had serious intentions.

Like the Mini-Cooper S, the Fulvia HF coupé had front-wheel drive. Unlike the Cooper S, the HF was initially too heavy, but it had larger wheels and a great deal of development potential; furthermore, the team also possessed what appeared to outside observers to be almost unlimited funds for development and for payment of star drivers. The HF, with its light-alloy body panels, was only a 1.2-litre car at first, but 1.3-litre models were announced in 1967, and the definitive 1.6-litre HF car arrived in the autumn of 1968. This, allied to the use of the five-speed Flavia gearbox in the 1.6-litre model, and the hiring of drivers such as Ove Andersson, Rauno Aaltonen and Harry Kallstrom, meant that by 1967 Lancia were a force to be reckoned with.

It was the 140bhp (in rallying tune) 1.6HF which really turned Lancia into a winning team, though the team's debut in 1968 could hardly have been more disastrous. International regulations had changed, so the RAC Rally proper

The rear-engined Alpine-Renault started life as a fragile little 'special' useful only for tarmac events, but by the beginning of the 1970s it could tackle anything. In forestry rallying, and in 1.6-litre or 1.8-litre form, it could be a winner. This car, in fact, was driven by Andrew Cowan in the 1971 Scottish

could not accept much-modified Group 6 cars in 1968. The ever-resourceful Jack Kemsley, however, introduced a secondary event alongside the main rally, called it the 'European Club Rally' and attracted three 1.6HFs.

Even so, everything went wrong for Lancia in 1968, as Mikkola, Munari and Aaltonen all crashed, but in 1969 (by which time the 1.6-litre car was homologated) there was no mistake. This was a snowy event, so snowy in fact that there was doubt, until the very last hours, that the cars would be able to get through the Welsh section at all. Four Fulvia HFs started and two finished, with Kallstrom's car winning from

Orrenius's Saab by more than four minutes, and with Tony Fall's car taking third place.

A year later, Kallstrom did it again, not without drama, for his engine needed a major rebuild in Wales on the last night, and a front-suspension change was also required hours later when the Fulvia collided with a non-competing car almost within sight of a major control. On this occasion his was the only works Lancia to finish, and his winning margin over Eriksson's 1.9-litre Opel Kadett Rallye was less than three minutes.

Before leaving the RAC Rally and the cars that were so successful in the 1960s, I must mention two types of car which *could*, given luck, have won the event outright. One was Ford's Escort Twin-Cam, the other the Porsche 911.

The Escort's rallying history is now well known, as the car had a quite remarkable 12-year life, in one form or another, as a works rally car. Even though it started life, in 1968, with a theoretical disadvantage (it had a front engine and rear drive, at a time when such layouts were

The Triumph TR4 is British, but the rally is Canadian – Jean-Jacques Thuner's car at the start of the Shell 4000 in 1964

considered unfashionable for success in loose-surface events), and the Twin-Cam of 1968–1970 was only partly successful, it seemed to improve with every succeeding change, being a better and more competitive car at the end of its long life than ever it had been at the beginning!

In 1968, when brand new, it had a Lotus-Ford twin-cam engine (and, thus, logically enough, was called the Twin-Cam), and it immediately replaced the Lotus-Cortina for Ford's team drivers. It was a winner from the start. Roger Clark won four events in two months, including a runaway success in the Scottish Rally, which was a classic forestry-stage event. There were no full factory entries in the 1968 RAC Rally though the David Sutton team were loaned a Boreham-built Twin-Cam for Timo Makinen to drive; it retired with a blown engine.

By 1969, everything had started to go wrong

for the Escort. That year, the team's best RAC Rally result was fourth for Ove Andersson, but in 1970 things were even worse when no factory-built car finished in the top ten. Even in 1971, when the 16-valve engined RS1600 had taken over from the Twin-Cam, the team cars were suffering from a nasty attack of axle-shaft breakages, and it was Hannu Mikkola's turn to take fourth place. But in 1972 the team bounced back with astonishing vigour, in Africa as in Europe, and the revival of their fortunes is told in a later chapter.

The relative failure of the rear-engined Porsche in special stage rallying is an enigma. The cars, in whatever form, always looked good enough, and were certainly fast enough, to win, but they usually suffered from casual preparation by the works (who were never deeply committed to the sport, which they considered far inferior to sports-car racing) or had to be represented by semi-official teams from Scandinavia.

It was Vic Elford who, as we shall see, persuaded Porsche to become more serious

Roger Clark, still not at the height of his powers, in a Ford Lotus-Cortina on the 1966 Scottish Rally

about the 911, but within a couple of years he was lost to sports-car racing. After that it was Scandinavians – Bjorn Waldegard, Ake Andersson and Pauli Toivonen – who learned how to drive the heavy air-cooled car on forestry tracks.

Waldegard and Andersson had so nearly won the Gulf London Rally of 1967 in 2-litre 911s prepared by the Scania-Vabis team in Sweden, but transmission failures put them down behind Ove Andersson's winning Lotus-Cortina. In 1968, Ake Andersson made no mistake in the same event, beating his namesake into second place.

That was the last of the great Gulf Londons (an event in 1968, incidentally, which lasted for 81 hours with only a single three-hour halt for a rest at half-distance), but Porsche's success was never repeated on the more important RAC Rally. Vic Elford's 4-cam 911R did not start the

1967 event due to last-minute cancellation, and along with Tony Fall and Pauli Toivonen he was forced to retire from the 1968 event with transmission and suspension problems. In 1969 Bjorn Waldegard's Swedish-prepared 2.2-litre 911 led the event until the last day; Waldegard then went off the track on a snowy stage, and could only finish 12th. A year later, the unfortunate Waldegard led the rally for 24 hours in a 911S, until its transmission (apparently the 911's weak spot at the time) let him down yet again. Waldegard made one last valiant try in 1971 with another 2.2-litre car, but weather conditions were against him. Not even the combination of a Swedish genius in a factory-prepared Porsche could beat the magnificent driving of Stig Blomqvist in a Saab 96 V4 over a very snowy course in Scotland and northern England. With no further Porsche challenge, Waldegard defected, first to BMW and later to Lancia.

This was all somewhat puzzling, especially as Porsche's reliability in road-car guise was never in doubt. But apart from the factory's half-hearted attitude, there is also the fact that a Porsche was by no means as easy to drive as it looked. Britain's Roger Clark (whose business interests include a Porsche dealership) once told the author that rallying a 911 was much more difficult than in an Escort, and that he could quite see the problem.

By the start of the 1970s, therefore, forestry special-stage rallying had become the norm by which most other modern events were to be judged. Its development had made Scandinavian drivers (namely Swedes and Finns) famous all round the world, and it had also encouraged the development of rally cars that were stronger and more agile than ever before. It really is worth repeating that without the stimulus of preparing strong cars capable of careening over the gravel, mud and rocks of a British forest or a Scandinavian estate, some factories would never have had models worth entering in car-breaking events such as the Safari and the Acropolis.

While all this was taking place, however, the major events in Europe were enjoying something of an Indian Summer. Most of the European Championship rallies in the mid-1960s still found much of their fast motoring on public roads, and were as flamboyant and exhilarating to those involved as ever. It proved to be a final fling, but nobody who ever took part in one of the last 'road races' will ever forget it.

7 | The last of the Great Road Races

Before the end of the 1950s, top-class rallying in Europe seemed to take on new pace and urgency. It was almost as if the entire scene – events, cars *and* drivers – had shifted into overdrive. Already gentlemanly old-time rallying had been discarded; in the 1960s all traces of amateurism disappeared completely. It was no longer enough for drivers to be resourceful and enthusiastic – now they had to be dedicated, brave and willing to make a profession out of their sport. People actually began to be paid to go rallying. Though it was the factory teams which helped to bring about this change, the events themselves encouraged it as well. In the ten years that followed the end of petrol rationing in 1957, the tempo of rallying increased dramatically.

The consequence was inevitable. By pushing up their pace so obviously, open-road events

The one and only time that a Dyna-Panhard won a major event was in 1961, when the Monte Carlo Rally regulations were especially suited to it. This was Maurice Martin's winning car on the Monaco circuit at the close of the event

became much less popular with the public. For the rallying enthusiast it might have been an exciting experience to stand out in the dead of night, in the middle of a French or Italian village, watching highly-tuned cars racing through at very high speeds. The squeal of tyres, the thunder of exhausts and the flash of intense lighting might be music and choreography to some – but not to others. Police, local authorities and an indifferent general public became increasingly alarmed about the possible dangers.

Twenty, or even ten years earlier, there had not been much traffic on some of these remote roads; private cars might have had the lawful right of way, but drivers of rally cars (not yet decorated with sponsors' stickers) could usually elbow their way past without much drama. By the mid-1960s, however, the average motorist who had once merely ignored the exciting sport of rallying began to turn distinctly hostile.

To counteract this, the cars were routed over more and more secluded tracks, mountains and stamping grounds – yet there were still risks of clashing with the public. A big international rally, along with its attendant officials, pressmen,

The formidable combination of Ms. Pat Moss, Ann Wisdom, and an Austin-Healey 3000 – rushing up a speed test in the Tulip Rally of 1961

service cars, trade vehicles *and* ever-larger crowds of spectators, was too massive an occasion to be hidden away.

Motor racing accidents, though mercifully rare, made headlines, and the motor-sporting world grieved over them. It could so easily have happened, although it never did, on any of the classic open-road rallies.

Even in the 1950s, as described in the previous

Little man, big car, wonderful reputation – Eugen Bohringer and a 'works' Mercedes-Benz won many events in the 1960s

chapter, this 'image' problem had led to rallying being pushed off the open roads. Some countries virtually banned rallying, while others made sure that there was no competitive motoring at high speeds over public roads. Elsewhere, in the so-called 'Latin' countries, open-road rallying continued to develop, to get faster, and to take on many of the aspects of racing. In France, Italy and Jugoslavia, until well into the 1960s, there was a series of spine-tingling world-class rallies. By the 1970s, however, it was nearly all over; and by the start of the 1980s the sole survivor of the breed was the Tour de Corse. It is fitting, therefore, that this rally of all rallies should still be a World Championship qualifier.

Speed made for change. In the first place, several new and fast cars appeared to make a

From 1958 to 1963 the Rootes-prepared Sunbeam
Rapiers were truly formidable rally cars. 'Tiny'
Lewis is driving this 1962 model

In the 1960s, there was nothing quite as exciting as the sight of Timo Makinen and an Austin-Healey 3000 in full-flight. 77 ARX was one of a set of 1962 team cars, normally nicknamed 'Sunset Strip'. That is Bo Ljungfeldt's Ford Falcon trying to keep up

Right The supreme combination of the early 1960s was Erik Carlsson and his Saab. Here he is, on his way to third place in the 1964 Monte Carlo Rally

Three famous names in one picture—Paddy Hopkirk and Henry Liddon (1275cc Mini-Cooper S)—on their way to a famous Monte Carlo Rally victory in 1964

Even front-wheel-drive
rally cars get sideways—
Barbasio's Lancia Fulvia
1.6HF on the Col du
Turini in the 1972
Monte Carlo

If ever the Big Healey
had a successor! The
Datsun 240Z could win
where strength and long-
legged performance were
needed. Harry Kallstrom
in a 1973 model

Left The loneliness of the
long-distance rally driver
—an Alpine-Renault in
the French Alps

Slot-car racing—at very high speeds on ice and snow—by Hannu Mikkola in a 1973 Ford Escort RS1600. In the Monte Carlo Rally of 1973, Mikkola finished fourth behind three Alpine-Renaults

Was this the best rallying team of the 1970s? Sandro Munari and the Lancia Stratos won so many events that they almost seemed to be invincible. On this occasion, in the 1974 Tour de Corse, and in spite of a slight argument with a wall, Munari won outright

For more than 10 years, a Porsche 911 could have been a regular rally winner, if only the factory had properly committed themselves to the sport. On the 1978 Safari, Bjorn Waldegard led for a while, but suspension problems pulled him back to fourth place at the finish

A great combination— Walter Rohrl in a Fiat 131 Abarth, here seen winning the 1978 Acropolis Rally. Rohrl and the Fiat were World Champions in 1980

The outstanding car of the 1970s was the Ford
Escort RS. In 1979 Ford won the World Rally
Championship, and Bjorn Waldegard was Cham-
pion driver. They so nearly won the Monte Carlo
Rally, but were foiled by rocks placed by saboteurs

All the might of the BMC Austin-Healey team, resting at the bottom of the Mont Ventoux hillclimb on the 1962 Alpine Rally. It was car number 5, driven by the Morley twins, which went on to win the event outright – the second consecutive victory for a Big Healey

mockery of established schedules – cars like the lightweight Alfa Giuliettas, the Mercedes-Benz 300SLs and the Porsche Carreras. Next, the truly committed car manufacturers, having found speed with their sporting models, redoubled their efforts. To satisfy their own competitive instincts, they began to evolve a series of 'homologation specials' – cars that had a veneer of meekness but which were designed to sell only in limited numbers, and to do only

one thing. That was to win in competitions – racing or rallying – so that mechanical specification and performance took precedence over most other aspects of comfort and refinement. The last of the helter-skelter open-road events would see tremendous struggles between cars such as the Lotus-Cortinas and Escort Twin-Cams, the Mini-Cooper Ss, the Lancia Fulvia HFs and the Alfa Giulia GTAs.

Such cars demanded, and got, a new breed of driver. Until now, the typical rally driver tended merely to be experienced, competent and financially secure; in the 1940s and 1950s most of them seemed to mature in their thirties, and nearly all had a weakness for the fleshpots associated with success. True stalwarts, able to race and perform with the best – like Ian Apple-

The loneliness of the long-distance rally driver – one of the MG Midgets in the 1962 Monte

yard, Peter Harper, Maurice Gatsonides, Walter Schluter and a few more – were in a tiny minority.

For the last, desperately serious, species of road races, new, red-blooded professional drivers appeared – stars who matured and gained their reputation during the 1960s. Such as Erik Carlsson from Sweden, Paddy Hopkirk from Northern Ireland, René Trautmann from France, Rauno Aaltonen and Timo Makinen from Finland, and Britain's talented Pat Moss. There were also several dashing amateurs, like the rotund, balding little restaurateur from Stuttgart, Eugen Bohringer, or the quiet little farmer from East Anglia, Donald Morley. Later, young tigers like Vic Elford and Roger Clark from Great Britain, Bjorn Waldegard and Hannu Mikkola from Scandinavia, or Jean Vinatier and Gérard Larrousse from France, all came along to raise professional driving standards even higher.

The key to all this professionalism was practice – day upon boring day of training and route learning. Not only did the new drivers have to be the fastest ever, but they literally had to become paid servants of their sponsoring companies, going wherever money and marketing policies directed them, and enduring lonely weeks of practice in pre-event preparation. In the 1950s it had usually been considered good enough to drive once or twice over sections of the route on the way to the start. Ten years later, it was considered normal to spend at least two weeks practising for an Alpine or a Liège (and perhaps wearing out one or even more cars, even hire cars, in the process), and up to a month preparing for a Monte Carlo Rally. The great rally drivers learned to live much like owls, working all night when traffic was thin and sleeping most of the day.

Terms such as 'recces' and 'pace notes' crept into the language of rallying. Pace notes, which did so much to make rallying faster and safer, provide a detailed, concise and accurate way of recording every feature, the layout and hazards, of a particular stretch of road. They can make a remarkable difference to a crew's performance and confidence. Before they were devised, practice for a special stage or hill-climb was precisely that – a driver went over the same piece of road time and time again, trying to memorize its features. The note system made it possible for a driver even to leave initial reconnaissance to his co-driver, and simply to visit the sections in order to agree upon and refine the basic notes.

As already mentioned, the first famous example of a complete written record of a route, features, bends, hazards and all, appears to have been by Stirling Moss and Denis Jenkinson, with their Mercedes-Benz 300SLR, in the 1955 Mille Miglia, which they won so convincingly. Jenkinson, however, has told me that Lincoln devised a rudimentary form of notes for the Mexican Panamericana in 1953, which Porsche developed in 1954 and which he inherited from John Fitch (ex-Lincoln) at the end of that year. But then, as Jenkinson also remarked, he was already using a signalling system to Eric Oliver from the sidecar of a motorcycle combination at the Nürburgring in 1950!

Pace notes as an aid to rallying, however, seem to have appeared during the same period, initially in the BMC rally team, whose captain, John Gott, was such a precise planner of events and routes. Stuart Turner, that rallying sage and mastermind who spices his conversation with a dry wit, once told me that Gott 'used to tell us everything about a route in advance, everything from local milking time to the schedule of the Jugoslavian trains over unguarded level crossings', and suggests that pace notes evolved naturally from that sort of pre-event briefing. By the end of the 1950s, certainly, British crews had a monopoly of the art, in contrast to the French and Italian habit of marking up corners in advance with painted hieroglyphics on trees and walls; sabotage of such marks was obviously possible, and seemed to happen on many occasions!

An essential element of pace notes was the 'shorthand' which made it possible for every corner, brow, length of straight and special feature to be defined; once this had been done, the art of rallying became less a matter of bravery and balance, and more of applied science. The revolution in rallying methods and technology in the 1960s was as striking as that

In 1960, Mercedes-Benz taught the rallying world how to go about practising. They dominated the results of the Monte Carlo Rally, with this man, Walter Schock, driving the winning 220SE

Rover only ran a 'works' team for a few years in the 1960s. Their finest hour, without doubt, was in the 1965 Monte Carlo Rally, when Roger Clark and Jim Porter took this standard Rover 2000 to sixth place, and won the Group 1 category outright

Horses for courses? Racing driver Louis Rosier drove this 4CV Renault to a class win in the 1951 Monte Carlo Rally. Usually, though, these rear-engined saloons were under-powered for serious competition

In his first serious rally, Stirling Moss (crewed by John 'The Autocar' Cooper and Desmond Scannell) took second overall place in the 1952 Monte Carlo Rally in this works-entered Sunbeam Talbot 90

affecting Grand Prix racing in more recent years.

In addition to standard pace notes, a subsidiary form of note-taking was adopted for rallying over ice and snow, or in the event of significantly altered road conditions. Once again it was BMC who developed this refinement, by sending well-driven practice cars ahead of the events, just hours before sections were closed to non-competing traffic, so that any change in the hazards could be superimposed on copies of notes made in practice. Before long, indeed, there were two types of team drivers on the major events – those actually competing, and those (perhaps the up-and-coming men, or those surplus to the team at a particular time) entrusted with the preparation of the last-minute information.

I have stressed the use of pace notes, which were read out by the co-driver to his driver with the aid of intercom systems plumbed into crash helmets, because they made a startling difference to the pace of rallying over tortuous sections. On familiar hill-climbs the effect was not as pronounced, but on long and obscure special stages the use of notes could increase a car's average speeds by up to 10mph and could reduce the risk of accidents to a minimum.

Car-makers now began to take much more interest, and numerous factory-sponsored teams soon made the scene more competitive and colourful. The reason was obvious. In the past, few factories, however sporting-minded, had wanted to throw good money into an effort that might hinge on the vagaries of the weather or on the results of tightly marked, monotonous series of time-keeping contests. Now that the best, most prestigious rallies were developing into a true test of driving ability, with the speed, endurance and reliability of the cars themselves becoming important, there was certain publicity to be gained. The factories soon realized that it would be well worth the expense to advertise success in the Monte Carlo or Alpine rallies, alerting the sporting world to the fact that their cars were faster and better prepared than those of their rivals.

To match the performance of fiercer cars and professional drivers, the events, too, had to be revised. Even the Monte Carlo Rally, that most reactionary of all events which became the spotlight of attention every January, had to change its ways. As already described, throughout the 1950s the Monte involved competitors in thousands of miles of running round Europe, the accent being ever more concentrated on eliminating tests near the finish. With the development of studded tyres, accurate time-keeping became possible, and success or failure came to depend on the genius of a co-driver. Matters came to a head in 1960 when Mercedes-Benz completely dominated the event, taking the first three places in works-sponsored cars which had been practising for weeks in the mountains.

For 1961, therefore, a series of special stages were added to the normal route through the French mountains between Charbonnières and Monaco; but, true to form for this event, there was also a very complicated handicap based on engine size, tuning *and* the homologated weight of the cars themselves. Like the fabled example of the 'curate's egg', parts of this were excellent, for every serious rallyist loved the idea of special stages, even on ice and snow at speeds up to 100mph, but almost everyone hated the notion of a handicap. Having analyzed the formula, experienced observers had decided weeks in advance that a competently-driven Panhard Tigre saloon (which was large and heavy, with a small but efficient engine and front-wheel drive) was going to win.

And so it did, with Messieurs Martin, Loffler and Jouanneaux taking first, second and third places. Not even the remarkable Erik Carlsson, who drove a Saab 95 estate car on this occasion because it was heavier than the saloon, could catch the Panhards. René Trautmann (Citroën DS19) was fastest overall on the five special stages, with Carlsson behind him and Gunnar Andersson's Volvo third, but Trautmann could only finish 19th overall. There were, of course, the usual accusations that the whole thing had been rigged by the Monegasques in favour of French cars (not a very convincing argument, considering Trautmann's misfortune); but it is a fact that no Panhard driver ever won an important rally again.

Things improved subsequently, and the Monte gradually earned the winter ice-racing reputation which it has kept to the present day. Some of the younger members of the Monte's organizing committee would doubtless have loved to go for a full-blooded road race, Alpine Rally-style, but this was impossible as most of the really demanding routes used on the Alpine in summer were completely blocked by snow-banks between October and April every year. Achieving a result on the less difficult routes

Ford set out cold-bloodedly to win the Monte Carlo Rally of 1963 without any previous experience, and failed completely. In 1964, however, they came close, for this car, driven by Bo. Ljungfeldt was fastest on aggregate over the special stages, though a favourable handicap allowed Paddy Hopkirk's Mini Cooper S to win, and the Falcon was second overall

On one occasion, which Reliant fans will never forget, a team of Sabre Sixes actually won the big sports car class of the Alpine Rally (in 1963) after all the BMC Austin-Healeys had retired

which were open all winter, even at a running average of 60kph (37mph) – possible with the connivance of the French police – was out of the question. The advance in studded tyre technology meant that lack of grip was no longer the problem it had been in the 1950s; indeed, adhesion with the new studded tyres, which laid a carpet of tiny spikes on the ice or snow, was so good that on some cars the bogy of brake fade actually reappeared!

Handicaps of one type or another, however, continued to feature in the Monte Carlo Rally until 1967, and usually managed to cause confusion and controversy. The 'weight' factor was immediately abandoned after the 1961 fiasco, but another factor of comparison involving engine size and the car's state of tune (Group 1, 2, or 3, for example) persisted until 1965. These proved to be surprisingly ineffective. In 1962 Erik Carlsson and his remarkable little two-stroke Saab beat Eugen Bohringer's Mercedes-Benz 220SE, with two Sunbeam Rapiers driven by Paddy Hopkirk and Peter Procter behind him, while in 1963 it was Carlsson who once again triumphed over the handicaps and the weather (1963 was an appallingly difficult year) to beat Pauli Toivonen's big Citroën and Rauno Aaltonen's 997cc Mini-Cooper. Significantly, as far as the handicap was concerned, all these cars were in pseudo-standard – i.e. Group 1 – tune.

One of the great rally cars of all time – the Austin-Healey 3000 – garlanded after its victory in the 1964 Spa–Sofia–Liège, driven by Rauno Aaltonen and Tony Ambrose

By 1964, Ford of Detroit had decided that they were ready to buck the system. Their attempt in 1963 came to nothing, but in 1964 they homologated large and very fast new cars, Falcons, hired good drivers and spared no expense. They could not, however, overcome the handicaps, as Paddy Hopkirk's 1071cc Mini-Cooper S proved by beating Ljungfeldt's 4.7-litre Falcon, and once again Carlsson urged his 850cc Saab into the top places of a Monte Carlo Rally. Unfair? Perhaps, for Ljungfeldt's Falcon was 82 seconds faster than Hopkirk on the special stages and several minutes quicker than Carlsson's Saab.

There was still a handicap in 1965, though it had little effect on the results, in view of the very wintry weather. Adjustments to the handicapping 'formula' had shifted the balance slightly in favour of modified machinery, and the top five finishers were all in Group 2 or Group 3 cars. In the last few seasons, the Abingdon-prepared BMC Mini-Cooper S cars had started to win events outright all over Europe, so nobody was surprised that they repeated their 1964 victory in this Monte. The only uncertainty was which of the distinguished drivers would come out on top – and it proved to be Timo Makinen's turn. The real shock was that the resourceful little German, Bohringer, drove a Porsche 904 – a sports *racing* car, no less – into second place, with Pat Moss (or Pat Moss-Carlsson, as she had now become) taking third place in a Saab. Further down, in sixth place, one of the event's real sensations was caused by a young man named Roger Clark, who drove a Rover 2000 in a way that no Rover manager could have expected, and won the Group 1 (standard car) category; it was the first time Europe had really come to know of Mr Clark, but it would assuredly not be the last!

If 1965 was a great Monte year for the British, 1966 was a real disaster. By this time, the organizers had clearly become unhappy about the way the 'foreigners' were repeatedly winning an event that had traditionally favoured the French. For 1966, therefore, the handicap was arranged so as to make the use of Group 1 cars imperative. The significance of this was that none of the really competitive modern rally cars – BMC Mini-Cooper S, Ford Lotus-Cortina, Alfa-Romeo Giulia GTA, and Saab, etc. – were homologated in Group 1, which required proof that more than 5000 vehicles had been built in a consecutive 12-month period. Cars like the big

To win rallies, it is usually essential to take the shortest route. Paddy Hopkirk (Mini-Cooper S) couldn't possibly improve on this at the Gasworks hairpin on the Monaco GP circuit. He was confirming his victory in the 1964 Monte Carlo Rally – the Mini's first

Events like the Alpine encouraged the strangest cars to compete. This was a Porsche 904, complete with racing exhaust, entered in the 'prototype' class

Citroën DS, on the other hand, undoubtedly qualified, and it appears certain that the organizers made their decision for 1966 in order to give these big front-wheel-drive cars an even chance of success.

What happened between publication of the regulations and the start of the event is now well known. BMC and Ford both moved every possible organizational mountain to get their cars homologated in Group 1 (BMC may, indeed, have built 5000 cars in 1965, but Lotus – who assembled the Lotus-Cortina for Ford – most certainly did not!), and turned up on the event with their usual, though standard, rally cars.

This would not have been so frustrating if the cars had not been competitive, or if the practice and note-making processes had not been so thorough. In 1966, of all years, BMC introduced

Rootes's Imp was always a good contender for class wins, but occasionally a favourable handicap could produce startling results. In 1965 Rosemary Smith, here seen starting the Col de Fouchy hillclimb, won the Tulip Rally outright

their 'ice notes' crews – much more of a 'secret weapon' than any form of 'illegal' engine tuning or car-swapping could have been – which enabled the drivers to choose the ideal tyre equipment for each stage, regardless of conditions in the service compound where they had to make the choice. Their overall performance was so good that on some stages they even beat Group 3 cars like Gunter Klass's Porsche 911 (which had no ice-notes crew, and no front-wheel-drive transmission); and at the end of the event, *on the road* the Minis were in the first three places (in the order Makinen-Aaltonen-Hopkirk) with Roger Clark's Lotus-Cortina fourth. The best Citroën standing, at that point, was Pauli Toivonen's car in fifth place.

Every possible accusation was hurled at the British teams by the chauvinistic French press, who alleged that BMC were cheating by sub-stituting identical-looking cars on the special stages, or that their cars, at very least, did not comply with Group 1 regulations. How was it that 'standard' Minis could beat Porsches and big Citroëns on scratch times? The predictable consequence was that the scrutineers ordered the Minis to be stripped, quite literally, to their component parts; and a desperate search commenced for something – anything – that might provide grounds for a disqualification. Nothing of consequence was found, except that BMC (and Ford) had 'illegally' altered their headlamp dipping arrangements so that the latest quartz-halogen single-filament bulbs could be used. This incredibly flimsy reason was made the excuse for disqualifying the British cars. Citroën, therefore, got their Monte 'victory' after all. Pauli Toivonen was reputedly so disgusted by what had happened, and by his team's attitude to the whole affair, that he vowed never to drive for Citroën again – and he kept his word. Toivonen was acclaimed for that decision, and Citroën's sporting reputation was never the same again.

The only certain way for BMC to kill the accusations of cheating was for them to return next year, in 1967, and to win again, which they duly did. This was the last time the Monte Carlo Rally featured a 'handicap' factor – the very simple one of limiting each car to the use of eight tyres on each of the two long loops from Monaco – tyres which had to be chosen *before* even starting out on that loop, and which were branded by the organizing team (with the competition number) and carried in the car at all times. Inevitably, this was viewed as a further attack on BMC, whose Mini-Cooper S, with their 10-inch wheels, were notoriously heavy on their rubber.

It was the sort of technical challenge which BMC and Stuart Turner relished, one which involved months of preparation, and one which I had the pleasure of chronicling afterwards for *Autocar*. As early as the previous October, BMC sent Timo Makinen tyre-testing with a variety of new Dunlop covers, chose a compound with a much-improved life potential (and better stud retention), and used it as the basis for their assault in January 1967.

The event was a resounding triumph for BMC, even though the unfortunate Makinen was eliminated during the last hectic night when his car ran into a huge rock which had mysteriously found its way onto a narrow road not far from Nice. It was a typical Monte 'road race' of the 1960s. Long concentration runs from eight starting points as far apart as Oslo and Athens, Warsaw and Lisbon, led to Monaco, to be followed by what was known as the 'Common Route' – Monaco to Monaco via Chambéry, 800 miles in 21½ hours, and six long special stages. After another night's rest, the 60 leading cars tackled the now-famous and traditional Mountain Circuit of 380 miles in 11 hours, including a further six special stages (of which three were repeated crossings of the Col du Turini); that schedule was so tight that it has sometimes been described as 'one long special stage, from Monte to Monte'.

After the Common Route, completed in almost spring-like weather, Vic Elford's factory-prepared Porsche 911S led the three 'first team' Minis by just over half a minute, and there were two 1.2-litre Lancia Fulvias behind them. The hectic Mountain Circuit altered all that, for mechanical mishaps were compounded by sudden and heavy snowfalls. Elford's Porsche lost ground, Makinen's Mini hit the rock, and Paddy Hopkirk's Mini dropped back, but Rauno Aaltonen (partnered by Henry Liddon,

MGAs were still active rally cars at the start of the 1960s. This 1600 Mk II de Luxe, to give it its full title, won a Tulip Rally class for Rauno Aaltonen in 1962

who had co-driven the winning car in 1964) hung on to beat Ove Andersson's Lancia Fulvia by a mere 13 seconds.

It was the final vindication, and almost the final fling, of the 'Mini era', for by 1968 these cheeky, bright-red little cars, were being over-

The MGB was a solidly reliable car in the 1960s, and good enough to win the GT category in the Monte Carlo Rally when driven by Donald Morley

The top of Mont Ventoux really is as bare and desolate as all that, as Simo Lampinen's 1.3-litre Triumph Spitfire discovered on the 1965 Alpine Rally

The Renault 8 Gordini, when developed into 1.3-litre form, was a good competitor for, but not as fast as, the BMC Mini-Cooper S. It had remarkable traction on snow-covered roads

hauled by several rivals as they reached the handling and traction limits imposed by front-wheel drive and 10-inch wheels. The next three Montes were completely dominated by Porsche, so much so that everyone was surprised when a Porsche did *not* win in 1971, after achieving the hat trick!

In 1968 Vic Elford (in a Stuttgart-prepared 911T) won one of the driest-ever Montes, beating team-mate Pauli Toivonen in an identical car, but not without a dramatic struggle against Gérard Larrousse's works Alpine-Renault, which was only eliminated part-way through the final night when it crashed on fresh snow reputedly shovelled into the road on the Turini by drunken spectators. BMC Cooper S team cars finished third, fourth and fifth (Aaltonen, Fall and Hopkirk), and beat the Lancias from Turin once again.

Elford, that most dedicated and determined of drivers, might have won again in 1968, for his 911S was leading the event with only three special stages to go, but crashed head-on into a tree *after* the finish of the Turini section. That left victory to Bjorn Waldegard's factory-prepared Porsche 911S (from Larrousse's sister

Peter Harper was still Rootes's fastest driver in the mid-1960s, as he often proved in the 4.2-litre Sunbeam Tiger. Although number 1 in this Tulip Rally, he actually finished third overall, and won the GT category

Vic Elford matured, as a rally driver, with Ford, but was often let down by his cars. In the 1966 Alpine, he led for a while, but soon after he climbed the Mont Ventoux hillclimb, his Lotus-Cortina's engine let go

car), a performance which the same two drivers and cars repeated in 1970. It was significant that BMC did not even compete in 1969 and 1970 (policy, from British Leyland, having changed considerably), while Alpine-Renault finished third on each occasion (Jean Vinatier in 1969 and Jean-Pierre Nicolas in 1970). Ford, too, made their mark, with fourth overall for Jean-François Piot in 1969 and fifth for Roger Clark in 1970. ·

Although Ford had done so well in 1970, their management was far from satisfied. Stuart Turner had left BMC in 1967, spent two years out of the sport, but returned in 1969 to take charge of competitions at Ford. It was his organizing genius that had led to the Escort's resurgence after a decline in 1969, but his hope that Twin-Cam 'ice-racers' could win a Monte Carlo Rally in 1970 was dashed. Almost at once this led Ford to start developing a special mid-

engined rally car, one which would spark off other important contenders in the next few years.

At the beginning of the 1970s, therefore, the Monte Carlo Rally had regained its place as one of the world's most important road events. In ten years it had transformed itself, not without trauma, from something of an over-commercialized trek around Europe into one of the most concentrated ice-racing road rallies ever known. Ten years earlier precise navigation had been all-important, but by 1970 the accent was firmly on driving skills, car preparation and widespread (and expensive) team organization.

Nevertheless, while the media might still love the Monte, the *real* experts – drivers and team managers – tended to prefer a more demanding if less publicized road race – the French Alpine Rally. We have followed the story of this rally up to the end of the 1950s, just as the great

You should normally never *let a Mini understeer as much as this, but Rauno Aaltonen has just struck a patch of gravel on a very wide corner and is fighting his way out of trouble*

speed-up began, and as the faster, more rugged cars put in their first appearance. The great years of the Alpine were yet to come. Although the highest target average speeds remained at 60kph (37mph) on all road sections, even until the last rally of all, held in 1971, this did not imply that

Svengali and Trilby? No – merely team-manager Stuart Turner giving advice to Timo Makinen at a tyre changing session on the Monte Carlo Rally of 1967. Makinen didn't win that one, but another Mini-Cooper S did

the maintenance of an unpenalized run and the gaining of a *Coupe des Alpes* became progressively easier. On the contrary, by a combination of route changes, involving even more obscure mountain roads, and the unashamed use of 'pruning scissors', winning a *Coupe* seemed to get more difficult every year.

Although 'pruning' was not strictly allowed, according to various local laws and authorities, and the use of rough or even damaging tracks was perfectly acceptable, it goes without saying that drivers, even those in factory-prepared cars, much preferred to go very fast rather than batter their machines over unsuitable surfaces.

The professionals were well accustomed to the organizers' habit of raising average speeds by 'pruning'. This meant that a section was made more difficult rather than theoretically possible by cutting the effective time allowed for its completion. A 60kph average, of course, meant that one kilometre had to be completed every minute. If, however, a crew drove more than 40 kilometres into what was advertised as a 40-minute section, and found no control or official car anywhere in sight, they were not at all perturbed. They merely had to drive far enough, and fast enough, to find the next control, and satisfy the organizers that they had covered the necessary distance in the permitted time.

By the end of the 1950s, the latest generation of cars – such as the Austin-Healey 3000s and the lightweight Alfa-Romeos – were not only very fast uphill but also remarkably rapid and stable downhill, for their powerful disc brakes and radial-ply tyres gave them what appeared to be extraordinary grip and control. A few years back, the timed ascent of one of the high passes in the Alps between Chambéry, Briançon and the Mediterranean coastline at 60kph had been difficult enough. Later it became necessary to make the ascent a speed hill-climb, and to carry on the descent of the other side as part of a *selectif* or tight road section; and before long the time allowances for that valley to valley sector had to be slashed. It was highly questionable, highly demanding, and the authorities undoubtedly knew exactly what was going on; nobody seemed to mind.

Although the Alpine's route changed somewhat from year to year, its pattern soon became familiar. The first night's motoring, out of Marseilles, usually included a speed hill-climb all the way up the spectacular slopes of Mont

Jean Rolland was a very resourceful Frenchman who habitually got more out of an Alfa Romeo Giulia GTA than did the Italians. He has just won an Alpine Rally, and is feeling very happy about it

Ventoux and the first of a series of tight road sections in the hills behind Cannes and Nice, before the really big passes north of this area were tackled. The second of a three-phase Alpine often included *selectifs* and speed sections farther north, towards Chambéry, Annecy and Geneva, but the second rest halt always preceded a final high-speed assault on just about every high, narrow and sinuous road which the organizers could find. A typical 'last night' might begin from Aix-les-Bains and take in the Cols of Iseran, Glandon, Croix de Fer, Galibier, Izoard, Vars, Allos, Cayolle, Restefond and other less famous ascents before there was any respite, and before daylight had properly arrived. Then followed a full morning of serpentine wriggling around narrow, broken-down, and incredibly tortuous little roads around Entrevaux and Puget Theniers, before the pace finally slackened and the very depleted field made for the finish,

usually in Cannes, Nice, Monte Carlo or Menton. There was, quite literally, nothing like the Alpine, despite what less experienced rally drivers might suggest; the only 'night' to compare with it is perhaps the final section of the Rallye do Portugal, or (in rather different weather and surface conditions) the last, hectic, thrilling rush through the Kielder Forest in the Lombard-RAC Rally.

Even though Ken Richardson's works Triumph TR3As defeated the Abingdon-built 'Big Healeys' in the 1958 and 1959 events, the Alpine Rallies held between 1958 and 1965 might justifiably be called the 'Healey years'. Teams of red cars with white hardtops, always magnificently and quite unmistakeably prepared by the same team of mechanics, were entered every year. Managed first by Marcus Chambers, and later by Stuart Turner, they were up in the lead most of the time and actually took outright victory on two occasions in their eight years of competition. It was mechanical misfortune that robbed the Morley twins of their richly deserved *Coupe d'Or* in 1963, and in the next two years they were only defeated by a combination of

If there's no weight on the inside wheel, you might as well hang it over the edge. Tony Fall's Mini-Cooper 1275S in the 1966 RAC Rally

handicaps and the presence of Alfa-Romeo TZs.

Although there were handicaps in all these Alpines, nobody seemed to care, because it was obviously done for the proper reasons. On all the normal road sections the same target times applied for all competitors, but on the even more difficult *selectifs*, small cars were allowed two or three minutes more than large cars, and the Group 1 competitors were not expected to go as fast as the Healeys, Porsches, and Alfas in the Group 3 category. This, in fact, was a carefully calculated (and successful) attempt to give everything from a Saab Sport to a Porsche 904 the chance of winning an Alpine *Coupe*. General classification and class positions, however, were still settled by referring to scratch times achieved on the speed tests and hill-climbs. On a few occasions, as performance and schedules persistently rose, the organizers got it slightly wrong. Only one *Coupe des Alpes* was awarded in 1961 (and that was to the outright winner), while in 1965 every GT car lost time on one or

other of the very fast *selectifs*. It was for that reason, more than for any other, that everyone was so delighted when Erik Carlsson's Saab Sport won a *Coupe* in 1964 – a performance which had hitherto been considered impossible.

Until 1962 the route of the Alpine struck deep into Italy, with near-impossible sections over the Gavia and Vivione obligatory, not to mention a timed climb of the Stelvio, but from 1963 onwards the event was concentrated mainly on the south-eastern corners of France, with short forays for linking purposes into neighbouring Switzerland and Italy. In all this time, and despite the good intentions of the organizers, the Alpine was generally won by a GT car, though things became a little difficult in later years when the results were published in different categories.

In 1959, however, it was a well-handicapped factory-prepared Renault Dauphine (driven by Condrillier) which scooped the pool, from Kuhne's two-stroke DKW, and Paddy Hopkirk's Sunbeam Rapier, while Ford won the team prize with their much-improved Zephyrs, and Triumph made something of a meal of the GT category, with class wins for 2-litre *and* 2.2-litre TR3As. A year later, there was an outright win for de Lageneste's beautiful little Zagato-bodied Alfa-Romeo Giulietta, and a really splendid drive into second place by Pat Moss and Ann Wisdom in their Austin-Healey 3000; they also made up one of the members of the Austin-Healey team which took the team prize. Trautmann's DS19 took its class, and this year it was Peter Harper's turn to be best of the Sunbeam Rapiers. All hopes of a Triumph team prize disappeared in Marseilles itself, when Rob Slotemaker's TR3A broke a half-shaft only yards after the start. Erik Carlsson, however, once had even worse luck, when his Saab's engine blew up on the way to scrutineering!

If 1960 was a difficult year (with only six cars – two GT and four Touring – unpenalized on the road), 1961 was even tougher, for the only *Coupe* to be awarded was to the outright winner, Donald Morley, in his Austin-Healey 3000. Even the very talented Frenchman, Jean Rolland, in a Zagato-bodied Alfa-Romeo, lost one minute, and Paddy Hopkirk (Sunbeam Rapier – third again) lost two. Morley, however, did not have it all easy, for in the first part of the event he was headed by Hans Walter's Porsche Super 90, which finally dropped a valve on the main road climb of the Col de Grand St Bernard. The horror section, near the end of the gruelling

At the end of the 1960s, there was nothing quite as hideous as a Citroën DS 'Special' . . .

last stage, was the 68 kilometres from St Auban to Les Quatre Chemins, set at an honest 60kph for the fastest cars (no pruning was needed), which was extremely demanding for all concerned. Variations, embellishments and repetitions of this section became traditional in all future Alpines; Les Quatre Chemins, even though it means nothing more significant than 'the four roads', became an instant rally legend – a type of road section which could always be relied upon to cause trouble.

Having done it once, the Morleys did it all again in 1962. By this time five new works Austin-Healeys had been built, stronger and lighter than before, and by now equipped with 210bhp engines having light-alloy cylinder heads and triple Weber carburettors; for the next four years, the 'Squealeys' were as competitive as any other GT car in rallying. Triumph, for their part, had undergone something of a revolution, changing competition managers (the author taking over from Ken Richardson) and cars (fast-improving TR4s

instead of the old TR3As, which had always been virtually standard), while 1961 European champion Hans Walter had a new Porsche Carrera, complete with a four-cam 2-litre engine. An interesting runner on this event was Henri Oreiller's Ferrari 250GT Berlinetta, which gave the big Healeys a fright until it disappeared in the Italian sections. By comparison with 1961, it was an 'easier' year, in the sense that five crews (two in Austin-Healeys – Pat Moss was third – Mike Sutcliffe's TR4, Walter's Porsche and Trautmann's big Citroën) all kept a clean sheet on the road sections.

In 1963 there were enormous upsets, not least because Ford had begun to expand their rallying activity considerably, having 'bought' Pat Moss, David Seigle-Morris and Peter Riley from BMC. BMC, for their part, were rapidly developing their Mini-Coopers *and* their Scandinavian drivers. In its very first event, a 1071cc Mini-Cooper S, driven by Rauno Aaltonen, won the Touring car category outright, while Rolland's astonishing 1.3-litre Alfa-Romeo Giulietta SZ was the best Grand Tourer, just as similar cars had been in 1958 and 1960. The Morleys lost their chance of a *Coupe d'Or* when

All sideways, but well under control – Jean-Luc Therier's Alpine-Renault on the way to second place in the 1971 Monte Carlo Rally. His teammate, Ove Andersson, was the outright winner, and Andruet's Alpine-Renault was joint third with Waldegard's Porsche 914/6

The new and the old – rally cars, that is. The Porsche 911 was already an established winner before Ford's Escort Twin-Cam came along. On this occasion Pauli Toivonen drove a 911 to win the 1969 Acropolis Rally, while Roger Clark's Escort was second

their Austin-Healey 3000 unexpectedly broke its rear axle on the last night of the event, all the other Healeys retired, and the class was won by the slow, unwieldy Reliant Sabres (for whom Roger Clark was having his very first works drive); all three TR4s, too, fell by the wayside. Greder's vast Ford Falcon hit a mountain and retired when second (the same combination had just won the handicap-ridden Tulip Rally with a remarkable effort), while Vic Elford confirmed his Tulip effort in a TR4 (third overall on scratch times) by harrying the much larger Austin-Healeys until a little over-exuberance put him off the road and out of the event.

By 1964, Ford had made their Cortina GTs competitive, Rover were in rallying with their 2000s, Triumph were beginning to turn their Spitfires into fast little GT cars, BMC had homologated the 1275cc Mini-Cooper S, and Alfa Romeo had produced the noisy but very effective 1.6-litre GTZ. All had an effect on the Alpine of that year, and once again it was Rolland (in the GTZ) who dominated proceedings, with Vic Elford (who had 'transferred' from Triumph to Ford) taking the Touring car group in his Cortina GT. For all that, however, the Morleys quietly and efficiently won their *Coupe d'Argent* in an Austin-Healey 3000, while of the seven cars to be unpenalized, three were

One of the raucous but very rapid 'works' Alpine-Renaults rushing down a French mountain on the way to a Coupe des Alpes *in the Alpine Rally of the late 1960s*

Mini-Coopers and one was Carlsson's Saab. Ford survived a crushing blow near the end when Seigle-Morris's Cortina suffered engine failure, but his lead was taken over by the determined Elford.

1965 was the last Alpine appearance for the Austin-Healeys (rule changes for 1966 would effectively outlaw these splendid cars), and it also introduced a full-blown category for prototypes. Among the latter were road-equipped flat-six Porsche 906 coupés, Matra-Bonnets, and the fully-developed fastback Triumph Spitfires which were using prototype 1.3-litre engines. Ford had Lotus-Cortinas (now reliable, with their leaf-spring rear suspension), Lancia had the ugly but fast Flavia sport Zagatos, and Rootes entered Peter Harper in a Sunbeam Tiger.

Rolland and Aaltonen both hoped to win *Coupes d'Or*, but neither was lucky. Alfa-Romeo, however, were rewarded with a GT win for Consten's GTZ, while Trautmann's Lancia won the Touring car group after Elford's Lotus-Cortina electrics collapsed near the finish, and Lampinen's Spitfire was the best of the pro-

totypes after most of the racing-type Porsches failed. The real tragedy, however, was that Peter Harper's V8-engined Tiger was the best of all the GT cars, but was disqualified at post-event scrutineering, on a technicality regarding engine specification; it would have been the only GT car to gain a *Coupe* in an incredibly fast and demanding event, and it is worth recalling that on this occasion the Morley twins, in a works Austin-Healey 3000, were beaten in a straight fight.

Thereafter, the Alpine became even more of a road race than ever, with the pruning technique well and truly in evidence, and with even greater use of minor roads, and tracks, so that a true 'homologation special' was needed to be competitive. There would be just five more Alpines. (The 1970 event was cancelled due to a clash of possible dates with the Tour de France and because of the first really strong anti-rallying protests from police and local authorities; and the 1971 event was a mere shadow of the usual rally standard.) None of the remaining rallies were won by anything even remotely approaching 'production car' specification.

That gritty and consistent French driver, Jean Rolland, won the 1966 event outright, from Roger Clark's Lotus-Cortina and Rauno Aaltonen's Mini-Cooper 1275S; Rolland's car was an

Alfa-Romeo GTA, which might have been carrying French plates, but was works-blessed in most respects. Once again Vic Elford (Lotus-Cortina) was forced out with engine failure when in the lead – one of several misfortunes in 1966 which led him to sign for Porsche in 1967. Nine factory teams and a single Porsche 911 (for Gunter Klass) all tried their hand on this occasion; of 81 starters, only 19 made it back to the finish in Cannes, and seven *Coupes* were awarded. BMC were claiming that their Mini-Cooper S cars were now every bit as quick as an Austin-Healey 3000, and they attracted a much more favourable handicap; the cars were certainly very powerful by this time, and normal radial road tyres rarely lasted for more than 30 *minutes* when used by a bold Scandinavian driver on a tight Alpine test! For the first time the Alpine's date had been moved back to September to avoid the worst of the French holiday tourist traffic, and to minimize police protests.

If the Alpine had been fast in 1966, it was positively hair-raising in 1967. I can do no more than quote my own copy from *Autocar's* report of the event: 'Brave drivers had blanched and team managers winced when they studied the layout of this new-style Alpine. . . . By chopping many minutes off already infamous Alpine road sections (in some cases setting speeds of more than 70kph in the mountains) and scrapping the handicap system altogether, there was no hope for the smaller cars. . . . The much-coveted *Coupe des Alpes*, once awarded for unpenalized runs on the road sections, were now to be awarded only to those cars having total penalties within two percent of the winner's times. . . .' For very obvious reasons, therefore, several factories entered Group 6 'prototypes', which included Weber-carburetted Mini-Cooper S cars from Abingdon, a lightweight four-cam Porsche 911R for Vic Elford and 'works' Renault Gordinis with 1.5-litre or even twin-cam engines.

Even so, and in the face of enormously strong opposition, BMC finally achieved their ambition – to win the Alpine with a Mini. Paddy Hopkirk took his Group 6 car, complete with light-alloy body panels and a reputed 125bhp engine, to victory over the Alfa-Romeo GTAs of Bernard Consten and J. C. Gamet; Harry Kallstrom's Renault 8 Gordini 1300 was fourth and Andruet's Alpine-Renault took fifth place. The pace was so fast and furious, right from the start, that at the first rest halt, Alpe d'Huez after 900 miles, Hopkirk's car was in seventh place, and Consten's Alfa was not even in the top ten! Gérard Larrousse's Alpine-Renault 1500 was then leading and looked uncatchable until the last night, when its engine failed; and five of the six crews leading Hopkirk at Alpe d'Huez retired. Only the top four cars gained *Coupes*.

For enthusiasts, this was a wonderful spectacle, but for private owners the financial prospect was horrifying, so in 1968 the entry was well down, with no BMC entries (for the first time since the early 1950s), and only three Fords – the Escort Twin-Cams then enjoying a successful first season. It was a year in which speeds were higher than ever, in which Alpine-Renault finally won the event for the first time after years of trying, and in which René Trautmann won his fifth (non-consecutive) *Coupe*, this time in a 1.4-litre Lancia Fulvia HF. The delighted Jean Vinatier led a mere 12 survivors back to the finish in Antibes, only three of which gained *Coupes* (Barailler's Alfa GTA gained the third).

It was all very exciting, but unlikely to endear itself to the public for long; consequently, the 1969 Alpine was really the last of the top-class 'road-racing' Alpines, and therefore the last in the world. It attracted factory teams from Ford, Lancia, Alpine-Renault, Alfa-Romeo, Citroën and Daf, of which the first three seemed most likely to be fighting for outright victory. The Fords were a varied collection of Group 6 prototypes (Stuart Turner had just taken over control at Boreham, and was still shuffling present and future possibilities of the design), one of which was a 2.3-litre Taunus V6-engined car for Roger Clark.

It was the Alpine-Renaults, however, which dominated proceedings, and in the end, at Juan-les-Pins, they took first, second, third and sixth places (for Vinatier, Andruet, Jorma Lusenius and Jean-Pierre Nicolas), with Trautmann and Kallstrom fourth and fifth in Lancia Fulvia HFs. Trautmann's fine performance, incidentally, gave him his sixth *Coupe*, a feat which no other driver ever equalled.

By then, however, the days of unrestricted high-speed rallying on open roads, even in remote country districts, were almost at an end. Probably only because of its exalted place in the sporting world, the Alpine Rally had been allowed to carry on years after other such events had been hounded off the scene, to continue on private ground. No matter how popular – and

Just about as high as one can go in France – Roger Clark and his Group 6 Ford Escort Twin-Cam near the summit of the Col de Restefond in the 1968 Alpine Rally

there was never any doubt about that, for every straw poll among professional rally drivers of the 1960s inevitably showed it to be their favourite – the Alpine Rally was living on borrowed time. In 1970, as already mentioned, it was cancelled, and in 1971 approval was only given at such a late stage that a mere travesty of an event was hastily cobbled together. There were so many last-minute route and timing changes that several crews backed out in disgust, and only 34 cars faced the starter. This, therefore, the last of the once-famous Alpines, was notable only for the fact that Jean Vinatier, finishing second, gained his third consecutive *Coupe*, and therefore a *Coupe d'Or*, though Darniche's Alpine-Renault won the event, and Jean-François Piot's Escort RS1600 was third.

By this time, alas, the greatest of all the long-distance 'rough-road' races – the legendary Liège – was also dead. Whereas the Alpine Rally had survived somewhat uneasily until

1971 because the local club was effectively using local roads, the Liège was a Belgian event which had never used Belgian roads for its rallying. Until 1955 it ran down to Rome before turning for home, but from 1956 it began to make deeper and deeper excursions into the Balkans.

Even though rallying in general began to speed up considerably towards the end of the 1950s, this really had little effect on the character of the Liège–Rome–Liège Rally, which had always been a really fast open-road event for brave drivers and rugged cars. Even when the route covered many miles of Italian roads, on the way to and back from Rome, the pace was always considerable. The Royal Motor Union began to direct its event into countries and regions where average speed restrictions were not as severe, with only light tourist traffic, and when this was combined with rough roads and the hot, dusty conditions of an Adriatic summer, the effect on the crews could be quite devastating.

After the Liège abandoned its traditional turning point at Rome, there were to be two further exciting phases in its development. From 1956 to 1960 it went nowhere near Rome, although retaining its original title, and it in-

Two of the great characters of the 1960s – Tony Fall (left) and Mike Wood. In the mid-1970s, Tony Fall became Competitions Manager of Opel in Europe

cluded a destructive loop of some 12 hours into Jugoslavia from the Italian border north of Trieste. From 1961 to 1964 – and these were really the most memorable of all 1960s rallies – it abandoned sections in France altogether, and sent its crews on a mad dash to and from Sofia, in Bulgaria; there were variations on a name, but this last breed of event is now affectionately

The most effective combination in Porsches was Vic Elford (left) and David Stone. Elford was one of the very few drivers successfully to make the transition from rally to racing driver. Not only did he win the Monte Carlo Rally in 1968, but he also won the Targa Florio and many other World Championship sports car races for Porsche

remembered as the Liège–Sofia–Liège. The challenge of the event, incidentally, was not merely that it was long, fast, tiring, and often run over rough roads, but that there was really no provision at all for the crews to rest. In 1961 there was, praise be, a four-hour rest halt in Sofia (and a massed start of surviving cars from the 'out' control), but this was soon reduced to a mere one hour – just sufficient, at the half-way point in a four-day marathon, for a shower and a snatched meal!

It is worth pointing out, too, that although the Jugoslavian and Bulgarian authorities were happy to welcome this somewhat anti-social event into their countries, they were worried about the impression the wealthy Western capitalists would take away with them. They would have wished for the visitors to sample their best hotels and finest tourist facilities; as it turned out, most rally crews merely remembered the rocks, the dust and the destruction wrought to their cars by the primitive back roads chosen.

In 1959, *Autocar*'s Peter Garnier (who competed in the event with Jack Sears in a works Austin-Healey 3000) described the event as 'the most devastating rally to date', and noted that of 97 starters, only 14 survived. Though there was still very little mileage in Jugoslavia, it already included the breaker's-yard sections around Rijeka, hundreds of gruelling miles in the Italian and French Alps, and some very fast sections made even faster by use of the pruning technique. The winning combination of Buchet and Strahle (1.6-litre Porsche Carrera) astonished nobody, as the crew were experienced and Porsche had already won twice before; the real surprise was that two highly modified factory-prepared Renault Dauphines (driven by Feret-Monraisse and Mairesse-Desse, respectively) took second and third places. Although the ordinary Dauphine was considered to be a pretty, if slow and rust-prone, family car, this performance, together with earlier outright wins in the Alpine and the Monte Carlo Rallies, proved that the basic engineering was certainly very sound.

A year later, however, BMC were no longer to be fooled by the 'official' mileages quoted by Maurice Garot's organizers. Having entered a very strong team – of four Austin-Healey 3000s, driven by John Gott, David Seigle-Morris, Peter Riley, and Pat Moss – they not only got three of them back to the finish (only 13 of the

82 starters could manage that) but also won the team prize *and* took outright victory. That was remarkable enough – what was even more so was that the win was taken by the incredibly talented crew of Pat Moss and Ann Wisdom, and that this win on the world's most demanding rally was the first ever achieved by the Big Healey.

Although the Jugoslavian section occupied a mere 12 hours, it reduced the field abruptly from 68 cars to a mere 28, and it also produced one of the 'classic' sections of the modern Liège, from Novi on the Adriatic coast to Vrbovsko in the hinterland behind it – a section that had everything from steep gradients to fantastic views (if only one had had time to look), over rocky tracks and occasionally through ramshackle villages. Rally drivers feared it, but the public thought it was all great sport. This rally, too, stretched from Liège to Jugoslavia and back, but the effective rallying started on the Austro–Italian border, and ended not much more than two days later at Chambéry, north of the 'classic' Alpine rally passes which the Liège still used. The whole four-day event, mark you, was run without a single rest halt.

The remarkable Miss Moss, be it noted, not only beat all her team-mates (a feat which, apparently, they had all been expecting for some time, for she had already finished second overall in the Alpine Rally of that year) and won the rally outright, but she did it in spite of considerable mechanical misfortune; this included a hasty gearbox change in France, which delayed her so long that she had to tackle the speed hillclimb of the Allos after the unfortunate officials had thrown it open to the passage of everyday traffic. As Marcus Chambers, her competition manager, wrote in his book about rallying (*Seven Year Twitch*): 'The girls made the last and fourth fastest climb . . . passing 18 very shaken Frenchmen on the way; these same Frenchmen had just time to mutter some suitable imprecations when they in turn were passed by the Austin service car being driven by Erik Carlsson as no Austin had ever been driven before!'

Miss Moss beat the Sander brother's Porsche by more than six minutes, but an equally remarkable performance was by John Sprinzel, who urged one of his own much-modified Sebring Sprites into third place, less than two more minutes behind the Porsche. In many ways, this was the lanky, introspective Sprinzel's best-ever drive.

The most exciting Italian rally cars of the late 1960s and early 1970s were the lightweight front-wheel-drive Lancia Fulvias. In 1968 this was Rauno Aaltonen, corner-cutting at Ingliston in the RAC Rally

After this breakneck event, however, the French took the invasion of their Alps rather badly, politely declining to welcome the event in future years. For the final, tremendously exciting years, therefore, it had to change its character. Mindful of his success in decimating the field of the 1960 Liège in only 12 hours of Jugoslavian rallying, Maurice Garot routed the major part of all future marathons through the Balkan countries, and they really became high speed battles for survival.

The latter-day marathons were not merely fast, unsophisticated rough-road events; indeed, to jack up the effective target average speeds even further, the organizers introduced whimsical timing methods which demanded great intelligence and foresight from co-drivers and team managers. The cunning system they introduced theoretically allowed a sensible average speed between individual controls; the Road Book, however, also specified a precise period during which each control was open to a particular competitor, and as the event progressed these periods were moved gradually and persistently forward in relation to the theoretical average speed. This meant that a complacent (and unsuspecting) competitor, content merely to achieve target times, would eventually arrive at some control in the depths of Jugoslavia to find it closed, and the officials on their way back to Belgium. Indeed, had he persisted at this rate,

The British marathon to end all marathons was the Gulf London Rally of 1968, which in the early stages featured a battle between the Opel Kadett Coupés and Escort Twin-Cams. Well sideways at Oulton Park at this point was Ove Andersson, who went on to take second place

he would have arrived back in Liège 24 hours after the winner had received his garlands!

There was another endearing and (in motor-sporting terms) illegal wrinkle. Even at the end of August, the Italian authorities, somewhat concerned about the rally's impact on their precious tourist traffic, specified that the Marathon's average in the Dolomites should be no more than 50kph. The wily Garot agreed to this, offering little explanation but stating that he would make competitors go even slower on the main roads between the high passes and that *minimum* transit times would be set to ensure this. The Italians were delighted.

Competitors, on the other hand, were not. It took no co-driver, already wise to the crafty machinations of the organizers' minds, more than a few minutes to work out that if a 150km section set at 50kph (and perhaps with the four monstrous passes of the Croce Domini, Vivione, Gavia and Stelvio included) had very slow

'compulsory minimum time' sectors between the passes, then the pace required over the passes themselves was very high indeed! It was a perfect way to conclude a frantic and gruelling event.

Cars, drivers and pre-rally preparation were all improving during the early 1960s, as the results of the Liège indicate. In 1961, the first of the races to and from Sofia, there were only eight finishers, but in the following years there were 18, 20 and 21 respectively. Rumour has it that Garot sulked after the 1963 East African Safari produced as many as seven finishers, thus defeating all his best efforts, and it has also been suggested that he swore to produce a Liège with only one finisher.

The four heroes who won those last break-neck Marathons to and from Sofia were Lucien Bianchi (Citroën DS19), Eugen Bohringer (Mercedes-Benz 220SE and Mercedes-Benz 230SL), and Rauno Aaltonen (Austin-Healey 3000); but honour must go as well to the individuals who led some of the events for long distances before suffering mechanical disaster at a late stage – René Trautmann (Citroën DS19) in 1961, David Seigle-Morris (Austin-Healey 3000) in 1962 and Rauno Aaltonen (Austin-Healey 3000) in 1963.

Nevertheless, discretion usually proved to be the better part of valour, for in only one of those four years – 1964 – did the leader at the entry to Jugoslavia also win the event three days later, and that was the formidable combination of Rauno Aaltonen, Tony Ambrose, and the (by then) tank-like Austin-Healey 3000.

Nobody ever came near to 'cleaning' a latter-day Liège, though in 1961 (the year in which most of the event left the restart at Sofia in massed formation, as in a *real* road race) René Trautmann urged his Citroën out of the dust and congestion to re-emerge from Jugoslavia at the head of 12 survivors without penalty. He would certainly have kept that clean sheet if his battered car had not suffered from failed suspension in the ensuing Italian sections. This was truly a case of the tortoise beating the hare, for his team-mate Bianchi then took over the lead, winning with a total penalty of nearly 41 minutes.

Above all, however, I believe that these rough-road races will be remembered for the sheer consistency, cunning and expertise of Eugen Bohringer who looked much older than he was (doubtless due to his ordeal in a Russian labour camp after the Second World War) and who drove Mercedes-Benz cars like nobody else. In four years Bohringer won the Liège twice, finished fourth in 1961 after staying abreast of Trautmann all the way round to Novi, and took third place in 1964 when nothing and nobody could match the blistering pace set by Aaltonen's Austin-Healey 3000.

Bohringer was distinguished by his unique combination of driving ability and rallying 'craft'. Helped to a great extent by the sheer strength of his cars, he rarely ran first on the road if it could be avoided (most Liège accidents occurred at the head of the column, when a rally car met a truck, tractor or unsuspecting private car around a blind corner in the wilderness), and always seemed to keep clear of other runners' dust clouds. In 1962, indeed, he chose to run so far back at times that his rivals were convinced that he had miscalculated the complexities of the timing system; yet he still survived to win by 29 minutes from the Marang–Coltelloni Citroën. In 1963, on the other hand, he practiced assiduously in the new 230SL sports coupé (which was not at all rally-proved, though it shared the same basic chassis as the 220SE saloon) and won comfortably with a penalty of a mere eight minutes.

The front-wheel-drive Lancia Fulvias were at home on tarmac, in the loose, or on snow, as Harry Kallstrom demonstrates when scrabbling towards fourth place in the 1973 Swedish Rally

Other Liège heroes of this period included the tough and always competitive David Seigle-Morris, who completed three consecutive events in Austin-Healey 3000s between 1960 and 1962, Erik Carlsson, who virtually had to carry his two-stroke Saabs around Jugoslavia in 1963 and 1964, to finish second on each occasion, and John Wadsworth who, in 1964, became the only man ever to get a Mini to the finish of a Liège.

All except the last of these memorable events used a route which split the car-breaking sections of the Balkans into two parts, divided by a long trek down the Jugoslavian *autoput*. Some of the more devious teams were reputed to have arranged their service vehicles as 'sleeping cars' for this main-road run, so that their star drivers could be given a rest, with mechanics installed in their place in the rally cars. For 1964, therefore, in order to stop this and make the event even tougher, these easy sections were deleted – Rauno Aaltonen's achievement becoming all the more remarkable when viewed against the revised format. It

Not many people had time to study the purposeful nose of a 'works' Porsche 911 on a tarmac rally, as it was usually going very quickly indeed! Bjorn Waldegard used this example to win the 1969 Monte Carlo Rally with some ease. He repeated the dose in 1970

should be emphasised, incidentally, that Tony Ambrose (Aaltonen's co-driver) did quite a lot of the driving on that event.

Even the Liège, however, that most respected of all international rallies, eventually ran out of suitable terrain. During the short time that the event ran along the sun-drenched Dalmatian coast between Titograd and Novi, road surfaces and conditions improved dramatically, necessitating deviations over minor mountain tracks in the hinterland. It was no longer enough to rely on the tightening up of time schedules over familiar sections such as the Moistrocca Pass on

the Jugoslavian side of the border at Predil, or on the combination of high speeds, rough surfaces, fog and sheer fatigue, in that last surreal night's motoring in the Italian mountains. The disturbance to holiday and business traffic, even in Jugoslavia, was becoming serious, and the authorities had to inform the Royal Motor Union, however reluctantly, that they could no longer welcome the Liège to their countries.

No other remote and demanding territories remained (though a Liège to include other East European sections was once considered), and the rally was forced out of existence. After that, the Marathon de la Route continued, in name only, as a rather gimmicky 84-hour endurance race round and round the Nürburgring circuit in West Germany. The pity of it was that the classic to end all classics did not have a swift and clean death, for in that way its reputation among the rallying fraternity would have been untarnished.

The Liège needs no better epitaph than this –

A Porsche 911, if properly prepared, seemed to be able to win almost anywhere, and Bjørn Waldegard made a habit of proving that. His victory in the 1969 Swedish Rally, in this car, was a model performance

One of the exciting prototypes which rallied round France in the early 1970s was Bernard Fiorentino's Simca-engined CG. On this occasion he drove alone, in the Ronde Cevenole – and sometimes, in this open condition, the crew tackled snowy events!

that when the London–Mexico World Cup Rally organizers were looking for difficult sections with which to embroider their European sections in 1970, they turned to Jugoslavia. The first two *Primes* used old Liège territory, which made dozens of drivers positively coo at the prospects; nor were they disappointed.

This, however, was not a rebirth, only a temporary reprieve. By the beginning of the 1970s, the open-road rally was dead and the special-stage event held sway. What the Scandinavians had invented in the 1950s, and the British refined in the 1960s, was now the only acceptable type of rallying in Europe. That, and the arrival of sponsorship – of cars, drivers and events – meant that rallying had moved into 'modern times'. The private business of the 1960s was to become the public spectacle of the 1970s.

8 | Motoring Marathons

In view of the amount of well-planned bally-hoo created at the time, it would have been easy to assume that the London–Sydney marathon of 1968 was the first transcontinental event of any type, and therefore a great new invention. Should there be enthusiasts who still believe this, let me say very clearly that the first 'marathon' took place successfully in 1907. Furthermore, because of the enormous practical and geographical difficulties entailed in making the journey – from Peking to Paris – it could be argued that this still ranks as the greatest and most courageous 'rally' of them all!

A traction avant Citroën *at the start of the 1953* Redex Round Australia Trial *from Sydney*

The story of long-distance events, therefore, truly begins with the French newspaper *Le Matin* and Prince Scipione Borghese's Itala, rather than with Andrew Cowan and his Hillman Hunter: and while giving full due to the Ford Escorts, Citroën DS23s and Mercedes-Benzes which have performed so magnificently in modern marathons, I feel that they must all give way to the six-cylinder Itala 35/45 tourer which trekked so doggedly across Siberia in the summer of 1907.

The Peking–Paris event, however, did not spark off a rush of imitators, for it was recognized as being altogether too difficult for most to tackle. Apart from another, no less news-worthy, marathon held the following year (from New York to Paris, via Vladivostok), long-

distance motoring was left to eccentrics, explorers and individual publicity seekers until the 1950s. Apart from the fact that certain journeys were just not possible (North America, for instance, was first conquered by motorists in 1903, Australia in 1908 and Africa, north to south, in 1923), there was simply not the interest or, more important still, the money, to support organized events. Even in the 1950s the embryo marathons were designed more for individualists, so it was not until 1968 that modern rally machinery, supported by a vast 'umbrella' of service and by huge budgets, could become established. After that, world inflation and the perils (for a factory) of possible failure in such highly-publicized events, helped to stunt the growth of this most expansive sport, which is once again in eclipse.

As mentioned in the opening chapter, long-distance rallies really developed from the original series of town-to-town races between 1895 and 1903. A long journey by road from city to city, against the clock and against rivals was a real challenge in those days, and even more so if it spanned more than one country or continent.

The shock caused by the dramatic carnage of Paris–Madrid in 1903, however, took time to subside, and it was not until the beginning of 1907 that the renowned French newspaper, *Le Matin*, stirred the interest of the sportsmen. On 31 January, its front page announced:

PARIS–PEKING AUTOMOBILE
A Stupendous Challenge

The article made scathing remarks about events then being held on closed circuits, and said: 'The whole *raison d'etre* of cars is that they make possible the most ambitious and unpremeditated trips to far horizons. For this reason the general public fails to see the logic of making motor cars chase their tails in tight circles. . . .'

Le Matin went on to comment: 'What needs to be proved today is that as long as a man has a car he can do anything and go anywhere.' This remark, note, was made at the beginning of 1907 when motoring was still a hazardous business!

Then followed the vital question: 'Is there anyone who will undertake to travel this summer from Paris to Peking by automobile?'

The initial response was encouraging, but it was a false dawn. The first 'entry' came from the Marquis de Dion, who likened the *raid* to a Jules Verne adventure, and within a week there were, reputedly, ten works entries. The most

In rough going, or on snow and ice, the rugged Volvo PV544 had a remarkable rallying record. Here is Sjotvedt's car trying very hard on the mountain circuit of the 1960 Monte Carlo Rally.

Before he became known as the hard man who drove Porsches, Sobieslaw Zasada made a name for himself in the tiny Steyr-Puch 650 TR – taking third overall in the 1965 Geneva and second overall in the 1956 Polish Rallies, both on handicap. It must have been faster than it looks – especially if all those eight forward facing lamps were really needed!

Karl Kling's Mercedes-Benz 220SE, rushing through the Hoggar mountains in Algeria, near the end of the Rally Alger-Centrafrique in 1961, which he and the Mercedes-Benz team had dominated

significant acceptance, as it proved, was that of Prince Scipione Borghese, an Italian nobleman, who commissioned Itala of Turin to build him a special 35/45 model with a non-standard chassis.

Within weeks, the organizers had reversed the route, so that the cars could actually finish in Paris (which was excellent for *Le Matin*'s purposes), and by starting from Peking would escape the beginning of the Chinese rainy season; the 'roads', after all, were really nothing but tracks, which heavy rains would soon reduce to impassable muddy morasses.

Although more than 30 teams expressed interest, or even the intention to enter, many withdrew as they realized the enormity of the challenge. Several, including De Dion, Metallurgique and Spyker went so far as to write to *Le Matin* expressing their doubts, though it was ominous for the others that Borghese did not add his voice to the protests.

In the end only five cars mustered at Peking to make the epic attempt, north-west to Mongolia and the Gobi desert, followed by a passage over the wild, bleak and almost uncharted plains of Siberia, from Tomsk to Omsk, then on to Moscow, and finally, by relatively civilized routes, to Warsaw, Berlin and Paris. Borghese's Itala, backed by meticulous forward planning, was the clear favourite, his rivals being Charles Godard's 15hp Spyker, Georges Cormier's 10hp De Dion, Victor Collignon's identical model and, improbably, the frail 6hp two-stroke Contal tri-car. In view of the rugged, difficult and unknown nature of the route, the five agreed that they should stay in convoy and help each other out of difficulties until they reached Irkutsk, after which the event (which was, in effect, to be no more than an unregulated race) would really get under way.

Immediately after the start from Peking, on 10 June 1907, the event degenerated into something of a shambles. Agreement to stay together was soon forgotten, two cars lost contact with the others only minutes from the start, and by the time the Gobi Desert had been crossed the resourceful Borghese's Itala was already a full day ahead. Chinese road conditions were so appalling that all cars had to be dragged, by men or animals, up ravines, often with stripped bodywork and with all provisions removed. The Contal tri-car was not only underpowered but badly balanced, so that it could often not get grip for its single-driven rear wheel; within a week it was eliminated, not for reasons of mechanical failure but because it had dropped behind and had run out of fuel. Other competitors, by then, tired of supporting the Contal and carrying its provisions, refused to go back to search.

At Urga the Borghese Itala team forged ahead into the Siberian wastes. To describe their adventures would fill an entire book (one, indeed, has been written, but *The Mad Motorists*, by Allen Andrews is long out of print). It is enough to say that the Itala team had spent an enormous amount of time and money in preparing for their marathon journey, with supplies of fuel, tyres and provisions dumped at strategic points across Siberia well before they arrived. These had been placed by camel caravan – cars being literally unknown in most parts of Russia in 1907 – at intervals of between 150 and 600 miles. It was marvellously planned service, lacking (in modern terms) only the teams of mechanics; in Borghese's case these were actually employed to drive the car for him.

The cars were delayed by all manner of mishaps and adventures. The Itala, for example, plunged off a rickety bridge into a ravine and had to be winched out by a gang of Siberian railway workers, while the intrepid (and, frankly, crooked) Godard, driving the Spyker, was involved in so much intrigue, financial skullduggery and sharp practice that it was a miracle he did not spend the rest of his charmed life in jail.

The Itala, however, kept going somehow, and all Borghese's advance planning was vindicated. By Omsk he was 10 days ahead of the remaining three cars, and by Moscow no less than 18 days clear. The urbane prince actually stayed in Moscow for three full days before setting out over the last 'easy' 2500 miles to Paris, completed in only 11 days.

In an interview after the event, Borghese claimed to have driven 10,000 miles and to have spent 30,000 French francs on top of the sponsorship granted by the *Corriere della Sera* and the *Daily Telegraph*. The cost to Godard, who had urged his Spyker across Siberia by begging,

A Citroën DS19 was ideally engineered for use in the trans-African marathons due to the way its suspension could be raised or lowered. This car was driven by Olivier Gendebien and Lucien Bianchi in the 1961 event

borrowing and – yes – stealing everything from money to food and fuel, was much less. He was even arrested in Germany (accused by *Le Matin*, who wanted the De Dions to beat him!) on a charge of false pretences committed in China, but managed to get back into his car just before the finish.

The three stragglers, still together, arrived in Paris on 30 August, 20 days behind the Itala. For the Italian car it was a great triumph. Fame, however, is ephemeral. Along with the De Dions, the Itala was shown at London's 1908 Olympia Motor Show, but later, when being shipped to New York, it rolled into the dockside water at Genoa. Salvaged, and found to be badly damaged, it was virtually abandoned until the 1920s, after which it was restored, and is now on permanent display at the Museo Nazionale dell'Automobile in Turin.

Only weeks later *Le Matin* announced another *raid* – this time an event that would encircle the earth, from New York to Paris! The original plans were wildly impractical (for they proposed an overland journey through the west of Canada and Alaska, and a trip *over the ice of the Behring Straits* to Russia) and had to be modified, although the start from New York, scheduled for 12 February 1908, was left unchanged.

As before, in spite of much interest, there were few entries and only six cars actually started. An Itala entry from Italy was withdrawn when it became known that the organizers were going to handicap its time by a week! The makes involved on this occasion were De Dion, Motobloc, Sizair-Naudin, Protos, Zust – and Thomas Flyer. The Thomas was the only North American car to take up the challenge on its own territory. Driving the Motobloc was none other than the indestructible Godard! All six cars were substantially bigger, faster and heavier than the Peking–Paris competitors, and this time the 'runt' of the litter was the Sizair-Naudin.

Even before leaving New York State, and all the way across America, the cars had to struggle against appalling roads and a very severe winter. The Sizair-Naudin retired only 100 miles after the start with a broken back axle, while Godard's luck finally ran out (with his money and his reputation) when he put the Motobloc on a train and was promptly disqualified. All the organizers' good intentions, of shipping the cars to Alaska from Seattle on 10 March, vanished in the snow, and the leading car (George Schuster's works Thomas) left San Francisco for Alaska on

The first of the modern trans-continental Marathons was London-to-Sydney in 1968. There was a long sea journey linking the Indian and Australian continents

28 March. Alaska, as feared, was also quite impassable, so that at this point the four cars still struggling west and north were all rerouted to Vladivostok for a restart; the Thomas, having actually made it all the way to Alaska, and tested out the abandoned route, was granted a 'bonus' of 22 days in overall timing! Even then, the chaos was not over, as the surviving De Dion was withdrawn on the personal orders of the Marquis de Dion.

On 22 May the only three cars left restarted from Vladivostok, following much the same terrifying, hand-to-mouth pattern, of progress, complete with bridge-building, river-crossing and railway-driving (quite literally, along the permanent way) as had been the experience of the Peking–Paris cars. It was not until July that the cars joined the original Peking–Paris route at Verkhne-Udinsk, by which time the Zust was going like the wind, and the Protos was even farther ahead. After the difficult motoring of the earlier stages, the three surviving crews now behaved as if they were on the last lap, and, indeed, the run to Europe was much more of a real race than anything which had gone before.

It was at this point that low farce replaced high drama. *Le Matin*, realizing that a German car (the Protos) was going to reach Paris first, decided to fudge the rules so that some honour remained for the French Zust. The Protos would officially finish in Berlin and the Zust in Paris, while the long-suffering Thomas Flyer was instructed to trek to New York via trans-Atlantic ferry!

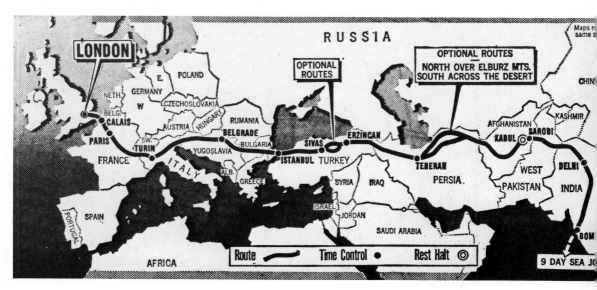

No-one took *Le Matin*, or the New York–Paris race, seriously after that. The Protos actually drove on from Berlin to reach Paris on 26 July, where it was greeted with embarrassed silence, the Thomas Flyer (still nursing its 22-day bonus) was four days behind, and the local favourite, the Zust, arrived weeks later.

In terms of total mileage completed, and time taken, there was no doubt that Schuster's Thomas Flyer was the winner, and the North American company made sure that the world got to know about it. (Unfortunately, the event had been going on for so long that the motoring press had by then virtually forgotten it!) On the other hand, the Protos had completed the Vladivostok–Paris section, where the weather was not a critical factor, in four days less than the Thomas, and its crew therefore claimed to be the moral victors of the *real* race. Only one thing was certain – the Zust was third, and last. Two of these cars have since been preserved for all time – the Thomas Flyer in the Harrah collection in North America, and the Protos (chassis only) in the Deutsches Museum in Munich.

Incidentally, although the Thomas was built only a few months after the Peking–Paris Itala had been made, it was much larger, more powerful and more rugged, which indicates the giant strides being made in car design at the time. Like the Itala, it featured final drive by chain and still had a large touring body with virtually no weather protection for its occupants, but the engine was a four-cylinder unit of no less than 9.4-litres.

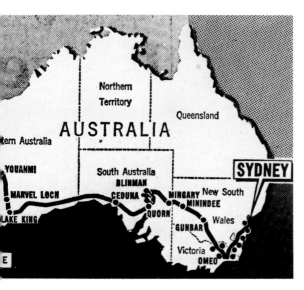

Sobieslaw Zasada's Porsche 911 showing the extremes to which competitors took their preparation before the 1968 London–Sydney Marathon. The cage was known as a 'Roo bar' – as it was intended to ward off collisions with kangaroos in the Australian outback

It is interesting to compare the two marathons in terms of time and distance covered: from Peking to Paris the Itala motored for 61 days and covered 10,000 miles (though some of that time was spent celebrating in Moscow and in Europe), while the New York–Paris Thomas Flyer covered about 13,500 miles in 170 days, of which 116 days were actually spent in motoring.

After the disorganized experience of these French-sponsored marathons, in which there were very few entries and even less interest from the press, it was hardly surprising that no further events of the kind were held for more than 40 years. In the 1920s and 1930s, however, there were several epic private and individual journeys across Africa and Asia, and it was probably only the outbreak of the Second World War which prevented the promotion of more organized events. The war, though tragically wasteful in terms of human life and property, in a sense helped to encourage later transcontinental motoring events, because a large number of new roads (or, at least, passable tracks) were constructed to enable military traffic to cross previously wild terrain.

Someone once called rallying a minority sport! This was the scene at the start of London–Sydney from Crystal Palace, in South London

After the war, however, there had to be an interval for peacetime readjustment, and it was not until the end of 1949 that the French magazine, *L'Action Automobile*, suggested a rally – across the Sahara – all the way from the Mediterranean to Cape Town. This sparked off a series of events, the last of which was held in 1961. The irony of it all is that the suggestion was made simply to prove that the journey was possible – which it was – and that ten years later the event had to be abandoned as impracticable because of political, rather than geographical, barriers.

In 1950–1, however, Africa was still at peace with itself, and 36 machines set out from Algiers, Casablanca or Oran to tackle the epic 9400-mile marathon to Cape Town. Although there were no famous rally drivers in the entry, there were also few false optimists. The team who entered a Bugatti can be dismissed as romantics; the *real* challenge came from drivers of Jeeps, Land-Rovers or Jeep-like machines being developed for the French army by Delahaye.

In many respects this was typically relaxed

transcontinental motoring, for it comprised no fewer than 40 daily stages, and a night's sleep at the end of each stage; but there was nothing easy about the itinerary which included two alternative ways across the Sahara, a common route from Kano to the Belgian Congo, and a fast finish across the plains and veldt of southern Africa. It had been hoped to use a new road south of the Congo, but this was not available, and the event was sent across to Nairobi before striking south to Lusaka.

Cars left the Mediterranean immediately after Christmas 1950, but none reached the Congo until the end of the following month. For much of the time a Land-Rover (driven by the French brothers Robert and Raymond Lapalu) was in the lead, but at the finish in Cape Town it was Captain Monnier's four-wheel-drive Delahaye which won the event, from a Jeep. The Land-Rover won its class, as did, significantly enough, a VW Beetle. The miracle, however, is that the event could be held at all, and that cars could battle their way through to the finish, as for at least 3000 miles of the journey there were virtually no roads of any description – conditions in the Belgian Congo being particularly primitive. Although Prince Borghese would have disputed the claim that it was 'the greatest rally ever to be organized in the history of motoring . . .', it was still a great epic – and more was to follow.

Surprisingly, there was no 1952 event, and the one held early in 1953, even though promoted by the AC de France, was thoroughly unsatisfactory. The event, indeed, was a farce, the rules were by no means clear, and the victory that was finally awarded to a Fiat 1900 (driven by the Italian B. Martignoni) came only after a great deal of squabble and protest.

That particular trip, therefore, became unfashionable for some years, but it was revived in 1959, with generous sponsorship by Shell. On this occasion not only did it attract one British crew (Peter Rivière, of *The Autocar*, and Gyde Horrocks, in a Land-Rover), but it was also graced by the presence of Karl Kling in a Mercedes-Benz 190D, and by Olivier Gendebien in a Citroën ID19. With a new name – Rallye Mediterranée-Le Cap – and with a route more than 9000 miles in length, it brought the marathon back into the limelight. Wisely, Shell limited the entry to a mere 30 vehicles – vehicles, incidentally, which were as various as a Porsche 1600 coupé and a Unic 10-ton truck!

Like the 1950–51 event, however, this marathon was still carefully sliced into daily stages, and for the first 800 miles out of Algeria it also had a military escort. Sections of the Sahara, south of Tamanrasset, were used as tie-deciding speed tests, and here Gendebien lost the event to Kling's Mercedes due to a navigational error in a blinding sandstorm. Compared with the early events, a route was now possible through the Belgian Congo, proving to be less serious than feared. Conditions, in general, were much less arduous than they had been in 1951, so it was not surprising that Kling's winning margin was a mere 16 minutes. The British Land-Rover entry was third.

There was no 1960 event, but for 1961 Shell supported a further, very exclusive marathon. Their organization had been so impressive in 1959 (and the route so obviously practicable for private cars) that for the first time there was genuine interest from works teams. Although only 16 cars actually started, six of them were Citroën ID19s, driven by notables such as Gendebien, Paul Frère, Lucien Bianchi and Annie Soisbault. Four Mercedes-Benz 220SEs were driven by Karl Kling, Michel May (with Peter Rivière), and other German drivers, while Auto Union 1000s were driven by Patrick Vanson and Mme Renée Wagner.

Lucien Bianchi (right) and Jean-Claude Ogier so-nearly won the London–Sydney Marathon, in their Citroën DS, but were eliminated by a main-road crash on the last morning

Paddy Hopkirk's Austin 1800 rushing through the scrub of the Australian desert in the London–Sydney marathon. The very experienced Irishman finished second overall to Andrew Cowan's Hillman Hunter

The major problem, for 1961, was that civil war was raging in the Belgian Congo, and this led to the abandonment of the route to Cape Town. Even though the event had to be halted at Bangui in the Central African Republic and retrace its steps to Algiers, it still totalled more than 7000 miles, involving two complete crossings of the Sahara desert, via Tamanrasset.

Speed, allied to strength and endurance, was the key to success on this particular event, which Mercedes-Benz tackled with their usual impeccable attention to detail. There were four long flat-out speed sections in the desert; on the 300-mile run from In-Guezzam to Agades, in Niger, Kling's 220SE averaged 75mph, and was cruised at more than 100mph on the hard and featureless sandy plains.

After 18 days and 7800 miles, it was something of a miracle that 13 cars made it back to the finish. Although it was a real triumph for

The best of all Marathons was the Daily Mirror London–Mexico *event of 1970, which was noteworthy for a 16,000 mile battle between Ford and British Leyland teams*

Mercedes-Benz, with Kling taking his second trans-African victory, and other cars finishing second and fifth; Citroën also had reason for pride, the Frère-Vinatier and Gendebien-Bianchi ID19s taking third and fourth place, and not a single car having to retire. Even Auto Union, whose cars were too small and slow to contest outright victory, had something to shout about. Eiklemann and Kuhne won one class in their modified AU 1000, while Patrick Vanson won his in a standard car.

There was, however, no future for a trans-African marathon, not only because of the Congo fighting, but also as a result of the political upheavals affecting Africa throughout the 1960s. Such turmoil made it impossible for a further event. In 1967, for example, when Ford mounted a single-car publicity 'race' from Cape Town back to Great Britain, with a Corsair 2000E against the *Windsor Castle* liner – a journey which had to be completed in 12 days – not only was it eventually necessary for the Corsair to be airlifted for more than 1000 miles to avoid politically sensitive 'no-go' areas, but the support crew, landing in the Congo ahead of the car's arrival, were arrested as South

Would Sir Henry Royce have approved? I think not. This was Ray Richards's Rolls-Royce Silver Shadow, as prepared by Bill Bengry for the London–Mexico World Cup Rally, and seen leaving Wembley Way after the start

African spies, and spent several harrowing days trying to talk their way out of jail.

No such obstacles, howevere, interfered with the long-distance trials promoted in Australia in the 1950s, variously sponsored by Redex, Ampol and Mobilgas. Although strictly not transcontinental – all the routes being confined to the same vast country – the Round-Australian Trials were worthy representatives of the 'marathon breed'. It all began in 1953, when Redex sponsored a 6500-mile event in August–September, which started and finished in Sydney, covering the whole eastern seaboard as far as Darwin, followed by a desert crossing of the outback, and a set average speed of at least 40mph. No fewer than 192 cars started the event, almost all of them private cars, and there was very careful pre- and post-rally scrutiny to ensure that standard components were used throughout.

Although a British Austin A40 led at first, once the going got rough – as it certainly did in the outback – cars like the Peugeot 203 and VW Beetle forged ahead. The really testing sections – Townsville to Mount Isa in Queensland, Alice Springs to Kingoonya and on towards Adelaide – had mile after punishing mile of dusty, rocky or even non-existent roads, where cars and drivers became completely exhausted. Even so, it was necessary to have one final 11-mile tie-deciding 'horror section' near the finish in Sydney, where only 17 minutes were allowed, and no car came close to meeting the schedule. It was not yet an event for star drivers, but the winning Peugeot 203 was crewed by Ken Tubman and Jack Marshall, while racing driver Lex Davison's Holden was only three points behind, and the A40 finished second to Tubman in its class.

A year later, the Redex event was much more ambitious, for the route had been stretched to 9600 miles, involving no fewer than 55 Australian Holdens, 41 Fords, 28 Peugeots and 22 Standard Vanguards. This time there were 246 starters, and the event was held in July, during the depths of what in Australia qualifies as

The truly international combination of a Jugoslavian driver in a French Peugeot 404, competing in the World Cup Rally stretching from Great Britain to Mexico

winter. As previously, it started and finished in Sydney, but in addition to touching Darwin, it also visited Perth on the west coast. In every way it was a full-scale marathon.

Endurance was an important factor, too, with several hot and dusty nights being spent out of bed. Tiredness – real, dragging weariness, took its toll, and many cars crashed or were damaged because drivers were not alert. Only one car – that driven by 'Gelignite' Jack Murray and Bill Murray (not related) kept a clean sheet all the way round the continent, and this, incidentally, was in a six-year-old Australian Ford V8. Second was Patterson's Peugeot 203 with nine penalties, and a Holden took third place, 14 points behind the Murrays. It was an event full of incident – with Jack Murray having to use his famous sticks of dynamite to throw ahead of cars in front of him in the dust, to explode, attract attention and warn of his approach, and another driver claiming to have been ambushed

and robbed by Aborigines! In many parts of Australia roads were non-existent, so drivers often had to practise straight-line navigation (by the stars!), and manoeuvre their way along dried-up river beds. The Queensland 'horror section' towards Mount Isa was used again, the route including 104 cattle-grids, 194 river crossings *without* bridges, and a large number of detours. Even so, 125 cars completed the course.

After that, Redex's interest seems to have waned, for the 1955 event – scheduled to be even longer, at 10,500 miles – was submerged at the finish under a smokescreen of protest and counter protest. Cars had to be much more standard than in previous years, and the organizers also proposed to impose penalties for accident damage. It was a recipe for sure disaster, as many more cars were forced out of the event, and – as has been proved so many times on other events – the 'damage' clause caused great resentment. Only 60 of the 176 starters completed the course, many in pitiable condition.

Right from the start, the lead was contested between VW Beetles, Holdens, Peugeots, Standard Vanguards (called Spacemasters in Australia) – and Jack Murray's venerable Ford V8.

Two VW Beetles, driven by L. Whitehead and by Eddie Perkins, finished first, but were then penalized for damage, whereupon a Vanguard Spacemaster (Malcolm Brooks) became the provisional winner. After that, the sparks began to fly, and although for a time Kennedy's Peugeot 203 was also declared the winner, it took months for the various organizing bodies to decide that the Beetles had, indeed, won the event!

Redex, of course, were not interested in sponsoring such a badly organized shambles, and withdrew from the scene. For 1956, therefore, the marathon scene split itself into two events – an 'official' event sponsored by Mobilgas, and a 'pirate' event sponsored by Ampol. Despite all sorts of legal action threatened against the Ampol by the CAMS (the Australian governing body), it duly took place in July over 7000 miles, to be won by a Peugeot 203; a month later the 8750-mile Mobilgas event took place, with fewer entrants. The result, which was to become rather familiar to watchers of other rough-road events in the 1950s and 1960s, was a win for a VW Beetle, driven by Larry and Eddie Perkins, with a Holden second and another Beetle in third place.

A year later, with the Mobilgas event increased to the original 'Redex' length of 10,000 miles, both trials were won by VW Beetles – the Mobilgas by Whitehead (who had won the 1955 Redex marathon), and the Ampol by Jack Witter. However, some idea of the general level of competition in the Ampol is suggested by the fact that a stately 1927 Rolls-Royce limousine, driven by Mrs Blanche Brown, finished fifth overall!

No more was heard after that from Ampol, and in 1958 even the 'official' Mobilgas Trial was just a shadow of its former self. Only 68 cars started the event, and continuous storms made much of the route virtually impassable, which more or less guaranteed victory for the ubiquitous (and near-amphibious!) VW Beetles. This time it was Cussack's Beetle which triumphed, with only three marks lost, followed by Eddie Perkins's car, and with Harry Firth third in an identical model. Mobilgas then decided, like Redex, that they did not want to be associated with such a volatile event, and withdrew, pleading future worldwide concentration on Economy Runs as their excuse.

For much of the 1960s, rallying fashion was firmly on the side of the no-nonsense high-speed 'road races', in which European manufacturers (who had most of the expertise and nearly all the good drivers) invested heavily. The lust for adventure, however, could not be wholly suppressed, and it was wonderful to hear the news, in January 1968, that two famous newspapers – the British *Daily Express* and the Australian *Sydney Telegraph* – were to sponsor a real transcontinental event in the autumn of that year – from London to Sydney.

Motoring might have come a long way in recent years, with cars *and* driving conditions having improved dramatically, but this – longer than any event promoted since New York–Paris in 1908 – promised to be an unusually exciting challenge. Better still, it reverted to the original idea of a genuine transcontinental marathon, not merely a long event which wound its way around, or across, a single continent, but one that included Europe, the Middle East, the Indian subcontinent and Australia. What made it all the more fascinating was that it soon became known that several powerful works teams and their drivers would be competing.

Nearly all the problems forecast when planning the ambitious route – wars, revolutions and political blockages – failed to materialize, though the route planners (Tony Ambrose and Jack Sears) had to abandon their hopes of taking the event all the way overland to Singapore before shipping them to Australia; the problem was

Service for the BL Triumph 2.5PIs, at Monza in the World Cup Rally of 1970. Numbers have been covered up because of Italian requests regarding open-road motoring. Brian Culcheth's car finished second overall, and Paddy Hopkirk's car was fourth

Rosemary Smith's Austin Maxi, brightly painted but lonely, in Italy in the 1970 World Cup Rally. This crew won the Ladies' award

that Burmese roads were thought to be unsuitable, and apparently Thailand just did not want to be associated with such a decadent western event.

The break point, therefore, came at Bombay, and judging by the schedule set it would still be quite a hectic dash. For the first time ever there was no question of placing rest halts along the way – this was to be a *real* marathon, with a start from London's Crystal Palace on 24 November 1968, and a scheduled arrival in Bombay on 1 December, just 171 hours later! The dash across Australia, from Perth to Sydney, was to occupy 68 hours – less than three full days. By comparison with this, nine days spent on board ship from Bombay to Fremantle was going to look very pedestrian indeed.

The London–Bombay sector, with only ten

intermediate controls, was much less difficult than at first appeared, while the 19-control run across Australia was even more testing than the works teams had feared. This marathon, however, was the first in which works teams, backed by comprehensive service and support organizations and by a lot of pre-event practice, had taken part, and was run off in a frenzy of publicity, fast cars and tiny penalty margins. From London to Bombay, in spite of the high set average speeds, only two sections proved impossible.

BMC (with three Austin 1800s), Ford (with no fewer than five Lotus-Cortinas), Rootes (with a couple of Hillman Hunters), Citroën (DS21s), and Ford Germany (V6 Taunuses) all had works teams, while a strong Australian challenge came from Holden and Ford-Australia. Furthermore, individual entries from notable personalities like John Sprinzel (MG Midget), Rob Slotemaker (Daf 55), Sobieslaw Zasada (Porsche 911S) and Keith Schellenberg

(1930 8-litre Bentley) all helped to make up a fascinating field. There was even a team of Moskvich cars from Russia.

Before the 72 surviving cars (of 100 chosen entries and 98 starters) reached Bombay, it was clear that much of the adventure promised in a transcontinental marathon had so far been missing. The rally leaders (Roger Clark and Ove Andersson, in their factory-entered Lotus-Cortina) had lost a mere 11 minutes – six minutes in Turkey and five over the Khyber Pass – while second-place man Gilbert Steapelaere (Ford Taunus 20MRS) had lost 20 minutes, and Lucien Bianchi (Citroën DS21) 21. The 'top ten' was fascinating, with only 25 minutes separating the leader from the tenth place, and with six different types of car involved. The run through Europe to Turkey had been long and boring, while that through Afghanistan was over remarkably good roads. The Sivas-Erzincan run (in Turkey) had effectively been one long loose-surfaced special stage, and the principal problem in the Middle East and India was that of the huge crowds.

The Australian run, however, was different. Apart from the flat-out dash across the Nullabor Plain, at the height of the hot Australian summer, there were to be hundreds and hundreds of miles of intricate navigation over rough tracks, before reaching relative civilization once again on the eastern seaboard. It was the sort of climax which only a romantic publicist could have dreamed up, and it was never to be repeated on a modern marathon. First of all, Clark's leading Ford Lotus-Cortina faltered, and needed a major engine rebuild, then Simo Lampinen rolled the Staepelaere Ford Taunus, Clark's axle failed, and Bianchi's Citroën (which had taken the lead at Port Augusta) hit a non-competing car head-on. Suddenly, in the Flinders Mountains, only hours from the finish, it was the Rootes Hillman Hunter (crewed by Andrew Cowan, Colin Malkin and Brian Coyle) which emerged to lead from Paddy Hopkirk's BMC Austin 1800. After well over 10,000 miles, six minutes separated Cowan from Hopkirk and the lead had changed three times in the last couple of days.

Everyone except Ford and Citroën seemed delighted with the event, and arrangements for more marathons were eagerly discussed. There was a lot of airy talk, of course (people were talking about a Peking–Paris revival in 1969, and it still hasn't happened), but not much

A valiant effort in the 1970 Daily Mirror World Cup Rally *was by the Martin family in their well-used Rolls-Royce Silver Cloud. They did not make it to the finish*

concrete planning. It was left to another British newspaper – the *Daily Mirror* – and a major sporting event – the 1970 football World Cup, to inspire the 1970 marathon from London to Mexico City.

This was the most competitive and difficult, of all modern marathons. Designed as a link, in spirit, between London (the site of the 1966 World Cup) and Mexico City (where the 1970 event was to be held), it was a gruelling 16,000-mile thrash which took in most of Western Europe and all of South America, with a couple of long sea voyages thrown in. Two major differences from the London–Sydney marathon were that there were several rest halts (absolutely necessary in view of the huge distances involved), and a number of incredibly long special stages, timed so that there could be no question of 'clean sheets' making a definite result impossible.

There were two major sectors – the first from London to Lisbon, via Vienna, Sofia, Jugoslavia, Monza and northern Spain, the second from Rio de Janeiro to Buenaventura (in Colombia) by way of Montevideo, Buenos Aires, Santiago, La Paz, Lima and Cali. After that, the 'short' 51-hour run up Central America led to Mexico itself. If London–Sydney had been something of an unknown adventure, at least in prospect,

The Marathons attracted strange entries. This 8-litre Bentley, owned by Keith Schellenberg, tackled several of them. In 1974 his assault on the UDT World Cup Rally was thwarted by a broken transmission on the edge of the Sahara desert

Andre Welinski (right), Jim Reddiex (centre) and Ken Tubman won the 1974 UDT World Cup Rally, which crossed the Sahara desert twice during its route. Their Citroën DS23 was self-prepared

the works teams treated this as no more and no less than a huge European type of rally. The route and regulations (masterminded by John Sprinzel) were published nearly a year in advance, practising began almost immediately afterwards, and before April 1970 every serious crew had a detailed knowledge of the whole itinerary. The problem for the organizers, as in 1968, was that they had to provide sea transportation for the cars – this time from Lisbon to Rio de Janeiro. The crews, however, did not have to accompany their cars on this occasion. Many opted to stay in Portugal for a short holiday, but some flew ahead to carry out some last-minute route surveys, while Citroën even sent some of their drivers away to tackle (and win!) the Moroccan Rally.

As in 1968, the battle was going to be between Ford and British Leyland. Ford entered seven push-rod-engined Escorts, while BL produced four Triumph 2.5PIs, two Austin Maxis and a single Mini 1275GT which they regarded purely as a 'sprint' pace-maker for the first part of the route. Facing them were four works-prepared but privately entered Hillman Hunters, a massive team of six Citroën DS21s, five Mosk-

The individual stages were sometimes immense – the longest being from Cuzco to Huancayo, all in Peru, mostly at more than 12,000 feet altitude, set at well over 50mph average speed, and more than 560 miles long! It was the kind of event for which factory teams set up service and refuelling halts *in the middle of a stage*, and where drivers and mechanics carried oxygen supplies for the high-altitude sections. For what it was worth, South America was in its 'winter', which meant that although it was sometimes cold and snowy up in the mountains, the weather was pleasantly warm most of the time and very hot in equatorial areas.

Right from the start it became clear that fast cars, rather than strong cars, were going to win. By Lisbon, after five stages and seven days, René Trautmann's Citroën DS21 led the event, with a mere five minutes penalty, from Hannu Mikkola (Ford Escort) on seven minutes, and Verrier's Citroën on nine minutes. There were four Citroëns, four Escorts and two Triumph 2.5PIs in the top ten.

The story, though more drawn out, was no different in South America. Ford had air-freighted mountains of spares into each country ahead of the rally, while British Leyland hired a big Bristol Britannia turboprop aircraft to carry the spares round for them. 'If it's Tuesday, this must be Uruguay . . .' was the attitude of organizers, drivers and service crews. Trautmann's Citroën soon crashed out of the lead, which was then taken over by Hannu Mikkola

Christine Dacremont produced a stupendous drive in the 1974 UDT World Cup Rally, to take second place overall, ahead of Robert Neyret and Claudine Trautmann, also in Peugeot 504s

vich 412s, representative entries from many of the South American countries, and – as usual – a few romantically inclined private entries. The most bizarre of all was the VW-based Beach Buggy, and the grandest were two Rolls-Royces – a Silver Cloud entered by the Martin family and a Silver Shadow entered by Ray Richards but driven for him by Bill Bengry and David Skeffington.

The *Daily Mirror* World Cup Rally was in every way the biggest and best so far. Starting from London on 19 April, and with a break of 12 days for the transatlantic crossing, it was due to finish in Mexico City on 27 May, incorporating seven intermediate rest halts and 17 special stages on the way. Routes ranged from the car-breaking tracks of Jugoslavia, the autobahnen of Germany and the 'Alpine Rally' sections behind Nice, to the featureless pampas of Argentina, the yawning emptiness of Chilean desert, the air-gasping heights of the Andes and the steaming jungles of Colombia. From London to Lisbon took seven days, Rio to Buenaventura occupied 13 days, and there was a three-day sea voyage to Panama City before the last dash to Mexico City.

and never challenged, while Brian Culcheth's and Paddy Hopkirk's big Triumphs moved purposefully up the field. Some of the glamour disappeared when Prince Michael of Kent (co-driving the Huzzars' Austin Maxi) had to retire, after which, nothing daunted, he joined the organizing team. Neither Rolls-Royce lasted long in South America, and many privately entered teams fell out due to sheer fatigue. Seventy-one cars restarted from Rio de Janeiro, but only 26 made it to the Colombian port of Buenaventura, and 23 to the finish in Mexico.

Citroën's challenge faded early in the South American run, the Rootes Hunters were handicapped by sketchy factory support, and eventually the big battle was between Ford and BL. Five of the seven Escorts survived, as did two of the big Triumphs – the Escorts occupying first, third, fifth, sixth and seventh places. There was tragedy in Panama when Marang was killed in a Citroën smash, and near-tragedy in the

Shekhar Mehta (right) and Lofty Drews, normally more famous for their participation in the Safari, took this Lancia Fulvia HF, prepared by the factory, on the UDT World Cup Rally of 1974, but they suffered mechanical breakdowns in the Sahara

Argentine mountains when Andrew Cowan put his Triumph 2.5PI off the road in thick dust.

It was, by any standards, the best-ever marathon, which made the *Daily Mirror* a lot of friends; as, indeed, it should have done, for they spent more than £200,000 in sponsorship! The problem was, as Ford's competition chief Stuart Turner commented afterwards: 'After this little log, the London–Sydney Marathon becomes just another rally!' In other words, what could possibly follow London–Mexico, and be bigger and better?

The short and simple answer was – nothing. Three more marathons – London–Munich in 1974, London–Sydney in 1977 and the Round South America event of 1978 – all suffered from absence of works entries, poor organization or, somehow, lack of glamour. Yet all of them, in one way or another, should have been major talking points for enthusiasts and drivers.

The 1974 World Cup Rally – from London to Munich, via the Sahara desert and Kano in Nigeria – was ill-starred from the beginning. Even though it attracted generous sponsorship from UDT, the British finance house, its regulations were late in arriving, its route details sketchy in the extreme and its timing badly hit

by the 1973 Yom Kippur war and ensuing Middle East crisis. Original plans were for the event to reach Kano across the Sahara, then strike east to Khartoum, up through the Middle East, all the way north to Moscow, and back via eastern Europe to Munich. But after the Middle East countries had been cut out and Moscow, too, eliminated, the final route was a relatively tame double passage of the Sahara, and a rather complex scramble around the Balkans.

Antipathy between Wylton Dickson, who conceived this event, and various works teams, resulted in the 70-car entry being entirely made up of private competitors. Hottest favourite was Andrew Cowan, driving an Escort RS2000 lent to him by Ford, but the best prepared team came from Australia – and included Ken Tubman, who had already driven in the Redex events and the earlier marathons of 1968 and 1970.

After the Channel crossing, the route led down to Algeciras, at the southern tip of Spain, the restart being from Tangier, and the southernmost point in the event being Kano. London to Kano was scheduled in six days; the return trip, via Tunis, Sicily, southern Italy, Greece, Turkey and Jugoslavia, was to take 12 days, including no fewer than four ferry passages. As with the 1968 London–Sydney marathon, rest halts were few and far between, being dictated only by ferry schedules and the need to collect stragglers.

This time the route length was 10,800 miles, but only 52 cars actually started, some as bizarre as ever, including Schellenberg's 8-litre Bentley, which had no more luck than it had had in 1968, a 1957 Hillman Minx, and several robust four-wheel-drive vehicles. Stirling Moss was in a Mercedes-Benz 280E and Innes Ireland in a Jeep Cherokee.

The experiences of the 1950s had not led anyone to expect a 'massacre' in the Sahara, but this was partly caused by bad visibility in sandstorms, and a poor road book at critical points. Of 40 cars which actually set out into Algeria and into the desert, only eight made it to Kano, while another 13 struggled into Tamanrasset, days late, and were permitted to rejoin the column on its way back to Tunisia. From that moment the rally was effectively over, with the Welinski-Tubman-Reddiex Citroën 110 minutes ahead of Shekhar Mehta's Lancia Fulvia coupé, and the rest nowhere. Six of the eight 'full-distance' crews returned to Tunis, by which time the Citroën's penalty was 10hr 8min, and only five of them reached Munich.

Outwardly one of the most suitable vehicles for a rough-road marathon is a US Jeep, but they have rarely achieved any great successes. This one was at the start of the 1974 event

The event which finally convinced Daimler-Benz that they should re-enter rallying was the 1977 Singapore Airlines London–Sydney Marathon, won by Andrew Cowan and Colin Malkin in this 280E

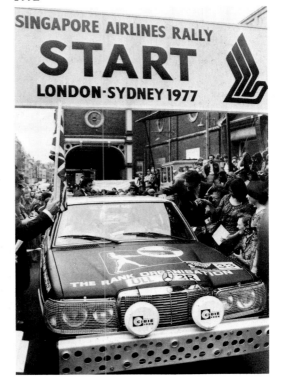

Paddy Hopkirk came out of retirement to drive this Citroën CX on the 1977 London–Sydney Marathon, and was rewarded by third place in what seems to have been a chaotic event

In the meantime, there had been many hair-raising tales of bravery, resource and near-disaster. Stirling Moss reckons that he came near to death when his Mercedes broke down and was stranded in the desert. Andrew Cowan's Escort suffered a bent axle, so that co-driver Johnstone Syer had to make a fruitless return flight to Europe for new half shafts. The Bentley had a major rebuild on the approaches to the Sahara, rejoining in Tunisia; and Mehta's Lancia blew up on the return towards Tamanrasset, thus robbing the contest of any interest.

Second place, in the end, was taken by a Peugeot ladies' crew, headed by Christine Dacremont, who was a full 28 *hours* behind the Citroën in overall penalties. In this context, therefore, the special stages were quite pointless; as a matter of record, however, Andrew Cowan and Sobieslaw Zasada (Porsche 911S) were each fastest on five occasions. It was Zasada, indeed, who led the rally as it turned away from

civilization in Morocco towards the Sahara.

In 1977 Singapore Airlines were persuaded to lend generous sponsorship to Wylton Dickson's next extravaganza, which was a repeat of the original London–Sydney marathon. Although there were no works teams (costs had escalated so far, and publicity returns were so doubtful, that most teams were reluctant to commit themselves to one big event that might be as expensive as half a season of World Championship rallies), the shambles of the 1974 UDT affair appeared to have been forgotten, and there were semi-official teams from Mercedes-Benz, Peugeot, Citroën and Fiat. The diesel-engined Fiat entry was significant, but most professional of all were the five factory-prepared 280E Mercedes-Benz cars, looking ominously efficient, fast and strong.

The second London–Sydney event was longer than the first, with 17 controls (and no rest halts) between London and Madras, a short section in Malaysia (to keep the sponsors happy), and a much more concentrated 7000-mile run through Australia, starting from Perth, but visiting Alice Springs, Darwin and most of the famous old Redex and Mobilgas marathon country. The total distance was well over 18,000 miles, with 11 days allowed for the London–Madras section, and 9 days in Australia. Apart from the British cross-channel ferry trip, there were sea crossings from Madras to Penang, and from Singapore to Fremantle; as before, Burma and Thailand were not available to long-distance rallying.

In less than ten years marathons had changed so much – and experience had shown that roads and cars were now far too good for penalties to be extracted merely by setting long distances – that the 1977 event had to be turned into something of a rough-road endurance contest. Starting from London's Royal Opera House, Covent Garden, on 14 August, the journey to Madras in high summer would be a hot, dusty and exhausting experience, while the complex journey through Australia promised to be nothing less than a full-blooded battle for survival.

Sixty-nine starters, including a Mini-Moke, a five-ton Leyland truck, a Bedford motor caravan and a 1927 Bean (which was discouraged from tackling the complete event), left London. One entrant arrived four days before the start without a car, bought a new Mercedes 280E, and set off in it, completely without preparation. Special stages were needed to split the well-

Range Rovers should be useful for rough-road Marathons, but none has – so far – picked up a major award. This was Taylor's Australian example in the 1977 London–Sydney event

organized crews, and at Teheran, after the first five stages, Achim Warmbold's Mercedes-Benz 280E led Zasada's Porsche 911 by 7 minutes, and Tony Fowkes's 280E by 12 minutes. Andrew Cowan, Colin Malkin and Mike Broad, top favourites in their 280E, were fourth, only another minute behind. Veteran Paddy Hopkirk, was sixth in the Australian-entered Citroën CX2400.

Before the rally reached Madras, and the first sea trip, there had been dramatic changes in the order. Warmbold, clearly sent out as the 'hare' to tempt other competitors into indiscretions, broke a half shaft in the middle of a 250-mile stage in Iran, which marooned him for hours. Another stage, even longer at 350 miles, saw Zasada's Porsche 911 take the lead, although it suffered enough battering to need a lot of suspension work at the next service point. At Madras, therefore, Zasada's Porsche led a phalanx of three Mercedes-Benz 280Es – Tony Fowkes's car being second (eight minutes behind), Cowan's car third, and Alfred Kling (no

relation to Karl Kling) fourth – followed by Hopkirk's Citroën CX2400, and one of the reliable Peugeot 504s.

The 680-mile run through Malaysia was short by marathon standards, but one special stage in a rubber plantation, requiring a great deal of careful navigation (and badly signed by the local organizers) caused chaos. Several top contenders, including Zasada and Cowan, temporarily lost their way, there were several cases of head-on meetings in the bush, and at one point the stage was cancelled before being reinstated by the stewards. The outcome was that Fowkes became the new leader, from Zasada by 150 seconds, with Cowan's Mercedes third. This ill-stared rally then suffered another blow when the ship scheduled to take the 52 surviving cars to Fremantle was found to have a bent propeller shaft, and alternative transport had to be obtained. Cars would arrive two days later than planned, and part of the arduous Australian section would have to be cut.

The Australian run, though shorter, was, if anything, even faster than planned, and virtually all rest was cut out. 'Eight days motoring, with just five hours rest out of the car' is how Andrew Cowan described it at the finish, and this was not eight days of fast touring, but a week's battering

Timo Makinen's smart Mercedes-Benz 450SLC at the start of the 1978 South American marathon . . .

. . . after a high speed roll it was no longer as sleek!

over the worst tracks and so-called roads that Australias deserts and outback could offer. It was sheer exhaustion that lost the rally for Fowkes and O'Gorman in their Mercedes (they were among the few two-man crews, which demanded extremes of stamina), when a miscalculation of control times cost them 20-minutes penalties.

In those eight days, the rally encountered everything from dust storms to floods, and hot weather to heavy rain, battling through mud and over rocky tracks. Andrew Cowan was in his element. By just keeping going, rapidly but without taking risks, conserving his car and relying on Mercedes-Benz engineering to do the rest, he emerged as the winner, with a total penalty of 2hr 42min. The unlucky Fowkes finished second, 55 minutes adrift after further trouble, while Paddy Hopkirk urged the Citroën CX2400 into third place, with Jean-Claude Ogier's sister-car a long way behind him in fourth place.

It was not, however, a harmonious event, for most of the organizers seemed to be at loggerheads with one another before the finish, and there were many protests about penalties, routeing, amendments and regulations. One of the biggest arguments was over the Australian police's delight in radar speed traps, and the fact that being caught meant penalization in the event as well. Only 13 cars finished the complete course, though 39 somehow qualified for a finishers' award by cutting out great chunks (many hours or even several days of the route) to get there. Warmbold's Mercedes-Benz never left India, while Zasada's Porsche challenge faded on the Hawker stage in Australia when he became stuck in the sand for more than three hours, and the rear suspension problems became serious; the unlucky Pole eventually finished 13th and last of the 'full-distance' runners. But although the rally was as much of a fiasco as the 1974 event, it proved that the best-prepared cars in modern marathons can only be slowed down by making use of every last mile of difficult terrain. Each car in the 'top ten' had less than eight hours of penalties, almost all of which were incurred on special stages which had been set at impossible target averages.

One other marathon was held in the 1970s, namely a very long journey in 1978 around the South American continent, starting and finishing at Buenos Aires. Although not billed as a 'World Cup Rally', it was effectively just that, for the football World Cup had been held a few weeks earlier in Argentina, whose automobile club was hosting the event, with sponsorship from the national bank! The Vuelta a la America del Sud was limited to Group 1 cars (which were allowed local variations to suit cars manufactured in South America), and was intended to be a survivable trip rather than a flat-out car-destroying race for seasoned professionals. For that reason, not only were there many special stages, but there were 25 overnight halts, and several extra rest days. Even though the only water crossings were the ferry trips to and from Tierra del Fuego in southern Argentina, the 18,000-mile event took five weeks to unfold, from 17 August to 24 September.

The entry, frankly, was poor, for only 57 cars started, and the only works team was a massive seven-car entry from Mercedes-Benz. The reason was not difficult to find – South America is (or was, at the time of writing) virtually a closed continent to cars made in Europe and elsewhere, so it made little sense for any firm to spend a fortune on winning the event unless they could capitalize on the success afterwards. Mercedes-Benz, at least, could say that they needed to win to help sell their trucks, which in truth seemed to be *everywhere* already.

August and September in South America count as late winter and early spring, meaning that there was snow and biting wind in southern Chile and down near Cape Horn; on the other hand, the hinterland of Brazil, the Amazon basin and Venezuela were extremely hot and mainly humid. As in the 1970 London–Mexico, rallying conditions varied immensely, taking competitors over hundreds of miles of sand and rocks, onto new super-highways, from sea level to more than 15,000 feet, from bleak Argentine pampas to dense Amazonian jungle, from the fleshpots of coastal Brazil to the incredible squalor and hopeless poverty of rural Peru and Bolivia, from the Atlantic to the Pacific, and from the tip of Cape Horn to the shores of the Caribbean.

The marathon proved to be a complete walk-over for Mercedes-Benz. Their seven cars – four 450SLC coupés and three 280E saloons – never looked like being challenged by any other car or team, and if their own drivers had not at times produced self-inflicted damage (Timo Makinen rolled his 450SLC badly, and spent the next three weeks having the car straightened out, while Daray's 450SLC suffered transmission damage in an off-the-road excursion), they might have finished in the top seven places. Mercedes-Benz team management allowed the drivers to scrap among themselves for the first half of the long (and, at times, tedious) event, but gradually began to impose team orders. Even at Lima, two whole weeks and well over 5000 miles from the finish, the orders were that Andrew Cowan and Colin Malkin, who were leading at the time, should stay at the front.

This, therefore, is what happened, in spite of various minor alarums, including a blown cylinder gasket on the leading car only two days from the finish of the event. As so often before, however, it was Sobieslaw Zasada who was unlucky; on this occasion he was in a works Mercedes-Benz 450SLC, but his car suffered the indignity of a collapsed battery which would not turn over the engine after a mid-stage re-fuelling halt high in the Peruvian mountains; and as these cars all had automatic transmission, there was no way that they could be towed or push-started. Andrew Cowan and Colin Malkin won their third marathon in 10 years with a penalty of 17hr 30min, which reflected the extremely high target averages on the stages rather than anything difficult about the road sections, with Zasada's 450SLC 21 minutes behind, and Tony Fowkes's 280E saloon third, 34 minutes behind Cowan. The unlucky Makinen took fourth place, and Ernie Kleint's 280E made it a 'five out of five' finish at the top for Mercedes-Benz. The best 'other rally' competitor was Recalde, in a 1.4-litre Renault 12TS, built in Argentina, who incurred 7hr 50min more penalties than Cowan.

It must all have cost Mercedes-Benz between one and two million pounds, for what was, in effect, a very hollow victory; which begs the question that marathons, after only 20 years or so of modern revival, may already be economically unviable for all but the richest teams. After this event, as before, there was airy talk about new delights for the long-distance rally driver in the 1980s. My own feelings, however, is that we may already have seen the longest and the best. The longest, for all its faults, was London–Sydney in 1977, and the best was certainly London–Mexico in 1970. As to the best driver – I can only emphasize that Andrew Cowan won three out of five modern marathons, crashed out of a fourth, and was robbed of almost certain victory in the fifth (London–Munich in 1974) by a faulty car.

9 | Modern Times

In the last ten years or so, although the actual sport of rallying has not altered very much, its public 'image' has changed out of all recognition. What was once a friendly, and only partly professional, sport has now become big business. When Sir Miles Thomas, a renowned ex-motor industry tycoon, wrote to *The Times* in the 1960s, complaining that rallying was all about 'grubby little men in grubby little cars', he had a point. For rallying, even at works level, was still essentially a private business, and its real dramas were known only to a restricted 'in-crowd'.

On its maiden event, the Mercedes-Benz 230SL coupé, driven by Eugen Bohringer, won the 1963 Liège–Sofia–Liège event outright

In the 1960s the general public thought it knew all about the Monte Carlo Rally, had certainly heard of the East African Safari, and had probably stumbled across the RAC Rally at one time or another, but that was about all. Although some people realized that Scandinavian drivers had come to dominate, they usually couldn't name them or the cars which they drove.

The 1970s brought a considerable change.

When Ford USA decided they could win the 1963 Monte Carlo Rally, they chose very special Ford Falcons as their weapons. Conditions, and bad luck, made sure that Bo Ljungfeldt, seen here on the Col du Turini, was not well placed, though he was fastest on the special stages

By 1965 the 'works' Triumph Spitfires were well-developed little cars. This is Robbie Slotemaker's car in the 1965 Monte Carlo Rally

One of the most remarkable drives of the 1960s was put up by Eugen Bohringer, who steered this racing-type Porsche 904 to second place in the 1965 Monte Carlo Rally (which was run in blizzard-like conditions), behind Timo Makinen's Mini-Cooper S

Ford won the team prize in the 1964 RAC Rally with these three highly-tuned Cortina GTs, driven (front to rear) by Vic Elford, Henry Taylor and David Seigle-Morris. They are on the Snetterton circuit in Norfolk

Events such as the Lombard-RAC Rally had become world-famous, and cars like the Lancia Stratos and the Ford Escort RS1800 were immediately recognizable, not only to motor-

ists, but to the general public as well, through coverage in national newspapers, on radio and on television. Nowadays, not only are drivers like Hannu Mikkola, Bjorn Waldegard, Markku Alen and Walter Rohrl turning into media stars, but most people even know how to pronounce their names. Events are reported at length, drivers are interviewed and lionized, and there has even been a TV programme about the life of a rally mechanic.

The transformation of rallying, from sport to big business, was sparked off, predictably enough, by the arrival of commercial sponsors. When rallying had still been a man-to-man, car-to-car, sport, and had owed no-one a living, there was very little razzmatazz, publicity, or overt marketing policy involved. European rallying regulations, in any case, made sure that this was so, for until the end of the 1960s sponsorship of cars and teams was simply not allowed.

An historic victory – Ford's first win in the RAC Rally of the 1970s, with an RS1600 driven by Roger Clark, in 1972. He won again in 1976

Fiat's first competitive rally car, after they joined the sport of rallying in the 1970s, was the 124 Spider, driven here by Simo Lampinen in Morocco. John Davenport is the co-driver

The display of trade, as opposed to commercial, stickers had been permitted for some time, and everyone was becoming used to that. Nevertheless, factory teams usually rallied in their own colours – BMC were habitually bright red, Ford were white or red (as were Porsche and Lancia), Alpine-Renault and Citroën were generally French blue, while Mercedes-Benz were usually a sober white. On the RAC Rally of 1970, therefore, it was something of a shock to be confronted by Timo Makinen's Escort Twin-Cam, liveried in red and white stripes, in honour of its links, on that occasion, with the London *Evening Standard*.

The sponsorship of rally cars, of course, followed that of Grand Prix cars, which first took on unfamiliar colours in 1968. Commercial involvement, in fact, produced immediate problems both in Grand Prix racing and in world-class rallying. The sponsors, because they were injecting sizeable amounts of cash in the hope of reaping advertising benefits, worked very hard to get their cars, and the events in which they competed, noticed by the media. The latter, for their part (and the BBC in particular) were often most reluctant to co-operate. There were occasions, in the early years, where any mention of team and product was taboo, causing several sponsors to withdraw in disgust. It was on colour television, where brightly decorated cars could put across such an unmistakeable message, that the problems were most serious. The BBC and ITV initially disapproved of the blatant display of livery on Grand Prix cars; but the Corporation eventually backed down, and nowadays they cover racing and rallying very thoroughly and with great success.

Sponsorship also helped to save many events, develop others, or even promote new ones. The Rally of Portugal, for example, did not exist until the 1970s, when it was regularly supported by that country's wine growers. Less worthy events such as the Tulip Rally faded away, and lost their standing. The true classics – like the Acropolis and the Safari – could stand on their reputations. The real benefits of sponsorship are shown in the case of Britain's biggest event, the RAC Rally. For many years it had been run with only modest help from Lombank, but in the mid-1960s it was taken up by *The Sun*, encouraged by its motoring correspondent Barrie Gill. The ebullient Gill helped to bring glamour to the event by persuading Grand Prix stars like

Jim Clark, Graham Hill and Denny Hulme to drive works cars; it was inevitable, but very gratifying, that media interest immediately mushroomed. *The Sun*, in due course, gave way

'Pit work' at more than 100 degrees in the shade – on one of the victorious Alpine-Renaults entered for the Moroccan Rally of 1973

By the early 1970s, an Alpine-Renault was competitive in the RAC Rally, where the conditions (and the 'secret' stages) did not truly suit it

The Datsun 240Z was exciting to watch, and exciting to hear, but the company's centre of operations was really too far away from the major events, and development was slow

Anders Kullang first came to prominence in 1972 when he urged this Opel Ascona to second place in the 1972 Olympia Rally

to the *Daily Mirror*, and by the late 1970s Lombard had retaken a major sponsoring interest in the event, not only injecting a great deal of welcome financial aid, but also providing a well-orchestrated publicity service. The event is now looked upon as one of the three most important rallies in the world (the Monte and the Safari are the others) and could not possibly have reached this pinnacle unaided.

At the end of the 1960s, encouraged by the sudden influx of marketing enthusiasm, there was a great surge of professionalism – involving teams, drivers, component suppliers and even the press. Suddenly there were rallying teams who not only practised for all events but had special development cars, and who tested assiduously at all times. The use of 'homologation specials' had begun in the 1960s, but a Mini-

Cooper S or a Renault Gordini was nothing compared with the eccentricities of an Escort Twin-Cam or a Lancia Fulvia 1600HF. There was also the remarkable Porsche 911 (which seemed capable of winning on tarmac, in the loose or on ice), and the incredibly light rear-engined Alpine-Renault, which now added strength and reliability to its high performance and remarkable handling. This, of course, was only the start – for every car mentioned already existed by the time the 1970s dawned.

All of a sudden, then, there was a living – and a very good living – to be gained by highly skilled, ambitious drivers who were prepared to become rallying professionals. Exclusive con-

One of Markku Alen's first famous drives was in this bulky Volvo in the 1973 1000 Lakes Rally, when he finished second

Jean-Pierre Nicolas won the 1973 Tour de Corse in a 1.8-litre Alpine-Renault in spite of unseasonal weather

As a Group 1 or Group 2 car, the Triumph Dolomite Sprint was always likely to be a category
winner. Brian Culcheth was BL's first-choice driver
in the years when the Sprint was in use

Although the two-stroke Wartburg 353s were never
anything more than class contenders, they usually put
up a reliable show in rallies of the 1970s

tracts were signed and large retainers were often
paid. Tyre companies developed special rubber
– not only by varying the treads, but also by
altering the compounds and the hidden con-
struction. Even the oil companies got more and
more closely involved, producing special lubri-
cants for highly-tuned engines and overstressed
transmissions. In case this increased involvement
went unnoticed, special press officers were
appointed to make sure that the world heard all

This is not night racing as such, but the massed start of the 84 Hour Marathon, held at the Nurburgring in the late 1960s, as a successor to the much-missed Liège–Sofia–Liège Rally

BMW were never serious about rallying, which perhaps explains why the 2002 Tii, like this one driven by Tony Fall on the 1972 Austrian Alpine Rally, did not win many events

the right things about a team and its performance.

It was a self-perpetuating process which speedily brought higher standards to world-class rallying, among teams, cars and events. Within a couple of years it had stimulated huge companies like Fiat and General Motors, who had previously stood aloof from rallying, to set up special teams and departments. Standards and expectations rose so far that smaller companies

Walter Rohrl, World Champion in Fiat 131 Abarths in 1980, won several big events for Opel in the mid-1970s. This is the 1975 Acropolis, and his co-driver was Jochen Berger

Rallying is often about driving fast alongside big drops – as Trombotto's Fiat 124 Spider is doing in the 1971 Sanremo

Toyota's Corolla coupé was theoretically not fast enough to win rallies outright, but it often confounded the observers. Hannu Mikkola used this car to win the 1000 Lakes in 1975, while team manager Ove Andersson is taking it to fourth place in the 1974 TAP Rally on this occasion

Stig Blomqvist, an acknowledged genius behind the wheel of a front-wheel-drive Saab, won the 1971 Swedish in this 96 V4 model. That was his first victory in the event – he was to win it four more times in the 1970s

Whoops – the late Jean-Francois Piot spinning his Alpine-Renault off into a snow bank in the 1973 Monte Carlo Rally. There was a happy ending – he recovered, and finished sixth behind several other identical cars

such as Triumph, Rootes-Chrysler and Volvo were virtually forced to back out as gracefully as they could.

By the beginning of the 1970s, it was abundantly clear that no firm stood a fighting chance of gaining outright victories in world-class rallies unless their directors could be persuaded to build 'homologation specials' in limited numbers, unless, of course, they already had a car (like the Peugeot 504) which was quite fortuitously suited to winning one particular event or type of event. Not even Porsche or Alpine-

A majestic line up of no fewer than six 'works' Lancia Fulvia 1.6 HFs in their new Marlboro sponsor's colours

cylinder heads at precisely the wrong moment.

It was Lancia (or, to be strictly accurate, Fiat – for Lancia had been Fiat owned since 1969) who took the bull by the horns and designed the Stratos, which was a purpose-built rally car from end to end. No other firm, not even Ford (who soon lost interest in their GT70 when they realized what sort of capital investment would be needed) could match that.

Ignoring the Stratos for a moment – and in the context of the 1970s that is extremely difficult – it was not so much the sound of rallying, but the look of rallying, which changed so much. At the beginning of the 1970s – when, in my view, the transition to 'modern times' began, the best, fastest and most exciting rally cars were nearly all sports cars or coupés; at the

On the Portugese TAP Rally of 1974, Rafaele Pinto performing a driving test in the Fiat 124 Abarth he drove to victory, with two other 124 Spiders second and third. . . . In 1975 the cars were even more impressive, further developed, and good enough for Markku Alen to take outright victory for Fiat

Sponsors' colour schemes could be very weird at times – this was Gilbert Staepelaere in a Boreham-built Escort RS1600, on the way to winning the 24 Hours of Ypres Rally in 1974

Renault (both of whom, after all, were campaigning modified production cars) could remain competitive for long. Previously successful companies who might have been tempted to build 'specials', if only they could have afforded it, were left behind – British Leyland being the perfect example. Other firms, with sturdy finances *and* an excellent engineering record (like BMW and Saab) were foiled by the rule-makers, who banned vital extras like optional

end of the 1970s they were virtually all saloon cars. At the beginning of the period the Monte Carlo Rally, the RAC, the Swedish and the Safari – four events about as different as could be imagined – were all being won by production-based coupés. If it wasn't Bjorn Waldegard and his Porsche 911s winning the Monte, it was a lightweight Lancia Fulvia HF winning the RAC, or a Datsun 240Z winning the Safari.

Compare that sight, and sound, with rallying ten years later, when the very special Fiat Abarth 131 and Ford Escort RS saloons were fighting for the much more valid 'World' Championship with the Opel Ascona 400, the Vauxhall Chevette 2300HS, the Saab 99 Turbo and the Datsun Violet 160J. Each and every one of those cars, however special, however costly, and however 'limited-production' were all four-seater saloons.

If I had to pick – say – four cars which meant so much to rallying during this period, I would nominate the rear-engined Alpine-Renault, the mid-engined Lancia Stratos and the front-engined Ford Escorts and Fiat Abarth 131s. There was an enormous amount of variety in

Last magnificent fling for the original-shape Ford Escort rally car – Timo Makinen/Henry Liddon in an RS1600 well tweaked-up in their speedy passage towards victory in the 1974 RAC Rally

their engineering, in their layouts, and in the methods of their sponsoring manufacturers, yet each, for the time, was right for the purpose. The story is simpler where star drivers are concerned, for drivers, unlike cars, remain competitive for so very much longer. At the beginning of the period the world's fastest drivers were all Scandinavian, and led by Timo Makinen, Hannu Mikkola and Bjorn Waldegard. At the end of the 1970s, all three were still driving, though the redoubtable Timo was now no longer in the superstar class. Mikkola and Waldegard, however, were not only the best but also the most successful and highest paid rally drivers in the world. The 1979 World Drivers' Championship had been fought between the two of them, and no young challenger

Story without words . . . Jussi Kynsilehto's huge accident on the 1975 1000 Lakes Rally. No one was hurt – the car retired!

who had come into the sport in recent years stood a chance.

During this period, too, the straight-line performance of rally cars increased considerably. At the end of the 1960s, when Ford introduced

Peugeot saloons were usually solid enough to win in really rough events – which is precisely what Hannu Mikkola was doing in the 1975 Moroccan event

the Escort Twin-Cam, they had been confident of being competitive with a 1.6-litre car producing about 150 or 160bhp, and weighing perhaps 800 kilograms. Within a year they realized that this sort of power/weight ratio was not going to be adequate for long, and began a series of development changes which continued until the end of the next decade. Not only did they increase the capacity of their four-cylinder engine to 1.8 litres, and finally to a full 2.0 litres, but they also pushed the power output to more than 180bhp, converting to 16-valve power with the RS1600 and its BDA engine, found about 205bhp in iron-block form, and finally achieved 2 litres with the light-alloy cylinder block, having about 230bhp at once, and gradually pushing that up to more than 270bhp at the end of 1979.

It is worth commenting, in passing, that the weight of their cars also crept up as the years passed by. If it was not for reasons of strength it was because of the addition of more equipment or fittings; whatever the cause, it is a fact that a late-model Escort RS weighed more than 1000 kilograms in 'rough-road' condition.

At the end of the 1960s, therefore, the rear-engined Porsche 911s, which could so easily have been completely dominant if only the factory had been bothered to treat rallying seriously, had 2.2-litre engines producing about 220bhp, considerably more than any other competitive car. The Escort, with 160bhp, and the very lightweight Alpine-Renaults with

about the same power but a much more favourable power/weight ratio, were much more representative of contemporary competitive rally cars, as was the Lancia Fulvia HF coupé, even though it had front-wheel drive allied to a narrow-angled V4 1.6-litre.

By the end of the period, there was much more conformity in the type and configuration of rally car which was – or, at least, should be – competitive. The mid-engined Lancia Stratos had been and gone and every truly competitive car had a front-engine, rear-wheel drive, nominal four-seater accommodation, and rather more conventional looks – conventional, at any rate, apart from the various engineering and aerodynamic aids which had recently become normal wear. To be a potential winner, it seemed, a car needed to have a four-cylinder engine of between 2.0 litres and 2.5 litres, with four valves per cylinder, a power output of at least 240bhp (preferably more than this, but some engines were incapable of such development) and a five-speed gearbox.

In little more than ten years, therefore, the 'image' of a winning rally car had been wholly transformed; and if there was one aspect of vehicle behaviour which was critical to such a change, it could probably be encapsulated in the word 'traction'. The weight of the cars likely to win seemed to change very little – it rose, perhaps, by about 100 to 150 kilograms (220 to 330 pounds), partly due to the standardization of heavy items like full roll-cages – but the power

available, and the speed at which the cars could be driven, increased dramatically. It would have been quite useless, however, to increase the power/weight ratio so much if the extra power were not transmitted to the often loose road surfaces. The conundrum posed by the need to maintain or even improve standards of traction,

When company policy dictates an unsuitable car, the drivers still try their best . . . Jean-Pierre Nicolas actually persuaded his front-wheel-drive Renault 12 Gordini to oversteer at one point on the 1973 Swedish – but then, studded tyres were banned that year . . .

Hannu Mikkola's victory in the 1975 1000 Lakes Rally in an under-powered 1.6-litre Toyota Corolla was a tribute to his meticulous practice and neat driving

Simo Lampinen was Finland's best Saab driver for some years – he took second place to Mikkola's Toyota in the 1000 Lakes Rally of 1975

handling and roadholding, and simultaneously to increase power and straight-line performance, was a dominant influence on the evolution of rally cars during the 1970s.

By 1970, with the honourable exception of Ford's new Escort Twin-Cam, almost every competitive rally car had its engine (and, therefore, a preponderance of the car's weight) sitting

on top of its driven wheels. Cars either had front engines and front-wheel drive – like the Saab V4s or the Lancia Fulvia HFs – or they had rear-mounted engines and rear-wheel drive – Porsche 911 and Alpine-Renault.

In every case, however, there were problems.

The Renault 17 Gordini, driven by Jean-Luc Therier, was a surprise winner in the 1974 Press-on-Regardless Rally in the United States

As 'homologation special' fever hit most factories in the early 1970s, Chrysler tried hard to make a 16-valve (BRM) engine conversion of their Avenger engine competitive, but it often had reliability problems. Colin Malkin used one in British events, with varied success

One excuse for going off into the snow on this Swedish Rally (1973), was the studded tyres were banned, and Per Eklund was lucky to find any grip at all. He finished second to his 'works' team-mate Stig Blomqvist

Ford found that as they pushed up the power output of their car, they also harmed the traction and roadholding of a car which never seemed to have enough weight over its driving wheels. No amount of development, of moving of components to the rear to alter the balance, or of sophistication in rear suspension (all of which were successively tried) seemed to retrieve the situation. The users of front-wheel drive cars were also having traction and roadholding problems, similar to those already experienced by BMC (and the Mini-Coopers) in the 1960s. Even though Saab used larger road wheels, which appeared to help somewhat, it seemed to be an inescapable fact that front-engine/front-drive cars with high-power/weight ratios could not solve the simple problem in rubber technology which accompanied the introduction of high torque and of steering efforts to the same pair of wheels; it was possible, apparently, to solve one problem at the expense of the other – better traction usually led to more understeer, and less satisfactory roadholding – but not both at the same time. It is amazing, incidentally, that certain manufacturers, who should have known better (like Fiat and Ford), spent a lot of money and wasted a lot of time, at the end of the 1970s, trying to solve the same problem. Only Saab,

The big and complex Citroën SM was never truly competitive in European rallying, but a hero like Bjorn Waldegard could make a difference – he was third in the TAP on one occasion

Stig Blomqvist winning his second Swedish Rally. It was all very relaxed – co-driver Arne Hertz even has time to spot and identify the photographer

whose wheels continued to be larger (with rubber contact patches, therefore, that were also larger than anyone else's), and whose engine power delivery was unique in character, were partially able to remain competitive. At the time, however, the rear-engined cars seemed to provide the best compromise of all. Their traction, certainly, was unrivalled, even if their rearward weight distribution could lead to high-speed roadholding problems. There was nothing faster up a slippery incline than a Porsche or an Alpine-Renault, but – according to the drivers, who might be assumed to know what they were

Timo Makinen launching himself into RAC Rally history, by winning the 1975 event in a new Escort RS1800. It was the Escort's fourth straight win, and Makinen's third consecutive victory

Once homologated, the mid-engined Lancia Stratos immediately established itself as the rally car to beat. It won its first World Championship event first time out – as driven by Sandro Munari in the 1974 Sanremo

talking about – there was nothing more difficult and delicate to drive fast downhill on low-adhesion surfaces than these same cars. Apart from this quirk of behaviour (which was much more serious and unmanageable with a Porsche, due to its considerable bulk), the rear-engined cars were fast, versatile and handy in nearly all conditions, even though the tail-out behaviour of an Alpine-Renault was often so extreme that it looked as if a spin would be inevitable at any moment.

The Lancia Fulvia HF won only one Monte Carlo Rally – in 1972, driven by Sandro Munari

At this time, therefore, the really dramatic sights in world-class rallying could be seen from Porsche, with Bjorn Waldegard, Gérard Larrousse, Pauli Toivonen, Vic Elford or Ake Andersson in charge, or from Alpine-Renault, whose drivers included heroes like Jean Vinatier, Jean-François Piot, Jean-Pierre Nicolas and Jean-Luc Thérier.

The users of conventional front-engine/rear-drive cars – apart from Ford there were the privately financed Swedish Opels, the BMWs and (from 1971) the Datsuns – were all in trouble. Not even these cars with independent rear suspension (BMW and Datsun) could find enough traction to match that of the rear-engined cars, and the gap in capability seemed to be increasing with every passing year.

Change could not, however, merely come about because the competition departments wanted it. Unfortunately, any new model had to sell successfully in order to be homologated. Production, even limited production, required

a certain amount of capital investment and commitment, from the company involved. Clearly, therefore, it was not financially possible for a company – say – like Saab to make a car with rear-wheel drive for rallying when their entire production effort was geared to the process of building cars with front-wheel drive.

There was also another, readily apparent, trend to be considered, that true rear-engined cars (i.e., those with engines *behind* the line of the rear wheels) were rapidly going out of favour with the general public, because of handling problems. In other words, it was one thing for JPN or Bjorn Waldegard to work miracles with a tail-heavy monster, but it was quite another to expect a novice to do the same. It seemed likely all over the world, that the cars of the future would either have front-wheel drive or the 'classic' front-engine/rear-drive layouts.

One manufacturer, however – Ford – was not to be put off. At the time their commitment to supremacy in motor sport was still total. By the end of the 1960s it was not enough for them merely to have a team in rallying, they wanted to win. Having already achieved supremacy in Grand Prix racing with the help of the Cosworth

Was he a one-make wonder? Sandro Munari, in a Lancia Fulvia HF or a Lancia Stratos, was just about unbeatable. But in a Fiat 131 Abarth it was a different story

Walter Rohrl, an Opel team driver when this picture was taken, went on to win his first World Championship, for Fiat, in 1980

Markku Alen, fast, fiery, but safe, may yet be World Champion in the 1980s. His career started with Ford in 1973, but he has been with Fiat since 1974

Hannu Mikkola, refuelling the inner man, during a hasty service halt in an event for Ford in 1979. The Ford team that year was the strongest in the world, and Hannu was arguably the fastest of the drivers

Lada occasionally emerge from behind the Iron Curtain and enter their cars in big events. This was the Girdauskas brothers in the 1976 1000 Lakes Rally

DFV engine, they had hoped that the Escort Twin-Cam would do the same job for them in world-class rallying. To add to the promise of a good car and excellent drivers, they had

persuaded Stuart Turner out of self-imposed retirement, to take over at Boreham in mid-1969. Under Turner, the Twin-Cam's specification was considerably improved. For the 1970 Monte Carlo Rally, Ford entered a team of four Twin-Cams which have since been described frequently as 'ice-racers'. It must have come as a considerable shock to all concerned, particularly the drivers, to find that the Escorts were

The ugly but effective Datsun Violet, fast enough for Harry Kallstrom to win the Acropolis Rally in 1976

Bjorn Waldegard, driving alone on a circuit test of the Swedish Rally in 1975, which he won in a Lancia Stratos

outpaced. Ford's best performance was by Roger Clark, who took fifth place, but this was little consolation as he was beaten by more than 9 minutes, with three Porsches and one Alpine-Renault finishing ahead of him. His only consolation was that he, in turn, outpaced the front-wheel-drive Lancia Fulvias.

Turner and Clark were so disgusted by this result that they virtually sketched out a new rally car on the flight back from Nice to London. Ford hired Len Bailey (a designer of several established Ford-powered racing sports cars) to produce a new mid-engined rally car. His brief was that he should use as many existing bits of Ford hardware as possible, including, for obvious reasons, one of the company's engines, but that he could design a new chassis and body, which had to be capable of small-scale production.

The result was the GT70, so exciting when revealed in January 1971, and so disappointing because it was never actually put into production. Here was a car with a simple pressed and folded steel-chassis frame, a glass-fibre body shell styled as a coupé with only two seats, and a mid-engined position for either the four-cylinder 16-valve BDA engine or the German Ford V6 power unit; in each case the engine was to be mated to a big five-speed ZF transaxle. There was all-independent suspension, by coil springs, with a few Ford parts, but mainly built from steel pressings and fabrications. Ford's rally drivers had reputedly helped to lay out the instrument panel and control locations, for the GT70 was to be a car built for only one purpose – to win in rallies.

Unfortunately, as is now well known, the project which had begun so optimistically in 1970, withered away and died in 1972, mainly because of Ford's parlous financial position following a long and bitter strike early in 1971, but partly because it became clear that the necessary number (400 would have been required for homologation into the appropriate group) could not easily be built without a substantial investment in even the simplest type of production tooling. That, and the inability of a very large concern to understand very small production numbers, made the scheme unworkable. The GT70 was rallied once or twice in European events, but never made much impression.

In other parts of Europe the mid-engined car was already in evidence, for Porsche were now building 914s (as VW-Porsches), some of them with flat-six 2.0-litre Porsche engines. Messrs Waldegard, Andersson and Larrousse all used 914/6 models on the same Monte Carlo Rally in 1971, at which the prototype GT70 made an appearance, but were all beaten by the 1.6-litre Alpine-Renaults, and – perhaps strangely – Porsche never persevered with this particularly rallying programme.

None of this deterred Fiat-Lancia, who were fast becoming *the* big spenders among the world's rallying teams. The Fiat side of the

Sandro Munari won the Monte Carlo Rally four times for Lancia – in 1972, 1975, 1976 and 1977. This was 1975, his first win in a Stratos

As in 1975, so in 1976, Peugeot won the Moroccan Rally – this time with Jean-Pierre Nicolas driving

Bjorn Waldegard's 1974 attempt to win the Safari for Porsche resulted in second place behind a Japanese Colt

partnership had only entered rallying at the beginning of the 1970s, and had, as yet, no really competitive car; Lancia, on the other hand, had developed their rally-winning Fulvia HF Coupé even before being taken over by Fiat in 1969.

A well-practiced Munari-Stratos combination was almost unbeatable. He made no mistake in Corsica in 1976

By the early 1970s, however (and notwithstanding their fine win, with Munari driving, in the 1972 Monte Carlo Rally) the Fulvia was struggling, not only because it had run out of progressive development, but because it was about to become obsolete in Lancia production terms.

How to win the event, and be sacked from the team. . . . Bjorn Waldegard beat Sandro Munari (also in a Stratos) in the 1976 Sanremo Rally, which displeased his chauvinistic team managers. The result was inevitable . . .

Roger Clark was almost invincible in an Escort RS1600 and RS1800 for seasons. He loved the new-shape RS1800, and won the 1975 Scottish Rally in fine style

Timo Makinen, arguably the best rally driver of all time, in action in a 1976 World Championship event in his 'works' Escort RS1800

It was at this time that Cesare Fiorio, Lancia's competition manager, started down the visionary path which was to lead to the all-conquering Stratos. It all began with a typical Turin Show 'special' by Bertone, a non-running wedge-styled mockup, theoretically powered by a Lancia Fulvia HF engine and gearbox. That car, as it stood, was unlikely to break many records, but Fiorio was so fired up by the whole mid-engined concept – the looks, the layout and the possibility of the design – that he persuaded both Bertone (who loved that sort of a challenge) and Fiat to allow him to work up a design for a proper rally car. Fortunately for posterity, Fiat not only owned Lancia by then, but they also had a half-share in Ferrari; the latter were already producing cars with transverse mid-mounted 2.4-litre V6 engines and transmissions . . . and the rest is now history.

Lancia and Bertone effectively designed a new car, still called a Stratos, still wedge-styled, and still with a mid-engine position. The definitive car of 1971, however, used the Ferrari Dino's engine and power pack, had a glass-fibre body shell wrapped around a minimum two-seater coupé package, and a simple but robust monocoque, tubular frame which Bertone could build on the very minimum of production tooling. It was not a quick and easy project – radical new ideas rarely are – but cars were on

test early in 1972, and Sandro Munari drove the first competition car in the 1972 Tour de Corse. (True, it broke its suspension, but then, most new cars fail on their competition debuts.)

Homologation and approval, for use in CSI events, did not come about until October 1974, by which time a large proportion of the

One of the sensations of 1977 was the new twin-cam 16-valve Vauxhall Chevette, which Pentti Airikkala drove so very well

In a very wet and muddy Safari of 1977, Rauno Aaltonen slogged away in this Datsun Violet to take second place behind Bjorn Waldegard's Escort RS1800

necessary 400 cars had been built by Bertone. In the meantime, however, Lancia had already started using cars all over Europe, wherever regulations allowed. Sandro used Stratos cars alongside his faithful Fulvias to win the 1973 European Championship, and even before homologation was gained in 1974 a further six outright victories were achieved.

A one-event wonder; Kyosti Hamalainen's winning Escort RS1800 drive in the 1977 1000 Lakes

Once approved, the Stratos's record in world-class rallying was remarkable, and its opening flourish quite sensational. It was homologated on 1 October 1974. On 6 October Munari's Stratos won the San Remo Rally outright, against some of the toughest possible opposition; on 20 October *two* victories were claimed (by Andruet in the Giro d'Italia, and by Munari in the Canadian Rideau Lakes Rally); and on 1 December Andruet took outright victory in the Tour de Corse. By comparison, Munari's third overall placing in the RAC Rally of November might have appeared something of an anti-climax – until one realizes that it was the Stratos's first-ever stages rally on unpractised roads, and that it was only beaten by Timo Makinen's Escort RS1600 and by Stig Blomqvist's Saab V4.

It was that RAC Rally performance, and Munari's second place in the 1975 Safari, which convinced impartial observers that this design was really something special. Not only did the Stratos look like, and sound like, a racing car, assuredly capable of winning almost every tarmac rally in the calendar, but it was also demonstrably very strong and – in the right hands – equally capable of winning rough-road events. Perhaps Munari was not quite the best driver in the world for rough or loose-surface events, but team-mates like Bjorn Waldegard (1975 and 1976), Markku Alen and Walter Rohrl (1978) certainly were.

For the Stratos was not only very fast, and possessed of excellent traction, but it was also strong and extremely versatile. From 1974 to

Antonio Zanini won the 1976 Firestone Rally out-right, in Spain, in his 1.8-litre SEAT

An unexpected victory for a popular guy – Jean-Pierre Nicolas won the 1978 Monte Carlo Rally in this privately-prepared Porsche 911

1977 was a good year for Andrew Cowan, for not only did he win the London–Sydney Marathon, but also won the Bandama Rally in this Mitsubishi Colt Lancer

Stig Blomqvist won the 1971 RAC Rally in a Saab 96, but his best performance in a 99 was with this EMS model in 1976, when he was second, behind Roger Clark's Escort RS1800

Markku Alen on his way to winning the 1978 Rally of Portugal, in the versatile Fiat 131 Abarth

1977 it was often seen in events when fitted with the optional four-valve cylinder heads, which pushed the power of the Ferrari 2.4-litre engines up to something like 285bhp; furthermore, it was available with short-travel (tarmac) or long-travel (rough-road) suspension, it could have aerodynamic aids, and it could be set low or high, lightweight or heavy. It was, in short, the all-can-do rally car which, in terms of results gained and 'image' established, paid back every little lira of the investment involved. The Stratos was one of those cars which could be extremely competitive even in private hands (provided those hands had lots of money at their

Even in enforced Group 2 form (because of regulations), the Toyota Celica coupé was a fine rally car, and often won the category. Ove Andersson was fourth in the 1978 Portugal Rally, and won the Group 2 category

BL had a great deal of trouble in making their TR7s handle properly, and Tony Pond is struggling for grip with this 4-cylinder example in 1976

Sandro Munari completed his personal hat-trick of Stratos victories in the Monte Carlo Rally of 1977. The magnificent car is here seen on full left lock, but on a right-hand-bend, at the top of the Col du Turini on the last night

By the end of 1978, Vauxhall had been through their homologation trauma, and had redeveloped a fine Chevette rally car. Pentti Airikkala on the 1978 RAC Rally

The Opel Kadett GT/E was a fine and competitive car in the Group 1 category in the 1970s. In the 1977 Swedish, Anders Kullang managed to take third place overall as well

disposal), and there is no doubt that it was a winner until the day that its homologation finally ran out. There can be no finer epitaph to the Stratos than to recall that Darniche's victory in the 1979 Monte Carlo Rally – over Ford and several other factory teams – was a private effort.

In factory-based hands, of course, the Stratos

was devastatingly effective. Cesare Fiorio once went on record as saying that he thought Sandro Munari was the world's best rally driver, which was certainly an exaggeration; but he might have been nearer the mark had he claimed that Munari *in a Stratos* was virtually unbeatable. In one of the many cars used by the factory (Martin Holmes, my distinguished contemporary, has identified no fewer than 27 works chassis) Munari won events all over the world, including a straight hat-trick of victories in the Monte Carlo, in 1975, 1976 and 1977.

Inevitably, perhaps, it was a Scandinavian, Bjorn Waldegard, who was fastest of all in a Stratos, and he proved it on several occasions, including Sweden in 1975 (his first event in a Stratos!), Sanremo (in 1975 and 1976), and the RAC Rally of 1975 (though he was disqualified for exceeding lateness limits on a road section). The trouble was that Fiorio seemed to want his protégé, Sandro Munari, to win everything. Consequently Waldegard was obliged to finish a 'team-managed' second place in the 1976

Monte, and his four-second victory over Munari in the 1976 San Remo was only achieved after he had been held back for four seconds at the start of the last special stage 'to give Munari an equal chance . . .'. This, finally, was too much for the brilliant Swede, who defected to Ford before the RAC Rally of that year, whereupon Lancia withdrew his Stratos entry in that event in a fit of pique.

The great days of the Stratos, when in full, raucous, unstoppable flow, were from 1974 to 1977. It was still obviously a potential 'winner' in 1978 and 1979, but joint Fiat-Lancia policy had then been directed to making the 131 Abarth a supreme rallying weapon. In 1978, however, there was still time for new-signing Walter Rohrl to win four European events in his Stratos, for Markku Alen to win the San Remo and the Giro d'Italia, and for Alen to excite us all with his RAC Rally drive at the end of that year. Bernard Darniche, with literally dozens of wins in European Rally Championship events, crowned his achievements with an inspired drive in the 1979 Monte Carlo Rally.

The Stratos was undoubtedly the most en-

One of the great shocks of the 1978 Monte Carlo Rally was the way in which 'works' front-wheel-drive Renault 5 Alpines took second and third places. This was Ragnotti's car, which finished second to Nicolas's Porsche 911

By 1978 BL had installed the 3.5-litre Rover V8 engine into the TR7, and made it a winner on tarmac. Tony Pond's car won the 24 Hours of Ypres and the Manx International in that year

Stig Blomqvist only drove a Lancia Stratos once – in the 1978 Swedish Rally, when he finished fourth overall having led the event for a time

thralling sight and sound of rallying in the 1970s – one which epitomized the transition of the sport to 'modern times' – but the two most significant teams, commercially, were Fiat and Ford. No other teams, not Saab, not Toyota, not Opel and not even Datsun, could match their achievements. Ford developed the basic concept of their Escorts from 1968 to 1979, and were rarely out of the hunt, while Fiat used two different cars – the 124 Abarth Spider of 1973–5, and the very competitive 131 Abarth Rallye of

1976–80. Saloon fought saloon, to the delight of the companies' sales staff; and from 1977 to 1979 there was really no other make of car in the hunt.

Ford lost ground at the beginning of the 1970s, but began to get back on terms with the 2.0-litre RS1600s in 1973. For the next three years, however, they suffered from budget constraints and a concentration on rough-road events, so that when they turned their attention to the World Championship in 1976 they were shocked to find that they were uncompetitive. A World Cup win in 1970 (Hannu Mikkola) and a Safari win in 1972 (Mikkola again) was not enough to ensure competitiveness in Morocco or in Aus-

Markku Alen took his first-ever victory in the 1000 Lakes Rally in 1976, in this Fiat 131 Abarth

Stig Blomqvist was the only driver ever to get the best out of a Saab 99 Turbo

Hannu Mikkola spent a couple of years – 1976 and 1977 – driving for Toyota, and took second place in the RAC Rally of 1977 with the 16-valve Celica

tralia. In 1977, however, they rebounded with a vengeance: Timo Makinen left the team, Bjorn Waldegard joined it, the RS1800 was progressively improved, and the Escort failed to win the World Championship by a mere four points, from Fiat. Just one other bit of luck

would have been enough – better tyres at San Remo, where the weather was unseasonably wet, or better sealed back axles in Corsica – but it was, in the final analysis, not their year. In September they were still ahead of Fiat, but Fiat then won three events in succession to make themselves safe.

In 1978 the Escorts were even more competitive, and the team was further strengthened by the arrival of Hannu Mikkola (from Toyota, whose cars had suffered a loss of performance when their 16-valve engines were banned due to changes in homologation). Once again they were favoured to win the World Championship

Dust, a very fast Escort RS, a Finnish driver, and large crowds in the stages were all typical of British rallying at the end of the 1970s

(what other team could boast a 'first team' of Hannu Mikkola, Bjorn Waldegard and Ari Vatanen, with the popular and experienced Roger Clark as 'first reserve'?), but another long strike lasting from September to November stopped all activity at Boreham, handing over the title on a plate to Fiat.

In 1979 there was no mistake, the only blot on an excellent year-long record being Waldegard's failure to win the Monte Carlo Rally (by six seconds, behind Darniche), after encountering sabotage in the form of rocks blocking a late special stage. Out of 12 World Championship events, Ford won five and finished second in three more; with only seven scores to count, they enjoyed the luxury of actually discarding a second place from their year-end total! It was a year in which Fiat were totally eclipsed (they were somewhat distracted by the fruitless effort

Tyres wear out less quickly if they spend time off the road! This was Jimmy McRae jumping the Vauxhall Chevette HS on the 1979 Phonepower Welsh Rally

The Vauxhall Chevette was an excellent 'tarmac' car, as Pentti Airikkala showed by winning the 1979 Circuit of Ireland

to make a front-wheel drive Strada/Ritmo into a winner) and in which Ford's main opposition came from the enormously strong, but otherwise uncompetitive single-cam Datsuns. At this point, knowing that the rear-drive Escort was about to be replaced by a new front-wheel-drive model, Ford withdrew from works competition, and the driving team was dispersed.

Fiat, the rallying novices of 1971 were, of course, *the* team to beat in 1977. Their first outright win was in 1972, when the 124 Spider won the Acropolis in Hakan Lindberg's hands, but as it was already clear that the car was not only underpowered but too heavy as well, it was decided to have Abarth (a Fiat subsidiary) develop a new car. This was done in true 'homologation special' style, for Abarth gutted the 124 Spider and designed a 16-valve derivative of the engine, independent rear suspension, and light-alloy body panels. Homologation was achieved early in 1973, and for the next three seasons the 124 Abarth Rallye, to give it its proper title, was a surprisingly effective weapon. Its best win was by Raffaele Pinto in the 1974 TAP (Portugal) Rally.

The Spider was, however, still not fast enough to guarantee Fiat's dominance in world rallying (they were second in the World Championship from 1972 to 1975 inclusive, usually behind

their team-mates, Lancia), so yet another special car was developed. This was the 131 Abarth Rallye, conceived in 1975, homologated in 1976, and a Championship-winning car in the next two years. As with the Spider, Abarth gutted

To win rallies in the 1970s, one needed about 240 to 250bhp from a 1000kg motor car, and this was how the Vauxhall Chevette provided the power

the basic two-door Mirafiori saloon shell, installed the 2.0-litre 16-valve engine, Colotti gearbox and independent rear suspension from late-model 124 Abarths, produced glass-fibre skin panels all round, and arranged for the necessary 400 'production' cars to be assembled. Being determined, on this occasion, to do nothing by halves, the Fiat competitions department reputedly took delivery of at least 50 cars, all at once, and were still working through them at the end of the 1980 season.

Not only was the 131 Abarth faster, lighter and nimbler than any previous Fiat (though it was by no means as rapid, in a straight line, as the Escorts or the Stratos), but it was also backed by a huge budget, a great deal of cunning and expertise, and a highly paid team of drivers including Markku Alen, Simo Lampinen, Jean-Claude Andruet, Bernard Darniche, Fulvio Bacchelli and Walter Rohrl. Nothing, seemingly (not even the bending or – occasionally – the breaking of regulations) was to stand in the way of this team effort. The 131 Abarth was originally supreme on tarmac but eventually became competitive in the loose as well. The result was that in 1977 Fiat won five World Championship

The 'office' of a factory-prepared Triumph TR7 V8

events, as far flung as New Zealand, Canada, Portugal, and their native Italy, an achievement matched exactly in 1978. In 1980, even with a car which they admitted had not been improved for two seasons, and which was coming to the end of an illustrious five-year career, Fiat were once again the dominant force in World Championship rallying.

The most interesting and significant, comparison with Fiat, Ford and Lancia is that of the activities of Mercedes-Benz. The German concern had supported rallying somewhat spasmodically in the 1950s and 1960s, as already detailed in earlier chapters, but until the late 1970s they had never allowed themselves to become involved in the colourful and commercial sport which was dominated by various 'homologation specials'.

Almost by default, however, they were slowly and insidiously dragged back into the sport. Cars were prepared for notable private entrants in the long-distance marathons, and a complete team of 280E saloons were built for London–Sydney in 1977. In spite of vigorous denials from Stuttgart, Andrew Cowan's winning car was dubbed a works machine, and brought much good publicity to the marque.

A year later, in South America, Mercedes-

Opel's Ascona 400 rally car finished fourth on its very first event – this one, the 1980 Monte Carlo Rally – then went on to win its second, the Swedish, outright. A fine start for a bulky but handleable car

Anders Kullang, Opel's star driver in 1980

Benz dominated the Vuelta a la America del Sud, after a disappointing (and once again 'private') show in the Safari. In 1979 they sent 5.0-litre 450SLCs to the Safari, and took second, fourth and sixth places; and at the end of the year a full works team of coupés dominated Bandama by taking the top four places. They took no chances here, incidentally, by hiring as drivers Hannu Mikkola and Bjorn Waldegard, who finished first and second respectively, Waldegard's performance clinching his World Championship crown.

This convinced Mercedes-Benz that they could win the 1980 World Championship with a concerted assault of 5.0-litre coupés, especially in the rougher events like the Safari, Argentina and Bandama. To their dismay, however, they

Bernard Darniche's ice-driving experience, and the sheer versatility of the privately-entered Lancia Stratos, allowed him to beat the might of Ford in the 1979 Monte Carlo Rally

found that their bulky coupés were not only too slow and unwieldy to keep up with well-prepared Escorts and Fiats but almost embarrassingly unreliable into the bargain. Since the powers-that-be at Stuttgart had always relied on the assurance from their engineers that relatively standard cars could be both fast enough and, as usual, bomb-proof, they were forced to rethink their entire policy to the sport during their first full season. Even so, they managed a 1-2 victory in the last event of the season – the Rallye Cote d'Invoire (the Bandama, renamed) – to add to a second place in South America, a third on Safari, and fourth in Portugal. It will be something of a comfort to lovers of rallying to realize that Mercedes-Benz found it much more difficult to break into the top ranks of rallying in 1980 than they had in returning to Grand Prix racing in 1954–5. They must have felt humiliated, for they withdrew from the sport

immediately after winning the Cote d'Ivoire, thus throwing their new signing, World Champion Walter Rohrl, out of work even before he could tackle an event!

By comparison with these teams, other marques were struggling. Opel, shackled by their pretence of only supporting private owners and dealer teams, started with the Ascona, went on to the unreliable Kadett GT/E, and finally produced the promising Ascona 400 for 1980. Datsun seemed to be able to win wherever it was rough, long and hot, though the more mundane Violets, strangely enough, were lastingly more successful than the very exciting

Daimler-Benz entered a team of five cars in the 1979 Safari, but failed to win. Hannu Mikkola drove this 450SLC 5.0 into second place behind Mehta's Datsun, and another 450SLC 5.0 was sixth
There have been only two truly great lady drivers in the 1960s and 1970s. Pat Moss was one, and the French girl, Michelle Mouton was the other. Mmle. Mouton drove this Fiat 131 Abarth to seventh place in the 1980 Monte

Vauxhall evolved the Chevette HS into the HSR for 1980, and it proved to be a splendid car for tarmac events. Jimmy McRae, seen here on his way to third place in the Rothmans Manx, won the Irish tarmac championship outright, and was then sacked by Vauxhall!

240Z coupés (Rauno Aaltonen, after his first drive in a 240Z, was quoted as saying: 'Wonderful, wonderful, it's the Austin-Healey 3000 all over again!'); Datsun, however, like many others, fell foul of a rule change for 1978, which banned the use of alternative 'accessory' cylinder heads, which in rallying terms had entailed several teams offering four-valve twin-cam heads as conversions to more ordinary engines.

BMW, when allowed to use 16-valve 2002s, were often competitive, and Toyota (through their European team, run so ably and pleasantly by Ove Andersson) were in a similar position. The 16-valve Celicas were almost a match for

the Fords when reliable – and when driven by stars like Hannu Mikkola – but in 8-valve form were no more than make-weights.

Saab were the nice guys of rallying, with a stable team, stable management and the consistent policy of using basically production cars with front-wheel drive. Their German Ford-engined V4s gradually slipped out of contention, though they were usually well placed on loose-road, secret-route or snow-covered section rallies, and especially if driven by that modest little man, Stig Blomqvist. As Blomqvist had never driven for any other team, it was not easy to know just how good he was, despite one RAC Rally win and a couple of second places behind the Escorts – not, that is, until he

A Mercedes-Benz might have been expected to win the Acropolis if they had amassed enough experience, but all the luck deserted them. Vic Preston Junior finished fourth in the event

Although the front-wheel-drive Renault 5 Alpines never won a World Championship rally, Ragnotti's car finished second in the 1979 Tour de Corse

Markku Alen's 1980 1000 Lakes victory was his fourth in five years – all of them in a Fiat 131 Abarth cars

On only its second event, Anders Kullang steered the Opel Ascona 400 to outright victory in the Swedish Rally of 1980

accepted an invitation to drive a 'works' Stratos on the 1978 Swedish! On that event he set 16 fastest stage times – more than anyone else in the event – and finally finished fourth in spite of several minor delays.

By the mid-1970s Saab were committed to using their bulky 99s, which had almost everything stacked against them. However, the dogged determination of the team at Troll-hattan to build good cars, and the sheer brilli-ance of Blomqvist (for no-one else ever mastered this car), enabled them to produce

occasional outright victories. Saab had an 'optional' 16-valve engine for 1976 and 1977, which was banned thereafter, but spent the next few years making an extremely competent (and extremely quiet!) Group 2 car out of the 99 Turbo. There was still, however, no way (literally) to circumvent the limitations of front-wheel drive.

As the sport developed, there were occasional flashes of brilliance from strange or otherwise unexpectedly competitive cars. When Renault took second and third places in the 1978 Monte Carlo Rally, with the front-wheel-drive Renault 5 Gordinis, everyone wondered if it was significant. It wasn't – even Renault were already developing a turbocharged mid-engined Renault 5, and *that* could be the shape of rally cars in the 1980s.

The 1978 Monte was won, most unexpectedly, by Jean-Pierre Nicolas in a rear-engined Porsche 911 which, until the end of the 1970s, was still a car that could have won many more events.

There were other debating points, too, such as the way Peugeot, with 504s in four-cylinder

Only Tony Pond could drive a Triumph TR7 V8 to its limit, and he dominated the Manx Rally from start to finish in 1980

Shekhar Mehta didn't let a lack of power from the single-cam Datsun 160J get in his way on the 1980 Safari, which he won outright. It was his third Safari win in a Datsun

Audi stepped up their motor sporting effort in 1979, with 'works' entries in many European events. Harald Demuth took sixth place in Portugal in this 80 GLE model

or V6 engined form, could win so many long-distance rough-road events, or – in stark contrast – why British Leyland should spend so much time and money on the brutishly powerful V8-engined Triumph sports cars and still not have a winning car at the end of five years. It was similarly strange that Talbot struggled to make sense of the 16-valve BRM-engined Avenger, yet had immediate success with the Sunbeam-Lotus, and that Vauxhall's big and unwieldy Magnum Coupés should be followed

Andy Dawson has been running the European arm of the Datsun rallying effort since 1978, and drove one of his own cars into fourth place in the 1979 Criterium Molson du Quebec. His team-mate, Tino Salonen, was second overall

by the very competitive Chevette 2300HS saloons.

In the same way that the mechanical scene was dominated by very few cars, the dozen or so years surveyed in this chapter – roughly, 1968 to 1980 – were dominated by very few drivers. There were changes, of course, but not dramatic changes, and the best, fastest and most highly prized drivers continued to be Scandinavian. Ever since the hugely popular and lastingly successful Erik Carlsson had burst on the international scene during the 1950s, and once European teams had begun to be thrashed on the

Bjorn Waldegard should have won the 1979 Monte Carlo Rally in this very special Escort RS model, but was held up by sabotage on a late stage, and lost the rally by just six seconds

During 1980 the Talbot Sunbeam-Lotus cars came to maturity, and celebrated the end of the year by winning the Lombard-RAC Rally. Earlier in the year, Guy Frequelin was third in the Rally of Portugal

A car rarely seen outside its native Italy is the Alfa Romeo GTV, which Mauro Pregliasco is driving well sideways in Elba during 1980

Per Eklund tried hard for two years to master the brawny Triumph TR7 V8, but was not quite as rapid as his team-mate Tony Pond

Tony Pond won the Tour of Ypres in 1978 in this Triumph TR7 V8, and repeated his victory in 1980

Only Stig Blomqvist would drive a Saab like this! He is entering a square right corner, and already he has put the car sideways, and is using a lot of left lock

Swedish and Finnish events, it had been quite clear that there was something special about Scandinavian rally drivers; yet not until Stuart Turner hired Rauno Aaltonen and Timo Makinen (in 1962), or until Simo Lampinen joined his first British team (Triumph, in 1965) did their prowess in almost *every* type of rally became obvious. By the end of the 1960s it was almost essential for ambitious teams to have at least one Scandinavian driver in their employ. The names which mattered most of all were Aaltonen and Makinen, Lampinen, Ove Andersson, Bengt Soderstrom, Harry Kallstrom, Bjorn Waldegard and Hannu Mikkola.

The last two drivers – Waldegard and Mikkola – were probably the fastest in the world at the time, and it is amazing to note that the first proper World Drivers' Championship was disputed between them, more than ten years later. Even as the 1980s get under way, they are still the targets at which other drivers aim their standards.

In the 1970s, other world-class performers appeared, all with their own particular talents. The true superstars were Markku Alen (such a raw and – frankly – uncouth talent in 1973–4, so very successful a few years later), Sandro Munari (though he never truly proved it in any car apart from the Stratos) and Walter Rohrl (brave in Opels, serene and successful in Fiats and Lancias); and one day perhaps we shall have to include Ari Vatanen and Henri Toivonen.

Some of the most successful drivers won many events by concentrating on their particular skills – Roger Clark (Ford Escorts) wherever 'blind' driving on loose-surfaced roads was the key to success, Bernard Darniche (Lancia Stratos) where meticulous practice and note-making would pay off, and Gilbert Staepelaere

(Ford Escort) where versatility, physical fitness and the great reliability of his works-provided cars could score. Other drivers were often supreme on their own territories – Jean-Luc Thérier, Jean-Claude Andruet and Jean-Pierre Nicolas in France, Raffaele Pinto and Fulvio Bacchelli in Italy, Shekhar Mehta anywhere in Africa, and Achim Warmbold in central Europe. It was not as easy as it looked to transmute skills and performances from tarmac to gravel, sunshine to snow, secret stages to pace-note events, and only a handful of drivers achieved it.

The rapid transformation of gentlemanly rallying into something akin to 'show business' was made clear, too, by the way in which a driver dressed and behaved. A rally driver of the

Perhaps the best Datsun drive of 1979 was by Timo Salonen in the Lombard-RAC, when he set many fastest times, and finished third behind two 'works' Escort RSs which had perhaps 80bhp more power

1960s might have worn overalls, but these would almost certainly have been of the loose-fitting, utilitarian variety, completely devoid of decoration. By the beginning of the 1970s his apparel was more stylishly cut, perhaps even flame-proofed, while his helmet would have built-in intercom equipment, and his 'out-of-car' kit would be in the team's 'image'. By the end of the 1970s his padded flame-proof overalls had begun to look like those of a Grand Prix driver, and were liberally splashed with advertising decals, his helmet looked as if it was a left-over from *Star Wars*, and his public 'image' was very definitely that of accomplished star performer.

The cars, of course, had become mobile advertising hoardings some years earlier. Sponsorship on an event-by-event basis had been common by the early 1970s; it is an interesting piece of inconsequential information that Ford's eight successive RAC Rally wins were achieved with the help of Esso, the Milk Marketing Board, Colibri Lighters, Allied Polymers, Cos-

Ford's mid-engined GT70 could have been equal to the Stratos if the company had truly believed in it, but it was dropped after only a little development

sack hair spray, British Airways and (twice) Eatons Yale fork lift trucks! Team sponsorship of the Grand Prix variety came later, and then only haltingly. Lancia were first to make a feature of this, with sponsorship from Marlboro cigarettes, later transferred to Alitalia and (on occasion) to Pirelli. Fiat also drew great support from Alitalia, and later from Olio Fiat, while Saab were often to be seen extolling the virtues of a Swedish make of caravan. On a 'one-off'

basis, or by sponsoring single cars for a particular championship, the commercial concerns usually made their presence felt. If they were not oil companies – Total, Mobil and Castrol were among the most active – they might be makers of toothpaste (Aseptogyl), of cigarettes (Rothmans, Colt, and Embassy, not to mention Marlboro) or of electronic equipment (Sanyo).

The sponsors, to their eternal credit, did not attempt to mould the shape of the events to their requirements, and there was no FOCA-style attempted take over by the constructors. The World Championship for Makes, won twice by Ford at the end of the 1960s without them really knowing about it (or appearing to care, either), became viable and significant after Alpine-

Russell Brookes was one of several British drivers who came to success and maturity in Ford Escorts. This is the Escort RS1800 with which he was so competitive in the late 1970s

The mid-engined Renault 5 Turbo was announced in 1979, and was rallied for the first time in 1980. It led the Tour de France and the Tour de Corse with ease until trivial failures forced it to retire

Renault had won it so convincingly in 1971 (with four outright wins) and 1973 (with no fewer than six wins), by which time Lancia had established their stranglehold on the points table in 1972 (with the Fulvias) and 1974 (with Fulvias, Beta Coupés and the Stratos).

To the Italians and the French, who always seemed to have competitive cars, the World Championship was always important, and became more so as the 1970s progressed. The British and the Germans only sat up and took notice when their cars started to figure strongly in the results. By the end of the decade, when cars, drivers and even the media had all helped to produce events which the ordinary enthusiast understood, the Championship was truly world-wide in scope and included events of a consistent type.

At that point, however, the sport's ruling body, based in Paris and not habitually known for taking advice and recommendations from the professionals, decided to change the whole basis of the homologation regulations. It threw almost every team into confusion, and put the whole future of rallying into the melting pot.

10 | The Future for Rallying?

The public image of international rallying changed dramatically – and encouragingly – in the 1970s. The almost apologetic and furtive operation of rallies in the 1950s gave way to the splendidly flamboyant and exciting sport of the 1970s. Cars which had seemed to slink about with the very minimum of identification took on spectacular colouring. The combination of terrific car performance and inspired driving, of colourful sponsorship and promotion, along with a massive increase in spectator interest, made top-class rallying a natural subject for media coverage, particularly by television. In the 1980s, however, even this may not be enough to sustain rallying as a popular world sport, for its future is inextricably tied up with oil, and with politics.

The arguments for and against the worth of international rallies have been ventilated many times. The 'antis' (and I am afraid that there are many of them) are of the opinion that *any* type of sport which involves motor vehicles and the consumption of oil must now be considered anti-social, and should therefore be banned. The 'pros' (whose ranks include, I hope, every reader of this book) recognize the problem, but suggest that there are many equally important balancing factors which help to sell the cars themselves or the specialist equipment installed in them.

Before noting the detailed arguments, however, let me make one of my opinions crystal clear – that I believe that *all* sport, no matter what its participants may say, is a self-indulgent process. So no matter what benefits are supposed to derive from international rallying, nearly all the drivers are only interested in fast driving (and the money and fame they can earn from this!) while most manufacturers are only truly interested in gaining publicity or marketing advantages for their cars.

Having admitted that (and many will not, because they can see the implications), one must recognize the fact that the arguments of the 'antis' carry weight. If rallying is mainly an outlet for energy and exhibitionism, there can be little justification for it to continue when oil starts running short; but if, as appears likely, oil continues to be freely available, though at a higher and higher price (so that rationing will effectively be by cost) there is no reason why rallying should not continue, just so long as its participants can afford to fuel its progress.

Where the 'antis' go wrong, of course, (and will never admit to it, even when corrected) is that they focus on motor sport because that very oil is at the heart of the action. If, on the other hand, it is pointed out to them that a great deal more oil is consumed by spectators taking their cars to football games, horse races and other types of sport, the force of their argument is destroyed. We know, too, that the total amount of fuel consumed on an RAC International Rally by competitors, service cars and officials is as nothing compared with a single day's flow, by private and public transport, of commuters into a large city, or by the flight of one half-loaded Jumbo jet across the Atlantic; but this, of course, is conveniently ignored.

On the other hand there are many peripheral advantages and 'plus' points to be claimed for major international rallying. The favourable publicity to be gained following a big win or series of wins is not disputed. One manufacturer alone – Ford – have proved that years of success with their highly tuned and very non-standard Escorts can bring enormous benefits to the image of what was, after all, a very ordinary family car; and their experience had been paralleled by BMC and the Minis in the 1960s. Nothing, I suggest, did more to transform the 'powder-puff' image of the large Austin-Healeys than the concentrated programme of rugged events undertaken by the works 3000s in the late 1950s and the 1960s.

Favourable publicity, of course, can often help to generate fresh sales of the standard product, which implies more business at all levels of the industry, more sales abroad, the chance of stable employment and even the creation of new jobs. If there were no rallying activity to encourage this, some other expensive type of promotion would need to be devised as

Audi are convinced that they can make their four-wheel-drive Audi Quattro into a rally winner, in spite of the unhappy experience of other constructors. No expense was being spared in development, and the car should certainly be fast enough in the 1980s

a substitute, and experience has shown that the same effect might be difficult to achieve.

Not every car manufacturer, of course, is able to manipulate that type of continuing publicity. While BMC, Ford, Saab and Fiat have all improved their corporate image with a consistent attitude, Rootes (or Chrysler UK, as they shortly became known) failed miserably to capitalize on their London–Sydney marathon success, while Lancia stopped using the phenomenal mid-engined Stratos partly because its victories were doing precisely nothing for the image of their front-wheel-drive touring cars.

Failure to live up to optimistic forecasts made when a rally car is introduced can have a very negative effect, as British Leyland found out with their aggressive but not very successful

Triumph TR7 V8, and as Audi discovered with their front-wheel-drive cars; Opel, too, came to realize that it was better to settle for dominating Group 1 with a near-standard Kadett GT/E than to lose so many battles for outright victory with highly modified and unreliable Group 4 machines.

Rally cars are now so very specialized that there is little contribution that current Group 2 and Group 4 cars can make to the technical improvement of the breed. Axle oil coolers, with thermostatically controlled oil pumps, may be extremely effective for a works Escort RS, but have no relevance to an everyday car, while mid-engined turbocharged Renaults do nothing to improve the run-of-the-mill Renault 5 except to resemble it in shape. Even a works Group 1 car, though supposedly 'standard', is usually so very special that it is virtually useless as an engineering test bed. There may, perhaps, be some minor component improvements still to be made, but this is now very unlikely since a modern full-blooded rally car uses components far removed from those suitable for family cars. Have the usual Ferodo competition brake pads and linings any relevance to cars used for commuting? Does a Dunlop, Pirelli or Michelin rough-road rally tyre really use carcase, tread-pattern or rubber compound which a road car might find valuable? And how do the 135bhp/litre engines with 5mpg thirsts accord with the economy-conscious motoring climate of the 1980s?

The future for rallying, therefore, depends entirely on its public image, its intrinsic value as a publicity and marketing medium, and its spectator potential. If the vast majority of people continue to find rallying, and rally cars, exciting to watch and to drive, then rallying may survive. If on the other hand, like bullfighting, more and more people turn against an exciting but potentially unacceptable sport, then it will die out.

Rallying in the 1980s will thus depend for its existence on the right type of event being promoted for the right sort of car. This book is being written at a time when the sport's administrators have just approved radical changes in regulations which may completely alter the type of competitive car. It is worth pointing out, however, that the spectators, the drivers and the media all want to see new regulations allowing extremely fast and demanding cars to be used. On the other hand, it is likely that the governing body, and the authorities which will have to approve future events, would rather see rules making the use of relatively standard production cars mandatory. The manufacturers, for their part, have to face both ways. They must appear to be socially and economically responsible by talking of using standard (or relatively unmodified) models which are in quantity production, in which case their colleagues in the sales and marketing departments will be delighted; on the other hand, teams like Ford, Fiat-Lancia, Opel, Vauxhall and British Leyland, all of whom have enjoyed developing 'homologation specials', will be very reluctant to give up their enormously fast, strong and agile monsters, which are only loosely derived from mass-production models but still recognizable as such.

Because all rally cars have to be homologated, and must be produced in certain minimum quantities (barring cheating, which was as rife in the 1970s as it had been in the 1950s and 1960s), the most successful rally cars of the mid- and late-1980s may have to be evolved from the new type of mass-production private cars which is now flooding the market. The technological tide is at present moving so swiftly in one direction, whether a car is being designed in Europe, in North America or in Japan, that this almost automatically means that some new rally cars will have to have front-wheel drive. As I have already made my own thoughts on the limitations of front-wheel drive very clear, I shall either be able to say 'I told you so', or be forced to eat my words.

Furthermore, I am completely convinced that the most versatile rally car, no matter how cleverly developed, cannot be one that has four-wheel drive. I would only temper that statement by including the important word 'permanent'; which is to say that I do not believe that a conventional four-wheel-drive car, where all four wheels are always being powered, can consistently be a winner. If, on the other hand, it is possible to gain approval for a car which could have rear-drive, front-drive *or* four-wheel drive according to a driver's instant whim, then I may be proved wrong again. Audi certainly intend to develop this type of car for the 1980s, but they are going to need drivers of considerable genius and adaptability to produce the results.

The format of future events, thank goodness, is rather easier to forecast. Special-stage events, already dominant in many countries, will gradually take over in the rest of the world as it becomes increasingly difficult to organize open-road events even in remote territories. Already we are seeing the last of the endurance 'road' events being held in Africa and in South America; and although alternatives could be found, it is still difficult to be sure of achieving a result without special speed tests. Modern Group 4 rally cars are so fast and so rugged that even the most appalling conditions fail to restrict their average speeds. Cynics who doubt the ability of something as fast as a Stratos, or as unbelievably strong as a big Mercedes-Benz, should visit the Safari to be convinced.

Even these countries are continuously improving their roads. A generation ago, in 1953, it was difficult to drive from Nairobi to Dar-es-Salaam (in Kenya) at *any* speed; nowadays, the same route, in the absence of heavy lorries, can sometimes be covered at averages of more than 100mph!

Reshaping a rally is not so much a question of accommodating changed conditions, as of satisfying the paying customer – the competitor. How else, for instance, can one explain a change in format for the Tour de France, which for more than 20 years had presented an intriguing mixture of road motoring, circuit racing, and timed hill-climbs, and which was transformed to the classic special-stage layout, with a good deal of flat-out rallying on gravel surfaces?

A special-stage event, given the availability of enough private land, or roads which can be sealed off for limited periods, can usually be arranged in most countries. It is a sad fact that this is likely to destroy the national character of an event, but it is at least one way to keep rallying alive in an area that might otherwise be opposed to it. Thus stages-events in France would be much like those in Italy, Germany, Czechoslovakia or Hungary. North American

Renault have taken another route. They have taken a small front-wheel-drive car and made it into a mid-engined, turbocharged 'bombshell'. The 5 Turbo should also be competitive in the 1980s

rallies might have multi-character terrain, and those in Sweden might be snow-covered. Events in Finland would probably be smoother and faster than those through British forests, while those in Australia and New Zealand might be longer and less crowded with spectators. Nevertheless, they would all entail high-speed motoring, in production cars and in relative safety, providing enjoyment for everyone concerned.

In many countries which have overall (and sometimes very repressive) open-road speed limits it would nowadays be quite impossible to organize an open-road event with sufficiently high target average speeds to ensure that cars were penalized for lateness. Anyone doubting this should study the way in which British club events have to be 'modified' to make certain that there is a nominal 30mph running average speed, and that competitors will be penalized!

Special-stage events, too, have many other advantages for enterprising organizers. Apart from providing a number of short, sharp speed

events (as one well-known British race organizer once said: 'What the spectator really likes is a lot of starts and finishes . . .'), they can be harnessed to the needs of the media, particularly of television, and, if suitably laid out, can also earn a good deal of money from paying spectators. In addition, of course, most competitors prefer this type of rally.

Within reason, a driver can rely on service and rebuilding facilities after each group of stages, or sometimes after each individual stage. There is nothing more reassuring than a quick nut-and-bolt check, and a wipe of the windscreen, even when everything is fine. Compared with this, the hours – sometimes days – of isolation on a transcontinental marathon, or on Safari – can be a lonely and worrying business. One puncture, or even two, can be shrugged off as an irritation rather than a major problem when stages are short, whereas a single breakdown in the bush, or even in a very long special stage, can end all hope of a good placing.

You might say that this sort of misfortune is what rallying *should* be all about, but virtually every top-class driver would disagree. They are paid, they say, to demonstrate their own abilities, and the performance of their cars, in the best possible way. To do this, and to enable teams to be compared under the same conditions, cars should therefore always be in the peak of condition. Major mechanical breakdowns, they say, are one thing, but if deterioration can be reversed by fettling, it should be allowed.

This philosophy, though controversial, is also one of the reasons for the declining interest in future motoring marathons, the others, of course, are money and politics. Both Ford (in 1968) and British Leyland (in 1970), discovered that there is no guarantee of winning such events, even after spending a fortune on support and back-up, if a car has an accident too far from its service crews.

The political problem of organizing future marathons is also much more serious than it was in the 1970s. It was all very well pointing to a temporary halt of border skirmishing in the London–Mexico marathon, or persuading the Pakistanis and the Indians to speak to each other for the first time in years so that the 1977 London–Sydney marathon could get through. These problems were as nothing compared with those likely to to crop up when organizing new marathons in Asia or South America.

To re-run the Peking to Paris event of 1907, using the same basic route, has been the dream of many enthusiasts, but has yet to be achieved. The latest scheme, by 'marathon man' Wylton Dickson, will surely never take place while relations between the Chinese and the Russians are so strained; indeed, it proved impossible to route the 1974 UDT World Cup Rally through the Soviet Union, and this at a time when that nation was actually making friendly noises to the West. As for routing any future viable event across Africa – you should ask Eric Jackson and Ken Chambers, not to mention their sponsors at Castrol, about their experiences in 1967 with the Ford Corsair 'race' against the Union Castle Line's *Windsor Castle*, from Cape Town to Southampton!

For the factory teams themselves, which tend to keep well clear of politics, the greatest deterrent to competing in future marathons is that of cost. It is surely significant that no factory has ever admitted how much it spent on a full-scale marathon assault. The Mercedes-Benz entry in the 1978 Tour of South America, even against almost non-existent opposition, must have cost a fortune even by their own prosperous standards; in the 1980s, for sure, nothing much less than £1 million would do the job properly. What team, given the imponderables and uncertainties of competing a transcontinental event, would want to budget on this scale?

In the future, as in the recent past, world-class rallying will probably continue as a colourful and well-publicized jamboree for sporting-minded manufacturers. No matter what the sport's administrators may try to do, with their regulations or directives, I am sure that the cars will be faster and even more exciting than before. And until the world's politicians ban the use of oil-consuming vehicles for sport, I shall continue to be an avid watcher and participant.

Photographic
Acknowledgements

As an illustrated history of the world of rallying the source of the photographs is interesting in itself. The majority of the contributions came from two sources – *Autocar* magazine for the 'historical' shots, photographer Hugh Bishop for the 'moderns'. Thank you.

The other suppliers, however, are no less important, often filling-in an otherwise unacceptable gap. Our thanks are extended to them too.

Below is a page by page listing of the credits:
Audi NSU, Auto Union AG; page 201.
Autocar (formerly *The Autocar*); pages 12, 13, 14, 15, 16, 18, 19, 21, 22, 23, 24, 25, 28, 29 (both), 30, 31, 32, 33 (both), 34, 35, 36, 38, 39, 40 (both), 42, 43 (both), 44, 47 (both), 48 (both), 49, 50, 51 (both), 52, 53, 54, 55, 56, 57, 58, 59 (both), 60, 63, 64 (both), 67, 68, 69, 70 (both), 75, 79, 80, 81 (both), 84, 85 (both), 89, 90, 91, 92, 95, 96 (both), 97, 98, 99, 100, 101, 102, 103 (both), 104, 105, 106, 107, 108 (both), 109, 110, 111, 112, 113, 115, 116 (both), 117, 118, 120, 121, 123, 125, 128, 131, 139, 144, 145, 146 (both), 147, 148 (both), 149 (all), 153, 163, 169, 198.

Autosport; pages 46, 127.
Hugh Bishop; pages 72, 73, 74, 75, 76, 77, 78, 119, 121, 135, 140, 141, 150, 151 (both), 152 (both), 153, 154 (all), 156 (both), 158, 159, 160 (both), 161, 162 (both), 163, 164, 165 (all), 166 (all), 167 (both), 168 (all), 170 (both), 171 (all), 172 (both), 173 (both), 174 (both), 175, 176, 177, 178, 179 (both), 184, 185 (both), 186, 187, 188, 189 (both), 190, 191 (both), 192, (both), 193 (both), 194 (both), 195, 196, 199, 203 plus all the colour except the first three shots.
BL Ltd; pages 61, 62, 71, 93, 99, 105, 106, 126, 177, 182.
Carerras Rothmans Ltd; page 180.
Daimler-Benz AG; page 124.
Ford Motor Co. Ltd; pages 72, 94, 122, 156, 157, 169 (both), 197.
LAT; pages 86 (both), 87, 101, 123 plus the first three colour shots.
Adam Opel AG; page 83 (both).
Graham Robson; page 142 (both).
Saab-Scania Automotive Group; page 82.
Colin Taylor Production; pages 129, 130, 132, 133, 134, 136 (both), 137, 138.
Vauxhall Motors Ltd; page 181 (all).

Index